About the Author

Michael Wilson is Emeritus Professor of Microbiology at University College London where he undertook research for more than 30 years. He has published 335 research papers and 12 books in the fields of Microbiology and Infectious Diseases. He holds 13 patents and in 1991 was given the "Inventor of the Year" award by Toshiba for inventing a device that could produce pure drinking water from sewage. In 2011 he was appointed Chevalier dans l'Ordre des Palmes Académiques by the President of France for his services to French culture.

D1600424

Dedication

For Andrew, Caroline, Edie, Fionn, Pippa and Sarah

Michael Wilson

INTO THE LABYRINTH: IN SEARCH OF DAIDALOS

AUSTIN MACAULEY PUBLISHERS™

LONDON • CAMBRIDGE • NEW YORK • SHARJAH

ISBN 9781528988148 (Paperback)
ISBN 9781528988155 (ePub e-book)

www.austinmacauley.com

First Published (2020)
Austin Macauley Publishers Ltd
25 Canada Square
Canary Wharf
London
E14 5LQ

TABLE OF CONTENTS

PREFACE

MOST PEOPLE KNOW ONLY one thing about Daidalos – he made a botched attempt to escape from Crete by flying and this resulted in the death of his son Ikaros. But there is far more to Daidalos than this simple story. As well as being considered to be the father of Greek sculpture, he was also a great inventor, scientist and engineer. His renown was so great that Socrates was proud to consider himself to be a descendant of Daidalos. The Greeks claimed him as one of their ancestors but he was also regarded as an important figure in ancient Crete, Egypt, Sicily and Turkey. He is associated with, and was instrumental in, some of the most important events in Minoan and Athenian history, yet he remains a shadowy figure. The aim of this book is to shine a light on this remarkable man and give him the prominence he deserves.

But how does one discover the truth about someone who is thought to have lived more than 3,500 years ago? Like many characters of the ancient past, there is considerable uncertainty as to whether or not Daidalos actually existed or is only a myth. This book is not an attempt to resolve this issue but assembles all that is known about him from ancient sources and tells his story. He was said to have lived in Athens, Knossos and Sicily and, consequently, what life would have been like in those places at the time of Daidalos is described. As a polymath, like Leonardo da Vinci, Daidalos has had a profound effect on Western culture. In this book, therefore, the ways in which he has been portrayed in art and literature, as well as his influence on science and technology are discussed. Daidalos has made an indelible impression on our society and this book is a celebration of him and his legacy.

Although there are many beautiful images in this book, many more have had to be left out because of copyright restrictions. However, these can be accessed on the websites that have been included in the text.

Chapter 1

WHO WAS DAIDALOS?

THE PRACTICE OF SCULPTURE, science, engineering, architecture and invention is a "slow-burn" i.e. results are rarely available immediately. In each case, the practitioner needs time and equipment to achieve their ultimate goal. Unless they are extremely rich, there is a need for financial support from some external source. When I started my career as a research scientist in the late 1960s I was lucky to have been given a research grant by the Science Research Council (SRC) but was too young to appreciate just how fortunate I had been (Figure 1.1).

Figure 1.1. The author as a research scientist. Taking a sample for microbiological analysis in 1972.

The SRC paid my university fees and I was given a salary of £550 per year which seemed a fortune in those days. It was enough to pay for rent, food, books, booze, tickets to see the Bonzo Dog Doo-Dah Band (Figure 1.2) at the students union and to get me to London to protest against the Vietnam War.

Daidalos (Latinised as Daedalus, Daedalos, or Dedalus) may likewise have been fortunate in his early years to have been supported by his family or some rich sponsor to engage in his sculptural and inventive pursuits, although we know so little about his youth that this can only remain conjecture. Later in my career, once I had become an academic researcher, I found myself entirely dependent on funds from research councils or commerce in order to investigate what I considered to be "great ideas". In my latter years, as a senior academic, I found that I

Figure 1.2. Bonzo Dog Doo-Dah Band on Dutch TV in 1968

was spending most of my time grubbing around trying to get financial support from a variety of sources and far less on actually carrying out research. Daidalos' career appears to have suffered from similar difficulties as one of the striking aspects of his story was his dependence on the largesse of a succession of kings to enable him to practice his many skills. I've therefore always felt a strong empathy with him. Despite the fact that Daidalos was a superb architect, scientist, sculptor, engineer and inventor, he was never in control, he always had to rely on some sponsor. He was never in charge of his own destiny. Nevertheless, he appears to have been a kind person and used his problem-solving abilities to benefit those, such as Pasiphae and Ariadne, who asked for his help. He did not use his talents for his own benefit, except once to escape imprisonment.

Every age appears to have some technological giant, but few have nurtured someone who, as well as being famed for their inventions and their ability to make useful devices or machines, is also renowned for their beautiful works of art. Leonardo da Vinci (Figure 1.3) immediately springs to mind as the obvious example of such an individual – a true polymath and Renaissance man. The European Renaissance of the 14th-17th century CE was an exciting time characterised by renewed interest in the learning of ancient times in terms of its science, art, philosophy and literature. Nowadays there are many examples of great scientists, inventors and artists but, as foreseen by C.P. Snow in *The Two Cultures*, the arts and sciences have become so divorced from one another that the likelihood of any individual making his/her mark in both disciplines has decreased significantly. To find another Leonardo da Vinci, we have to go back almost 4,000 years to come across someone of his calibre and that person is Daidalos. If Leonardo was the first "re-naissance man" then the equally-gifted polymath, Daidalos, should surely be known as the "naissance

Figure 1.3. Selfportrait of Leonard de Vinci. Print by Franciscus Bernardus Waanders (1840 – 1843)

man" as he was certainly the first great artist, architect, engineer, scientist and inventor.

Daidalos has intrigued, inspired and terrified people since the dawn of history. Most people have heard about his attempts at flying and the tragic consequence of his efforts – the death of his son Ikaros. This story has been an inspiration to aviators, writers and artists throughout the ages. And who has not been terrified by the story of the fearsome Minotaur who lived in the dark labyrinth made by Daidalos? But there is more to Daidalos than these two famous episodes and this book is an exploration of his life and times.

Trying to piece together the life of someone who lived almost 4,000 years ago is no easy task and perhaps the most we can hope for is that we can see "through a glass, darkly". Unfortunately, the earliest written records from Crete, where Daidalos lived for much of his life, are in scripts that have not yet been deciphered (see Chapter 2). Knowledge, at that time, was passed on orally. Later records that are in a script that has been deciphered (known as "Linear B") appear to be concerned mainly with keeping track of commodity transactions such as the number of sheep or jars of oil being bought or sold (see Chapter 2). The writing down of history or stories was not to emerge until more than a thousand years later. The Greek alphabet was invented in around 750 BCE and one of the earliest examples of writing is an inscription found on the famous "cup of Nestor" (Figure 1.4).

Early writing was in the form of poetry, and prose writing did not emerge until approximately 550 BCE. The oldest work of Greek prose to survive is *A history*

Figure 1.4. This is a drawing of the inscription on the Cup of Nestor which is a clay drinking cup found in a grave in the ancient Greek site of Pithekoussai on the island of Ischia, Italy. The cup is dated to 750-700 BCE. The inscription has been translated as: "Nestor's cup, good to drink from. Whoever drinks from this cup, him straightaway the desire of beautiful-crowned Aphrodite will seize."

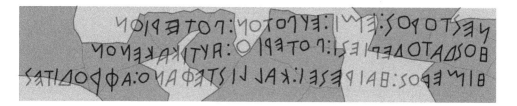

The Labyrinth

It is important right from the start to point out that there is tremendous confusion as to what is being referred to when the word "labyrinth" is used in the context of Knossos and the Minoan civilisation (Figure a).

Figure a. The Cretan labyrinth. Print by Hieronymus Cock (1551 CE). A group of hunters view the labyrinth from a hill. The labyrinth is located in a bay and is accessed through a drawbridge from the land. There is a town on the bay and a castle on the left.

The word has been used to refer to three different constructions:
    (i) the palace of Knossos itself which was built by Daidalos
    (ii) the prison built by Daidalos to house the minotaur
    (ii) the pattern of the dancing floor (choros) made for Ariadne by Daidalos

Some regard these as being separate structures while others think that the prison and palace are the same thing with the choros being just one part of this combined structure. All three possibilities will be described in Chapter 4.

Sir Arthur Evans, the discoverer of the palace of Knossos, believed that the palace itself was the labyrinth. The ancient writers do not really help us resolve this issue with some (Catullus and Pliny) suggesting that "labyrinth" refers to the palace while others imply that it refers to a separate structure – the prison in which the minotaur was kept. If the prison had been a separate structure, it could, of course, have been located near to, or underneath, the palace. There are relatively few mentions of the labyrinth in the ancient texts and the main ones are listed below:

"Then he turned back, unharmed, to great glory, guided by the wandering track of fine thread, so that his exit from the fickle labyrinth of the palace would not be prevented by some unnoticed error"[1]

"As a place in which to keep this monstrous thing Daidalos, the story goes, built a labyrinth, the passage-ways of which were so winding that those unfamiliar with them had difficulty in making their way out...”[2];

“So, Minos, moved to cover his disgrace, resolved to hide the monster in a prison, and he built with intricate design, by Daidalos contrived, an architect of wonderful ability, and famous. This he planned of mazey wanderings that deceived the eyes, and labyrinthic passages involved....So Daidalos contrived innumerous paths, and windings vague, so intricate that he, the architect, hardly could retrace his steps”[3].

“...there is no doubt that Daidalos adopted it as the model for the labyrinth built by him in Crete but that he reproduced only a hundredth part of it containing passages that wind, advance and retreat in a bewilderingly intricate manner. It is not just a narrow strip of ground comprising many miles ‘walks’ or ‘rides,’ such as we see exemplified in our tessellated floors or in the ceremonial game played by our boys in the Campus Martius but doors are let into the walls at frequent intervals to suggest deceptively the way ahead and to force the visitor to go back upon the very same tracks that he has already followed in his wanderings. This Cretan labyrinth was the next in succession after the Egyptian...”[4],

“Now the Labyrinth which Daidalos constructed was a chamber that with its tangled windings perplexed the outward way...”[5]

‘... these young men and women, on being brought to Crete, were destroyed by the Minotaur in the Labyrinth, or else wandered about at their own will and, being unable to find an exit, perished there...’[6]

“Philochorus, however, says that the Cretans do not admit this, but declare that the Labyrinth was a dungeon, with no other inconvenience than that its prisoners could not escape...”[7].

Figure b. Classical seven-course labyrinth. The labyrinth is described as being “seven course” because the path traces out seven concentric rings around the centre. A clay tablet showing the motif of the labyrinth was found in Pylos, Greece. This is the earliest datable representation of the seven-course classical labyrinth and it was recovered from the remains of the Mycenaean palace there which was destroyed by fire ca 1200 BCE.

of the Persian Wars written by Herodotus in approximately 440 BCE. So, we have no written record of events in the time of Daidalos (the 2nd millennium BCE) to fall back on and help us unravel the complex, and sometimes conflicting, tales that have been told about him. All we have are the stories written about him more than a thousand years later starting in the 6th century BCE (Table 1.1).

Table 1.1.

Ancient writers who mention Daidalos. The table shows only those writers who lived prior to the 2nd century CE. Many subsequent books were written about Daidalos but these were based on material from previous authors.

Writer	Book	Date of work
Homer	*Iliad*, 18. 587	Composed in the 8th or 9th century BCE but written down in the 6th century BCE
Bacchylides	*Ode 26*	ca 480 BCE
Pindar	*Nemean Odes*, 4.50	455 BCE
Herodotus	*History*, Book VII, 170	440 BCE
Euripides	*The Cretans* F988	435 BCE
Euripides	*Hecuba*, 786	424 BCE
Aristotle	*On Marvellous Things Heard*, 27.81	400 BCE
Aristotle	*Politics*, 1.9	400 BCE
Plato	*Hippias Major*, 282a	390 BCE
Plato	*Euthyphro*, 11; 15	380 BCE
Xenophon	*Memorabilia of Socrates*, 4.2.33	370 BCE
Heraclides Lembus	*On Constitutions*, 59	350 BCE
Aristotle	*Politics*, 1.9	340 BCE
Pseudo Scylax	*Periplous*, 112	335 BCE
Arrian	*Anabasis of Alexander*, 7.20	323 BCE

Writer	Book	Date of work
Clement of Alexandria	*Exhortations*, 4.13	195 BCE
Sallustius Crispus (Salust)	*Histories*, 2.9	ca 50 BCE
Diodorus Siculus	*Library*, 1.96.1; 1.97.1; 4.30.1; 4.75.5; 4.76.3; 4.77.1; 4.77.3; 4.77.5; 4.79.1; 16.9.1	49 BCE
Horace	*Odes*, 1.3; 2.20	23 BCE
Virgil	*Aeneid*, 6.1	19 BCE
Ovid	*Art of Love*, 2.30; 2.70	2 CE
Ovid	*Metamorphoses*, 8.152; 8.236; 8.260; 9.725	8 CE
Strabo	*Geography*, 6.3.2; 10.4.8; 14.1.19;	24 CE
Pomponius Mela	*Chorographia*, 2.112	43 CE
Petronius	*Satyricon*, 52; 70; 74	60 CE
Seneca	*Letters to Lucilius*, 90.14	65 CE
Pliny the Elder	*Natural History*, 3.16.2; 7.56.3; 7.56.7; 36.19.1	77 CE
Silius Italicus	*Punica*, 12.67; 12.96; 14.41	90 CE
Dio Chrysostom	*Speeches*, 12.45; 37.9; 37.10; 37.15; 80.8	98 CE
Pseudo-Apollodorus	*Library*, 2.6.3; 3.1.4; 3.15.8; e.1.8; e.1.12-15;	100 CE
Martial	*The Epigrams*, 4.49	100 CE
Plutarch	*Life of Theseus*, 19	110 CE
Dio Chrysostom	*Speeches*, 4.120-121; 37.15	112 CE
Juvenal	*Satires*, 3.21; 3.58	130 CE
Arrian of Nicomedia	*Anabasis of Alexander*, 7.20	130 CE
Hyginus	*Fabulae*, 39; 40; 44; 244; 274	150 CE
Pausanias	*Description of Greece*, 1.21.4; 1.26.4; 1.27.1; 2.4.5; 2.15.1; 3.17.6; 5.25.13; and many more sections	161 CE
Lucian	*Essays in Portraiture (Imagines)*, 21	180 CE
Lucian	*Dance (De Saltatione)*, 13; 47	180 CE
Clement of Alexandria	*Exhortations*, 4.13	195 CE

Unfortunately, relatively few of the books written about Daidalos and his era have survived the passage of time, many having been lost or destroyed, either accidentally or intentionally, during the intervening four millennia. One of the most horrendous acts

Herodotus

Herodotus (Figure a) was born in 484 BCE in Halicarnassus (present-day Bodrum, Turkey) a Greek city in southwest Asia Minor although he lived mainly in Athens and Thurii, a Greek colony in Italy. The date of his death is uncertain but is sometime between 430 and 420 BCE. He is the author of the second history to be produced in the ancient world *Historia* (*The Histories*) and is generally regarded as being the "Father of History". The first such history was written by Hecataeus of Miletus but only fragments of his works have survived. In one such fragment, he says: "I write down what I think is true, because the stories told by the Greeks are, in my opinion, ridiculous and countless."

Figure a. Marble bust of Herodotos (2nd century CE). This is a copy of a Greek bronze statue of the first half of the fourth century BCE.

Herodotus was widely-travelled and visited a large part of the Persian Empire, Egypt, Libya, Syria, Babylonia, the Dardanelles, Thrace, Macedonia and Scythia (Figure b). He travelled northwards beyond the Danube and eastward along the northern shores of the Black Sea to the Don River.

The main focus of his *Histories* is the wars between Greece and Persia (499–479 BCE) and what led up to them. It is divided into nine books: Books I–V cover the background to the wars as well as a description of the geography, social structure, and history of the Persian empire while Books VI–IX concentrate on the actual wars. However, it also contains many cultural, ethnographical, geographical and historical digressions thereby providing a wealth of information.

Although Herodotus made mistakes in his work, his *Histories* is generally regarded as being reliable and studies covering the many disciplines contained in his work (archaeology, geography, history, science, ethnology etc.) have substantiated many of his most important observations. Herodotus remains one of the leading sources of original information on the history of Greece, Western Asia and Egypt particularly for the period between 550 and 479 BCE.

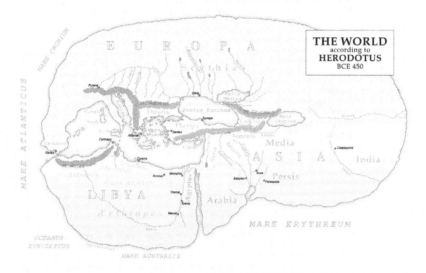

Figure b. Map of the world according to Herodotus

It is important to appreciate that, in addition to the written works of the classical authors, a valuable source of additional information is provided by the scholiasts. Scholiasts were usually scholars or school teachers who felt impelled to write about the ancient texts in order to explain the meaning of difficult passages or simply to comment on what the original author had written. The resulting "scholia" were sometimes written in the margins of the original texts or were published separately as short pamphlets or even as books. The first person to comment on Homer is thought to have been Theagenes of Rhegion who wrote during the period 529–522 BCE. Scholars at the Alexandrian Museum in Egypt (of which the famous library was a part) were particularly prolific as scholiasts as were their rivals at the Pergamon Library. The practice of commentating on classical texts continues, of course, up to the present day although modern scholiasts prefer to be referred to as "commentators".

of destruction was the burning of the Royal Library of Alexandria (Figure 1.5) which was the greatest library of the ancient world and was said to have contained as many as 700,000 books. This occurred in 48 BCE when Julius Caesar sided with Cleopatra in a war against her brother Ptolemy XIII. Caesar set fire to Ptolemy's fleet and, unfortunately, this spread and engulfed the Great Library[8]. Some of the library survived and was partially restored but was subsequently destroyed when the city was attacked by Emperor Aurelian (270–275 CE).

Figure 1.5. The Royal Library of Alexandria. The original image is a photograph of a 19th-century B&W artistic rendering of the Library of Alexandria by O. Von Corven, created based on some archaeological evidence.

Fortunately, a smaller library, based at a temple known as the Serapeum, survived both of these disasters. However, in 391 CE Emperor Theodosius I issued a decree sanctioning the demolition of "pagan" temples in Alexandria and consequently Theophilus (the bishop of Alexandria) attacked and destroyed the Serapeum and had a church built on the site. Unfortunately, such acts of vandalism are not confined to ancient times and have continued up to the present day.

In many cases, only fragments remain of the books

written about Daidalos. In trying to understand those books that have survived down the ages, we are faced with the problems that arise due to translation errors. Greek was obviously the language used in books written during the ancient and classical periods in Greece – for centuries it was the language of scholarship in the Mediterranean region. However, during the middle ages, the Islamic world became the dominant intellectual force in the Mediterranean and many works were translated into Syriac, Arabic and Persian and the original Greek versions were often lost. During the later Middle Ages, the Byzantine Empire started to collapse and many scholars went to Western Europe and brought with them some of the original Greek manuscripts. During the Renaissance, these Greek classics were then translated into Latin from Greek, Syriac (Figure 1.6), Arabic or Persian. Later still, the Latin texts were eventually translated into English. Any of the ancient texts that we read today in English may, therefore, have gone through a whole series of translations from Greek into Syriac, into Latin and finally into English. It would not be surprising, therefore, if the current version of any book differed significantly from what was written down by the original Greek author. This literary equivalent of "Chinese whispers" may have furnished

MS 577
Syriac Sertâ book script. Mt. Sinai, Egypt, ca. 11th c.

Figure 1.6. A book written in Syriac script from Mount Sinai, Egypt (11th century CE)

us with texts that are very different from what was written down by the Greek authors and the original meanings may easily have been lost or altered. Consequently, we should not be surprised when discrepancies arise between accounts of a particular event as related by different writers. Similarly, we can expect a lack of correlation between different writers when it comes to dates, lineages, locations, numbers etc.

(a) Marble Statue of Daidalos, found in Amman. This is a Roman copy (2nd century CE) of a Greek original (2nd century BCE) in the Archaeological Museum, Amman, Jordan.

(b) Statue of an artisan found in the sea off the coast of Algeria (1st century BCE). The figure can be identified as an artisan by his dress and muscular build. He has a pair of wax tablets tucked in his belt on which he would have written or drawn with a pointed stylus. It has been suggested that it represents Daidalos or possibly Phidias (a famous 5th century BCE Athenian sculptor) or the Homeric hero Epeios, who carved the Trojan horse.

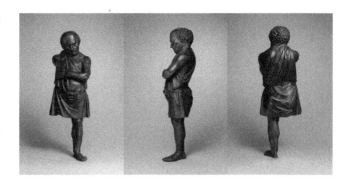

Figure 1.7. Statues of Daidalos

Daidalos in ancient literature

Daidalos (Figure 1.7) has been translated as meaning "cunning worker" or "skilful worker". But was he a real person, a hybrid of several historical figures or a character from mythology? It has been suggested that Daidalos might refer not to a specific individual but to anyone who was recognised as being a "skilful worker" i.e. it is a name associated with the activity of the individual. There is a similar debate as to whether "Homer" was one individual or a descriptive term applied to several ancient poets. In neither case has the issue been resolved.

The first reference to Daidalos is on a clay tablet (designated as "Fp1") found in the palace of Knossos in Crete (this building will be described in more detail in Chapter 2) which has been dated to approximately 1380 BCE. Translation of the Linear B writing (see Chapter 2) on this tablet has shown that it is, basically, a list of the offerings made in the month of Deukios i.e. September. Intriguingly, the tablet has the word "da-da-re-jo-de" written on it and this has been translated as "to the Daidalaion". The exact meaning of this phrase has been the subject of extensive debate and two possible interpretations have been suggested. One is that the Daidalaion refers to the choros (dancing floor) built by Daidalos for Ariadne that is mentioned by Homer and this creation is discussed in greater detail below. The other (suggested by Michael Ventris, who first deciphered the Linear B script) is that it refers to a shrine to Daidalos and the tablet is recording an offering made at this shrine: "The Daidalaion seems an appropriate name for a shrine at Knossos. At Pylos we find Iphimedeia, a semi-mythical figure in Homer apparently receiving divine honours."[9]. Linguistically, the second interpretation appears to be the most likely. This would imply that at some time after the construction of the palace a shrine was built in honour of the person who had constructed it i.e. Daidalos. The tablet records that an offering of 24 litres of olive oil was made to the Daidalaion in the month of September. This was significantly greater than the 12 litres offered to Zeus and indicates the great esteem in which Daidalos was held.

The next mention of Daidalos is towards the end of what is known as the Greek Dark Age i.e. approximately 1200 – 800 BCE. This occurs in Homer's *Iliad*, an epic poem composed in the 9th or 8th century BCE. A definitive version of the poem was written down in the 6th century BCE, although its contents were passed down orally for at least two hundred years before then. In this book, the goddess Thetis (the mother of Achilles) asks Hephaistos (Latinised as "Hephaestus"), the god of blacksmiths, sculptors, metallurgy, fire and volcanoes, to make a set of armour for Achilles (Figure 1.8). Hephaistos was a god with skills similar to those of Daidalos and was greatly venerated by Athenians.

Homer described in great detail the complex designs that Hephaistos carved on the shield (Figure 1.9) he produced. These were in the form of a set of concentric rings and one of these depicted young people dancing "...on a dancing-floor like unto that which in wide Cnosus Daidalos fashioned of old

Figure 1.8. Thetis receives weapons for Achilles from Hephaestus. A print by Franz Ertinger after a painting by Rubens (1679 CE). Hephaestus is shown giving a shield to Thetis, Achilles' mother. Achilles is standing between his mother's arms. In the background, two men are forging weapons, and other parts of the armour are brought in.

Homer and the Iliad

Homer (Figure a) is the author of the ancient Greek epic poems *The Iliad* and *The Odyssey*, which are the first works of Western literature. He is considered to be the earliest and most important of all the Greek writers and the progenitor of the Western literary tradition. Nothing definite is known about him and debate continues as to whether or not he actually existed. Some authorities think that the name should be regarded as a collective term for a number of individuals (this parallels the debate over the existence of Daidalos) who worked on the two poems over many years. Others consider him to have been a real person and he has often been portrayed as a blind, wandering minstrel. Of the many, often conflicting, legends about him,

Figure a. Portrait of the poet Homer by an unknown artist (1639 CE)

the most widely accepted suggests that he was born at Smyrna (present-day Izmir) an Aegean port and that he died on Ios, an island in the Aegean. There is also great uncertainly concerning when he lived, estimates range from the 11th-6th century BCE but most agree that it was probably between 850 and 750 BCE. The consensus is that the poems were transmitted orally for many years and were then written down at some point between the 8th and 6th centuries BCE. Tradition has it that Peisistratus, a tyrant of Athens, was responsible for producing the first definitive written version of Homer's works in the 6th century BCE.

The *Iliad* (Figure b) is a poem about the Trojan war which was a war that involved a 10-year siege of the Anatolian city of Troy (i.e. Ilium; present-day Hisarlik) by a coalition of Greek cities. The poem does not describe the whole war but is concerned with only a few days during the final year of the siege and focuses on a dispute between Agamemnon, the leader of the Greek forces, and Achilles.

Figure b. Hydria (water jar) with the Fight of Achilles and Memnon (575-550 BCE). Two of the Trojan war's greatest heroes, Achilles and Memnon, fight in front of their mothers, the goddesses Thetis and Eos. Each warrior has his chariot standing by. Inscriptions, in the Corinthian alphabet, identify the figures.

for fair-tressed Ariadne."[10] The fact that no further explanation was provided suggests that Cnosus (i.e. Knossos in Crete), Daidalos, Ariadne and the dancing floor (known as a "choros" or "coron") were all well known at that time: "Its very brevity suggests that audiences had an automatic familiarity with the legendary dances of Crete and their role in Ariadne's tale; otherwise the brief simile would have been intrusive and obscure"[11] This short phrase, dear reader, should not be glossed over because, as we shall see in subsequent chapters, it is central to the story of Daidalos and for centuries has been the subject of intense speculation with regard to its interpretation and implication. Critics, both ancient and modern, were scandalised by this passage because Homer had dared to imply that a god (Hephaistos) would imitate the work of a mere mortal (Daidalos).

Figure 1.9. Silver-gilt shield modelled after Homer's Iliad *by John Flaxman (1755-1826); manufactured by Rundell, Bridge, and Rundell, London*

Although Daidalos is not mentioned again in the *Iliad*, words derived from his name are used by Homer a total of 36 times in the *Iliad* and the *Odyssey*. The most frequently-used derivative is an adjective, "daidalic", which means "well-crafted", "intricately worked" or "skilfully wrought". It is also used as a noun "daidalon", although more usually in the plural form ("daidala"), to refer to well-made, admirable objects. The term daidalon also came to be applied to an object that had divine, exotic, animated or life-like qualities. This raises the interesting "chicken and egg" question of whether Daidalos was named because he was able to make daidala (Latinised as "daedala") or whether daidala were so-called because they were the type of objects made by Daidalos or a superb craftsman like him. Pausanias, a Greek writer of the 2nd century CE, believed in the former as he states in his *Description of Greece*, "I think that Daidalos was a surname subsequently given to him from the daidala and not a name bestowed on him at birth"[12]

The adjective, daidalic, and plural noun, daidala, appear many times in classical literature and a few examples of where they occur include *Oresteia* by Aeschylus, *Hekabe* by Euripides, *Idylls* by Theocritus, *Amores* by Lucian, *Protrepticus* by Clement of Alexandria, *Aeneid* by Vergil and the *Palatine Anthology* by unknown authors. The words are associated with a wide variety of objects including armour, clothing, textiles, furniture, jewellery, ornaments, musical instruments, equestrian equipment and ships

Another use of the adjective daidalic is in the phrase "daidalic sculpture", a term that was introduced in the early 20th century (see Chapter 4). This is used to refer to a particular sculptural style (characterised by Eastern, orientalising, influences; Figure 1.10), said to have been introduced by Daidalos and is not a comment on how well the sculptures had been made.

Confusingly, the plural noun "daidala" was also applied to small cult images, usually made of wood, as well as to the name of the festival in which such images were used (Figure 1.11). In contrast to being "well made", such cult images were usually very crude. These images became known as "xoana" as explained by Pausanias: "They conduct the festival known as 'Daidala', because long ago they used to call

Figure 1.10 Terracotta daidalic aryballos (container for scented oil) from Crete (675-650 BCE). This vase is in the form of a woman with her arms folded across her belly. The human head forms the vessel's spout and neck. Black paint was used to elaborate the figure, and traces of the original pigment remain on the eyes and hair, and in three bands on the body. Note the long, wig-like hair on either side of the face, the almond-shaped eyes and large nose – these are the main characteristics of the Daidalic style.

xoana, 'daidala'."[12] Such statues were used in two festivals known as the "Greater Daidala" (held every 60 years) and "Lesser Daidala" (held every 4 years) in Plataia, Greece.[13] [14] The wood for the statues came from a sacred grove of oak trees and these statues (i.e. daidala) were burnt, along with sacrificial victims, as offerings to Hera and Zeus.

Daidalos does not appear in any of the works of

Pausanias

Pausanias was a Greek traveller and geographer who was born in the kingdom of Lydia (present-day Western Turkey) in 110 CE and died in 180 CE. He travelled widely in Greece, Asia Minor, Syria, Palestine, Egypt, Macedonia, Albania and Italy. He used the information he gained from these travels to write his famous book *Periegesis Hellados* (*Description of Greece*). This is divided into 10 books and takes the form of a tour of Greece starting from Attica, the peninsular on the South East of Greece that includes the city of Athens (Figure).

Map showing which parts of Greece each book describes in the Description of Greece by Pausanias.

The first book was completed between 143 and 161 CE. As well as describing each of the places he visited, he also says something about its history as well as the daily life, ceremonial rites, customs and legends of its inhabitants. His book is generally regarded as reliable and many of his observations are backed by modern archaeology. Sir James Frazer, the famous anthropologist and classical scholar, said of Pausanias: "without him the ruins of Greece would for the most part be a labyrinth without a clue, a riddle without an answer."

Hesiod, the other great writer of the period and a near contemporary of Homer. Towards the end of the Archaic Period (which comprises approximately 800 – 480 BCE), the Greek poet Pindar (522 – 433 BCE), mentions Daidalos in an ode. This makes reference to Daidalos' metal-working skills: "With the sword of Daidalos, the son of Pelias sowed the seeds of death for Peleus..."[15]. This is the only reference to Daidalos' ability to make weapons, which is rather odd as this would have been expected to have been one of the main activities of a master metal-worker in those days. Another poet of the Archaic Age, Bacchylides (516-451 BCE) refers to another of Daidalos' skills, this time as a carpenter: "... to Eupalamos' son Daidalos, most skilled of carpenters, she [Pasiphae] told her unspeakable sickness..."[16]

Herodotus, a Greek historian of the Classical Age (which comprises approximately 480 – 323 BCE), makes a brief mention of Daidalos when describing the history of Crete: "Now Minos, it is said, went to Sicania, which is now called Sicily, in search for Daidalos, and perished there by a violent death."[17]. This book was published in approximately 440 BCE and, interestingly, it enables an estimate of when Daidalos lived (see later in this Chapter).

After Herodotus, a number of Athenian writers and dramatists in the 5th century BCE mention Daidalos. These include Plato, Aristophanes, Sophocles and Euripides. In one of Plato's works of the 4th century BCE, a dialogue between Socrates and Alcibiades (a prominent Athenian statesman, orator and general) is related (Figure 1.12). During the course of this conversation, Socrates (who was a sculptor and the son of a sculptor, Sophroniscus) was proud to claim descent from Daidalos[18].

Daidalos is also mentioned by later writers including Xenophon (430-354 BCE) and Aristotle (384-322 BCE). Most of these writers refer to Daidalos' ability to make statues that are so realistic that they seem to be alive. However, Xenophon, in his *Memorabilia of*

(a) A xoanon in the form of a simple plank figure (2000-1900 BCE). Found in Cyprus.

(b) Terracotta xoanon from Cyprus (ca. 1900–1800 BCE)

Figure 1.11. Examples of xoana or daidala

Figure 1.12. Socrates and Alcibiades by Christoffer Wilhelm Eckersberg (1783-1853 CE).

Socrates (a collection of Socratic dialogues) written around 370 BCE, uses Daidalos' story as an example of wisdom not necessarily being a useful attribute: "But wisdom now, Socrates, that at any rate is indisputably a good thing; for what is there that a wise man would not do better than a fool? Indeed! Have you not heard how Daidalos was seized by Minos because of his wisdom, and was forced to be his slave, and was robbed of his country and his liberty, and essaying to escape with his son, lost the boy and could not save himself, but was carried off to the barbarians and again lived as a slave there? And how many others, do you suppose, have been kidnapped on account of their wisdom, and hauled off to the great King's court, and live in slavery there?"[19] This shows just how widely-known Daidalos' story was in those days.

The first detailed account of the life of Daidalos was written by Pseudo-Apollodorus (180-120 BCE) who also extends the skills attributed to him to include inventor, master-builder, director of works, architect, engineer, constructor, problem-solver and author.

Diodorus Siculus (1st century BCE), a Greek writer who lived in Sicily, gave a fairly detailed account of Daidalos' life in his 40 volume *Bibliotheca Historica* which covers the history of the world up to 60 BCE. He refers to Daidalos as being an architect, sculptor, stone-worker and inventor. He suggests that Daidalos' building skills (with respect to the labyrinth) and sculptural abilities were learnt from the Egyptians.

Daidalos also appears in books written by Roman authors. Virgil (70-19 BCE), in his *Aeneid*, describes him as a talented inventor, sculptor and builder and also briefly relates his life story. Ovid (43-17/18 BCE) also gives an account of Daidalos' life in his *Metamorphoses*. In his *Natural History*, Pliny the Elder (23 BCE-79 CE) talks about the labyrinth built by Daidalos. Interestingly, when describing the Cretan labyrinth, he points out that "We must not... suppose it to be a narrow promenade along which we may walk for many miles together; but we must picture to ourselves a building filled with numerous doors, and galleries which continually mislead the visitor, bringing him back, after all his wanderings, to the spot from which he first set out."[20] This implies that, rather than being a separate structure, the very temple of Knossos, with its many adjoining rooms and courtyards, may in fact be the Cretan labyrinth. Certainly, diagrams of the palace (Figure 2.25 in Chapter 2) show its complexity and labyrinthine nature.

Plutarch, a Greek who lived in Rome, mentions Daidalos in his story of Theseus in his book *Parallel Lives of the Greeks and Romans*. What he says about Daidalos is based on the writings of Cleidemus (378–340 BCE). Unfortunately, none of Cleidemus' works have survived and his story differs in some respects from that related by most other sources (see Chapter 3). In his extensive survey of Greek art and culture (*Description of Greece*), Pausanias discussed the life of Daidalos and many of his works. In this book, he not only described the buildings and objects he came across in his travels but also attempted to determine their underlying cultural and historical relevance. He was keen to separate the historical and legendary aspects of Daidalos and attributed to him the invention of sails as well as a collapsible chariot. He certainly considered Daidalos to be a real person. For example, when describing the colonisation of Sardinia by the Greeks he scoffs at the idea that Daidalos may have joined Aristaeus in this venture because they were separated by four generations: "It would be utterly irrational to suppose that Daidalos, a contemporary of Oedipus, King of Thebes, could have participated in a colony or anything else with Aristaeus..."[21]

All subsequent writings concerning Daidalos were based on these ancient sources.

It was not until the 3rd century CE that anyone actually attempted to describe what Daidalos might have looked like. Philostratus the Elder (190-230 CE) in his *Imagines* mentions, briefly, Daidalos' appear-

Apollodorus of Athens

Apollodorus was born in Alexandria in 180 BCE and died some time after 120 BCE. He was a librarian in the Great Library at Alexandria and was a scholar with a wide range of interests and wrote books on history, philology, geography and mythology. He is best known for his *Chronika* which is a four-volume chronicle of Greek history covering the period from the fall of Troy (12th century BCE) to 119 BCE. He also wrote a twelve-book commentary on the "Catalogue of Ships" mentioned in Homer's Iliad – most of this survives in the *Geographia* written by Strabo the ancient geographer.

For many years a book called the *Bibliotheca (The Library)*, which was a compendium of Greek mythology, was attributed to him. However, it was later shown that this was written in the 1st or 2nd century CE and the author of this is now known as Pseudo-Apollodorus. The author of the *Library* describes the myths without interpreting them and often draws on very old and conservative sources. The most important of these was Pherecydes of Athens, a 5th century BCE author who wrote a long work on Greek mythology. The *Library* preserves many variants of the myths and provides a picture of Greek mythology as it was in the archaic and classical period. It is, therefore, a very valuable source to students of Greek mythology, far better than books written much earlier.

Diodorus Siculus

Diodorus Siculus was a Greek historian born in Agyrium, Sicily (Present-day Agira), but the dates of his birth and death are not known. However, his works were written in the 1st century BCE. His most famous work is the *Bibliotheca Historica (Library of History)* which covered the period from mythological times to 60 BCE (Figure). He travelled in Egypt during 60–57 BCE and also spent a number of years in Rome. His history consisted of 40 books, of which only books 1–5 and 11–20 have survived. Books 1–6 covered the mythic history of Hellenic and non-Hellenic tribes up to the Trojan war; Books 7–17 ended with the death

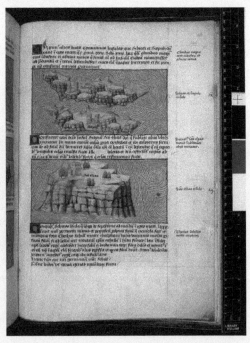

A page from the Bibliotheca Historicum translated by Poggio Bracciolini (1450-1460).

of Alexander the Great while Books 18–40 continued the history up to the start of Caesar's Gallic Wars.

He used the name *Bibliotheca Historica* to acknowledge that his work was derived from many sources including Hecataeus of Abdera, Ctesias of Cnidus, Ephorus, Theopompus, Hieronymus of Cardia, Duris of Samos, Diyllus, Philistus, Timaeus, Polybius, and Posidonius. His most important sources for Greek history were: (i) Ephorus who wrote a 29 volume book of Greek history covering a 700 year period up to 340 BCE – this has been lost and (ii) Hieronymus of Cardia who wrote a history covering the period 323–272 BCE but only fragments of this have survived.

Diodorus' *Library* is a very important source and what remains of it is the largest surviving collection of writings of any ancient Greek historian. Furthermore, books 11–20 are the only surviving continuous account of the Greek "classical" age. However, one criticism levelled at him is that he does not always distinguish between historical events and legends.

Lucius Mestrius Plutarchus

Plutarch (45-120 CE) was a philosopher who was born in Chaeronea, a city of Boeotia in central Greece. Although he studied in Athens (philosophy and mathematics) and also visited Rome and Alexandria, he spent most of his life in Chaeronea and nearby Delphi. During the last 30 years of his life, he was a priest at Delphi. He was a prolific writer and produced 227 books, approximately half of which were philosophical works while the rest covered theology, psychology, metaphysics, ethics, politics, education and history. His most widely-known book, *Parallel Lives*, compares and contrasts the lives of pairs of historical figures – one Greek and one Roman. A total of 23 of these pairs survive and, of particular relevance to this book, is the life of Theseus who is paired with Romulus.

Bust of Plutarch in Chaeronea, Greece

His works, particularly those on philosophy and education, have always been highly regarded and his biographies of historical figures have been used as source material by many writers including Shakespeare, Rousseau, Montaigne and Emerson.

ance while describing an ancient Greek painting from Naples: "Daidalos himself is of the Attic type in that his face suggests great wisdom and that the look of the eye is so intelligent; and his very dress also follows the Attic style; for he wears this dull coarse mantle and also he is painted without sandals, in a manner peculiarly affected by the Athenians"[22]

When did he live?

Figure 1.13. Oedipus and the Sphinx by Jean-Auguste-Dominique Ingres (1864)

The Sphinx, part lion, part woman, grimaces in horror as Oedipus solves her riddle: "What is that which has one voice and yet becomes four-footed, two-footed, and three-footed?" Oedipus replies, "Man, for as a babe he is four-footed, as an adult he is two-footed, and as an old man he gets a third support, a cane." The Sphinx then hurls herself onto the rocks below.

An important question that needs to be addressed is "when did Daidalos live?" Not surprisingly, given that we are talking about an era almost four millennia ago, this has proved to be a very difficult question to answer. The ancient writers give some vague pointers but, as we shall see, the time-lines of the participants in Daidalos' story do not match and this results in great confusion. Plato is rather vague about Daidalos' lifetime and says that this was "some one thousand or two thousand years"[23] before the writing of the Platonic dialogues *Laws*, i.e. 2350-1350 BCE.

Pausanias states that Daidalos was a contemporary of Oedipus (Figure 1.13), the King of Thebes[24]. According to a timeline constructed for the Oedipus trilogy (*https://www.preceden.com/timelines/33288-the-oedipus-trilogy-timeline*) this would place him in the 6th century BCE which is clearly far too late a date.

A more recent book has the confidence to be more specific about the time in which Daidalos lived – *The Cyclopaedia of Universal History*. This remarkable book is described by its editors (Isaiah McBurney and Samuel Neil) as consisting of "Tabular views of contemporaneous events in all ages from the earliest records until the present time arranged chronologically and alphabetically". It was published in 1855 and does not hold back from stating very specific dates for innumerable historical characters and events. This book has an entry for 1300 BCE in which it states "Daidalos, the sculptor, flourishes". Interestingly it says that Hercules was born in this year and King Minos was "active" (although there is also an entry for him in 1400, implying some editorial uncertainty). Other entries associated with Daidalos also feature in the book:

(i) 1257 BCE. Theseus unites the cities of Attica under one government

(ii) 1256 BCE. Minos the legislator extends his dominions by means of his naval superiority

(ii) 1240 BCE. Theseus and the Minotaur. Daidalos of Athens invents several mechanical instruments.

(iii) 1235 BCE. Aegeus throws himself into the sea. Theseus, his son, becomes the tenth king in Attica.

(iv) 1192-1183 BCE. Trojan War

Although, unfortunately, the original sources used by the editors are not stated, it is reassuring that at least it has Daidalos, Theseus and Minos as being contemporaries. As for the time stated – the early 14th/late 13th century BCE – this is not too unreasonable a suggestion as it is not too far off from the time period indicated by the archaeological evidence. However, it is the view of many modern archaeologists that Knossos, and the rest of Crete, was extensively damaged in approximately 1450 BCE (possibly by a natural disaster and/or invading Mycenaeans) and was probably occupied by Mycenaeans from then until it was finally abandoned in approximately 1375 BCE. Consequently, it looks as though the early 14th/late 13th century BCE is unlikely to be the era of Daidalos.

What we do know is that Daidalos lived under the protection of King Minos and that Crete, at that time, was a major power in the eastern Mediterranean (Figure 1.14).

So, can we give a date to the reign of King Minos? Herodotus, tells us that the Trojan war (Figure 1.15)

Figure 1.14. Map showing the extent of Minoan influence in the 16th century BCE. This is shown in red and includes those islands named in red.

occurred two generations after the death of King Minos: "...and in the next generation but one after the death of Minos came the Trojan war, in which the Cretans proved not the most contemptible of those who came to assist Menelaos"[25]

Figure 1.15. The Burning of Troy with the Flight of Aeneas and Anchises by François Nomé (1593-1644 CE).

Unfortunately, there is considerable disagreement with regard to when the Trojan war was fought and estimates range from 1334 to 1183 BCE. If we take the older year of this range and go back two generations, then this would place Minos' death to around 1394 (taking a generation as being 30 years). Although we don't know how old Minos was when he died, if we take a guess at 60 years then we can assume that he reigned during the last half of the 15th century BCE. This date, however, does not represent a time during which the Minoan civilisation was at its peak, it would have been very much in its decline and Knossos would probably have been occupied by Mycenaeans then. Here it is important to introduce the issue of whether the term "Minos" referred to a particular person or was a dynastic term, rather like "Caesar", and referred to a whole succession of kings. As will be discussed in Chapter 3, the latter is more likely as there appear to have been at least two kings called Minos each with a very different personality and reputation.[26] In support of this idea, *The nine books of the History of Herodotus* (translated from the text of Thomas Gaisford) by Peter Edmund Laurent published in 1846 has an interesting "Geographical Index". In this he writes: "Minos, eleventh king of Crete, was stifled in a bath at Camicus." It is difficult, therefore, to try dating Daidalos on the basis of him being a contemporary of King Minos – we don't know which Minos.

What about calculations based on Theseus (Figure 1.16) who, according to many writers, was a contemporary of Daidalos as well as being his cousin?

Figure 1.16. Theseus fighting a centaur. Engraving by Steinmiller after A. Canova (1757-1822).

Castor of Rhodes (1st century BCE) was a well-respected historian who produced a time-line of the Kings of Athens and placed Theseus as King during the period 1234–1205 BCE. This would mean that he reigned more than two hundred years after the abandonment of Knossos as a Minoan stronghold. Not only could he not have known Daidalos but this dating also precludes him (on archaeological evidence) from having had any dealings with Minos and either of his daughters, Ariadne and Phaedra.

Diodorus Siculus, Gaius Julius Hyginus and Apol-

Gaius Julius Hyginus

Hyginus was a Latin author (64 BCE – CE 17) who was born in either Spain or Alexandria. He was brought to Rome as a slave but freed by Augustus and appointed superintendent of the Palatine library. Of the many books he wrote, only two survive – one devoted to mythology (*Fabulae*) and one to those myths associated with the constellations (*De Astronomia* or *Poeticon Astronomicon*).

Unfortunately, the original texts of both books have been lost and all we have today are copies made by 2nd century CE writers. These versions are considered to be rather crude and one expert (Professor H. J. Rose) has described them as having apparently been written by "an ignorant youth, semi-learned, stupid". The *Fabulae* is a collection of approximately 300 myths told very briefly and crudely. They cover the major gods such as Zeus (Jupiter), and Poseidon (Neptune) as well

Gaius Julius Hyginus. A print by Hieronymus van Hensbergen (1674). Hyginus, in a toga, points to an arrangement of carved heads of ancient gods.

as their half god-half human (demi-god) offspring such as Minos and Theseus. Each fabula reveals the parentage of the particular god/demi-god as well as a summary of their life and history. The overall structure of the *Fabulae* is such that it provides a useful family tree of the gods and demi-gods. The book is a mine of information and is regarded as being of immense value in view of the fact that it is based on the works of many ancient writers that have been lost.

lodorus wrote that Daidalos was a descendant of King Erechtheus of Athens (see Chapter 3) who ruled the city from 1397–1347 BCE. Again, this puts Daidalos outside of the time period during which the Minoans were a dominant culture.

The early Greek writers have tended to confuse matters by, it has been suggested, trying to claim Daidalos as their own and attempting to shoe-horn him into their history and make him Athenian rather than Cretan (see later in this chapter). The absence of any archaeological evidence and the confusion arising from the ancient writers means that we cannot definitively suggest the time period during which Daidalos lived. All we can really do is conclude that it must have been at a time when the Minoan civilization was at its peak (a time known as the Neopalatial period), and archaeological evidence shows that this was between the 17th and early 15th centuries BCE. However, as discussed above, literary sources suggest that Daidalos' contemporaries (Minos and Theseus) were alive a few hundred years later i.e. during the 13th -14th centuries BCE. Taking this into account, and compromising on these two approaches, it is reasonable to suggest that Daidalos was alive sometime around the end of the Neopalatial period i.e. approximately the 16th century BCE. Throughout this discussion it is important to bear in mind that we are talking about events that happened way back in time, almost four millennia ago, so it is not surprising that discrepancies of a few hundred years have arisen in the historical records.

Muddying the waters: the Athenian appropriation of Daidalos

The 5th century BCE started off badly for Athens and the other Greek city-states because they were invaded by the Persians under Darius (Figure 1.17) and then his son Xerxes.

Much of northern Greece became part of the

Figure 1.17 Relief of Darius at Behistun, Iran

Persian empire (Figure 1.18). However, after a number of decisive battles on land (Marathon, Plataea) and at sea (Salamis, Mycale), often against overwhelming odds, the Persians were defeated and expelled from Greece.

Athens then became the dominant force in Greece (on account of the strength of its army, navy and financial resources) and entered what came to be known as its "golden age". This era was characterised by its economic and cultural vitality and it saw a flourishing of drama, art, architecture, historical writing, politics, rhetoric and philosophy. Athens was considered by its citizens to be the natural home of culture and democracy. In keeping with this, there was a desire to make its past as magnificent as its present so that its recent victories would be regarded as a natural and unsurprising continuation of its glorious history. Consequently, historians, dramatists and other writers produced works that hyped-up and glorified Athenian history. For example, at about this time a myth appeared that Poseidon and Athena were so impressed by the city that they competed for the honour of being recognised as its supreme

Figure 1.18. The invasion of Greece by Darius the Great. Illustration from History of Darius the Great *by Jacob Abbott, 1850. The text accompanying the figure reads "As they moved slowly on, they stopped to take possession of such islands as came in their way. ....The Persians destroyed the cities and towns whose inhabitants they could not conquer... The mighty fleet advanced thus, by slow degrees, from conquest to conquest, toward the Athenian shores. The vast multitude of galleys covered the whole surface of the water."*

THE INVASION OF GREECE.

Figure 1.19. King Kekrops, the legendary first king of Athens, who had a serpent's tail. A clay relief from Melos, Greece (460 BCE)

deity. Kekrops, the half-man/half-serpent first king of Athens (Figure 1.19), decided in favour of Athena.

Also, a whole new line of hereditary kings was invented to glamourise the Athenian past and the heroic deeds of one of these, Theseus, came to prominence – especially his adventures in Crete. At least seven known plays of the time portrayed Athenians as victims of Cretans although only one of these has survived intact – *Hippolytus* by Euripides. However, both Plato and Plutarch observed that the portrayal by these playwrights of Minos as being cruel was at variance with Homer and Hesiod who praised him as a lawmaker and judge. Were the playwrights talking about a later king Minos or were they indulging in racism? After all, Minos was descended from a Phoenician princess (Europa) and the Athenians had just defeated the Phoenician allies of the Persians at Salamis. Furthermore, Crete had refused to help the Greeks in this naval battle and so was certainly not the Athenians' favourite nation. As we will see in Chapter 3, Theseus was the hero who freed Athens from Minoan domination by killing the Minotaur and rescuing the Athenian sacrificial victims. Furthermore, although he was a king, he also became renowned for being the founder of democracy in Athens and so was greatly venerated.

A magnificent new building and restoration programme was undertaken on the Acropolis at this time and included the rebuilding of the walls and the Parthenon, the construction of the Propylaea (a monumental gateway), the Erechtheion (dedicated to Athena and Poseidon; Figure 1.20) and the temple of Athena Nike (Figure 1.21).

It was, therefore, important to show that Athenians had always been expert architects and sculptors and who better to encapsulate such skills than an "Athenian" Daidalos? Consequently, the newly-created "line of Athenian kings" was constructed to show that Daidalos was, in fact, a cousin of Theseus. Up until this time, all the available evidence (admittedly not a lot) pointed to him having been a Cretan. Daidalos, because of his fame as a craftsman and artist, was incorporated into Athenian history to show that it had always been a "centre of the arts". He also became a frequent subject of plays by 5th-century BCE dramatists including Aeschylus, Sophocles, Euripides and Aristophanes.

Figure 1.20. The Erechtheion on the Acropolis of Athens.

Figure 1.21. Drawing of the Acropolis from the West, with the Propylaea in the centre and the Temple of Athena Nike on the right. Thomas Hartley Cromek (1834). A row of columns stand in front of the gateway and a rectangular doorway can be seen in the centre of the stone wall of the gate.

Consequently, it was only in the 5th century BCE that Daidalos became identified as an Athenian, a relative of Hephaistos (a god particularly venerated in Athens) and a cousin of Theseus. This cultural misappropriation has complicated Daidalos' vague, fragmentary and tangled story. It has also been suggested that the adventures of Daidalos in Sicily and Sardinia (to be described in Chapter 3) were promulgated to establish a long-standing Greek presence in these regions and thereby legitimise Greece's later colonisation of these islands.

REFERENCES

1. Catullus, *Poems*, 64

2. Diodorus Siculus, *Library*, 4.77.3

3. Ovid, *Metamorphoses*, 8.152

4. Pliny the Elder, *Natural History*, 36.19.1

5. Pseudo-Apollodorus, *Library*, 3.1.4.

6. Plutarch, *Life of Theseus*, 15

7. Plutarch, *Life of Theseus*, 16

8. Plutarch, *Life of Caesar*, 49

9. Ventris M and Chadwick J, *Documents in Mycenaean Greek*. Cambridge University Press, 1959

10. Homer, *Iliad*, 18.587

11. Steven Lonsdale. A dancing Floor for Ariadne (Iliad 18.590-92): *Aspects of Ritual Movement in Homer and Minoan Religion*. In: *The Ages of Homer* edited by Jane B. Carter, Sarah P. Morris.

12. Pausanias, *Description of Greece*, 9.3.2

13. Eusebius, *Preparation of the Gospels*, 3.1.2

14. Pausanias, *Description of Greece*, 9.3.2

15. Nemean, *For Timasarchus of Aegina, Boys' Wrestling*

16. Bacchylides, *Ode 26*

17. Herodotus, *History*, 7.170

18. Alcibiades I, 121a

19. Xenophon, *Memorabilia of Socrates*, 4.2.33

20. Pliny the Elder, *Natural History*, 36.19.1

21. Pausanias, *Description of Greece,* 10.17.4.

22. Philostratus the Elder, *Imagines*, 1.16

23. Plato, *Laws*, 3.677d

24. Pausanias, *Description of Greece*, 10.17.4

25. Herodotus, *History*, 7.171

26. Diodorus Siculus, *Library*, 4.60.3

Further general reading

Ancient Greek Literature. K. J. Dover (Editor). Oxford University Press, 1997

Ancient Greek Scholarship: A Guide to Finding, Reading, and Understanding Scholia, Commentaries, Lexica, and Grammatical Treatises: From Their Beginnings to the Byzantine Period. Eleanor Dickey. Oxford University Press, 2007

Ancient Writers: Greece and Rome. T. J. Luce. Charles Scribner's Sons, 1982.

Daidalos and the Origins of Greek Art. Sarah P. Morris. Princeton University Press, 1995

Myth and the Creative Process: Michael Ayrton and the Myth of Daedalus. Jacob E. Nyenhuis, Wayne State University Press, Detroit, 2003

The Oxford Handbook of the Bronze Age Aegean. Eric H. Cline (editor). Oxford University Press, Oxford, 2012

Chapter 2

THE MEDITERRANEAN WORLD IN THE TIME OF DAIDALOS

AS WE WILL SEE in the next chapter, most of the stories about Daidalos centre on the three main places in which he lived – Knossos, Athens and Sicily (Figure 2.1). Some of the ancient texts also briefly mention trips he made to Egypt, the Elektrides Islands, Elis, Cumae, Sardinia and Daidala. It's therefore important to get a feel for what life would have been like in the three main locations where he spent most of his life. Unfortunately, as mentioned in Chapter 1, we only have a very rough idea of when Daidalos was alive. Consequently, in describing the three locations, we will encompass a broad time

Figure 2.1. Location of places in which Daidalos lived or visited. For specific locations in Sicily and Egypt see Chapter 4.

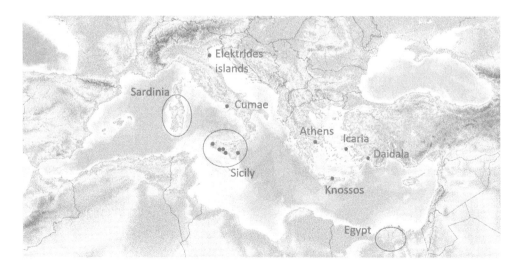

period from approximately the 17th to the 15th centuries BCE which is towards the end of the middle and the beginning of the late bronze ages.

Daidalos in Athens

Almost nothing is known about Daidalos' life in Athens, other than that he was famous as a sculptor and inventor before becoming a notorious child-murderer and blasphemer. Because of his fame, before his fall from grace, we can assume that he had a reasonable life-style. So, what would life have been like for him in Athens?

The period we are particularly interested in is known as the Late Helladic by modern archaeologists and this is deemed to cover the years 1600 - 1100 BCE. This is sub-divided further into 7 seven periods and Daidalos would have been alive at some time within the first two of these – Late Helladic (LH) I and LH IIA i.e. ca1600 - 1450 BCE. During the previous era, the Middle Helladic (ca 1900 - ca 1600 BCE), mainland Greece was largely agrarian. The wheel was introduced during this period and the dominant pottery style was known as Minyan (Figure 2.2) after the legendary King Minyas in whose city (Orchomenos) the pottery was first discovered.

Figure 2.2. Minyan Bowl made of clay (ca. 2500 BCE).

Towards the end of the Middle Helladic and the beginning of the LH periods, a number of power centres emerged (e.g. Mycenae, Athens, Corinth, Pylos and others: Figure 2.3) and these were dominated by a warrior elite ruled by a king who was known as a Wanax. These were typically centred around a palace which was often sited on a hill or rocky outcrop and was surrounded by defensive walls. This culture, and the LH period itself, is referred to as Mycenaean Greece after one of the best-known examples, the palatial complex at Mycenae.

Figure 2.3. Map of Mycenaean Greece showing the main palace sites. The location of Troy is also shown.

Mycenae was excavated by Heinrich Schliemann (Figure 2.4), a German archaeologist who was obsessed with establishing the historical basis of Homer's works. Here he uncovered evidence of an advanced civilization which supported Homer's description in *The Iliad* as being "rich in gold"[1]

Mycenaean culture was heavily influenced by the Minoans who they eventually succeeded to become the dominant power in the Aegean. But what about Athens in particular? This city is located on the west coast of the Attic peninsula which protrudes into the

Figure 2.4. Heinrich Schliemann in 1879, a pioneer in the study of Aegean civilization in the Bronze Age (1822-1890 CE)

Aegean Sea and is protected by mountains on three sides and by the sea on the remaining side. There is evidence of settlement there as early as 5,000 BCE and by the 16th century BCE it was an important centre of Mycenaean civilisation. The oldest remains found there are of the walls of the Mycenaean fortress on top of the Acropolis (Figure 2.5).

The Acropolis is a huge, flat 70 m high limestone outcrop which is 300 m long and 150 m wide. Such a natural feature would have appealed to early settlers as an easily-defendable refuge and a series of walls were built at different times to provide additional protection. Possibly the oldest of these is the Pelasgic wall which was 10 m high and 3.5-6 m thick, and parts of this are still visible near the Propylaea (the entrance to the Acropolis). The wall had two entrances, one in the North and one in the West.

Figure 2.5. The Acropolis

(a) A view of the Acropolis and Athens from the foot of Mount Anchesmus

(b) The Acropolis of Athens as it is today.

The walls were described as being "Cyclopean" because they were built from such massive limestone boulders that the Mycenaeans thought that only the Cyclops (a mythical race of one-eyed giants) could have moved them. The first King of Athens, Kekrops, is said to have reached the Acropolis in 1581 BCE and a three-dimensional reconstruction of what the city would have looked like at an early stage is shown in Figure 2.6.

The old entrance to the Acropolis was where it is now, just south of the Propylaea. At this point, two approach roads became footpaths at the summit and led into an open square with a guardhouse which commanded the path to the palace. This was destroyed in approximately 1000 BCE and only traces of it remain next to the temple dedicated to both Athena and Poseidon – the Erechtheion – on the north side of the Acropolis. The palace was on a raised platform and faced outward towards the gates. Like the one at Pylos (see Figure 2.10) it had side terraces with living quarters and storerooms. Two other entrances to the acropolis existed – one to the north-west and

Figure 2.6. Artist's reconstruction of the view from the southwest of the Athenian acropolis in its early Mycenaean phase. The palace is clearly visible but little remains of it today. It was situated where the Erechtheion now stands (see Figure 2.7). The Pelasgian wall is clearly visible around the top of the acropolis. The main entrance to the acropolis was a gateway (the Propylaea) and this is visible as a rectangular structure to the left, below the palace. Remains of the walls have been found near the Propylaea which was also the site of a later temple built to Athena Nike. The Propylaea, as well as an important water source, was protected by another wall (the Enneapylon) at the base of the acropolis.

Figure 2.7. The Erechtheion, dedicated to Athena and Poseidon) on the Acropolis of Athens.

Figure 2.8 Plan of the Acropolis showing the main buildings. The oldest structures (6th century BCE) are shown in orange while those built in the 5th century BCE, or subsequently, are shown in green.

the other to the north of the palace. The whole of the Acropolis was protected by the massive Pelasgian walls (or Pelargikon) which were said to have been built by ancestors of the Mycenaeans, the Pelasgians. The Acropolis could have accommodated 200-300 permanent residents within its walls while a larger population would have lived on its slopes or further away. During times of crisis, more than 2,000 people could have sheltered on the plateau.

In the 13th century BCE, an earthquake resulted in a 35 metre-long fissure in the marble near the northeastern edge of the Acropolis which revealed a spring. A well (called the Clepsydra) was dug here and a set of steps down to it. This was an important source of fresh water for the city and to protect it a nine-gated wall (the Enneapylon) was built at the foot of the Acropolis. Between 570 and 550 BCE, a temple dedicated to Athena Polias (the Hekatompedon) was built on the northeastern side of the hill, near where the Parthenon stands today. In the 5th century BCE, the Parthenon (dedicated to Athena), the Propylaea (a gateway on the Western end of the Acropolis), the Erechtheion (dedicated to both Athena and Poseidon) and the temple of Athena Nike were built (Figure 2.8). However, these buildings were erected

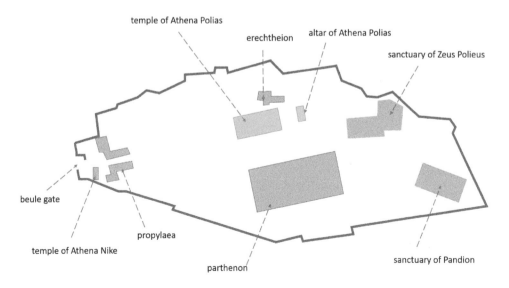

more than a thousand years after the time of Daidalos.

As can be seen in Figure 2.8, little remains of Mycenaean Athens.

The Minoans, being the dominant culture of the Aegean during the early LH period, exerted a strong influence over the Mycenaean palaces in terms of their social organisation, their technology and their arts and crafts. Like Minoan palaces, they functioned as administrative, ceremonial, production and storage centres. All Mycenaean palaces appear to have been very similar and, although very little remains of the one at Athens, it can be assumed to have been similar to those found at other sites. Unfortunately, little remains of any of the palaces of the LH I and II periods but they are thought to have been built around a long rectangular room known as a megaron. However, the remains of later (14th century) palaces have been found at many Mycenaean sites and we have a good idea of what they were like. The focal point was the megaron (Figure 2.9) which was a throne room containing a circular hearth surrounded by four columns which, like Minoan columns, were

Figure 2.9. Artist's impression of the megaron at Mycenae

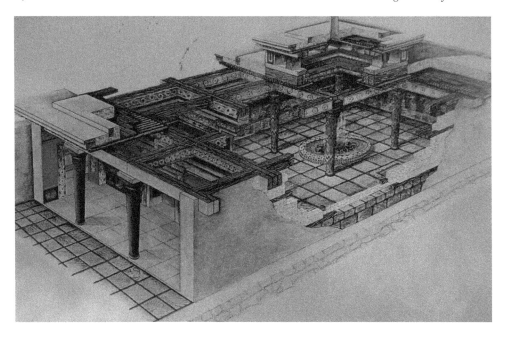

tapered so that they were wider at the top than at the bottom.

The megaron was not very large and would have easily fitted into the central court of the Knossos palace (see later). Internally, it was lavishly decorated with images of octopi, fish, dolphins etc. Access to it was via a monumental gateway (i.e. a propylon or propylaeum) and court. Around the megaron were courtyards which opened onto storerooms, workshops, reception halls and living quarters (Figure 2.10).

Unlike Minoan palaces, temples were not usually present in Mycenaean palaces, although small shrines have been found and these were often dedicated to Poseidon. Religious buildings and areas were often located outside of, but close to, the palace. A further significant difference from Minoan palaces was the presence of a defensive wall surrounding the palace.

Mycenaean society was very hierarchical. The wanax was not only the overall leader (king) but also had an important religious role as he presided over sacrificial feasts conducted in the palace. Beneath the wanax was the "lawageta" who was a military leader, landowner and also a religious official although, unlike the wanax, he did not make political appointments. Beneath the lawageta was a band of aristo-

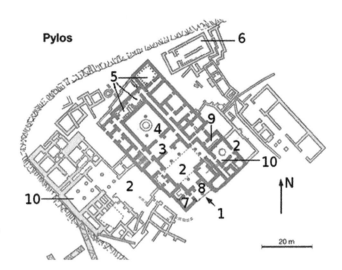

Figure 2.10. Plan of the palace at Pylos

1. Entrance, 2. Court, 3. Antechamber, 4. Megaron (main hall), 5. Storerooms with olive oil, 6. Storerooms with wine, 7. Archives, 8. Propylon, 9. Bath, 10. Small megaron

cratic warriors known as the "hekwetai" (followers) and a group of administrators known as the "collectors". It has been suggested that the rise of this elite class was attributable to the wealth derived from the booty brought back from military campaigns.

The lower strata included farmers, craftsmen and slaves. The palace housed records, mainly of business transactions, using the Linear B script on clay tablets. The text was inscribed on a damp clay tablet using a sharp stylus, usually made of bone or metal. The tablet was then left to dry in the sun. Fortunately for us, when the palaces were destroyed by fire, these clay tablets were baked and this enabled them to survive to the present day.

Agriculture was highly organised and the land used for agriculture was basically of two types – privately-owned (by the wanax and lawageta) and publically-owned. The main crops were wheat, barley, lentils, olives and grapes. Wool and flax were also produced while pigs, goats, sheep, and cattle were herded. The Mycenaeans traded widely (e.g. with Sicily, Syria, Egypt, Libya and Anatolia) and their fleets (Figure 2.11) dominated the eastern Mediterranean. Major exports included bronze weapons, jewellery, olive oil, wine, wool and stemmed drinking cups.

Figure 2.11. Reconstruction of a Mycenaean ship

Mycenaean Greece was a war-like culture as evidenced by the large number of weapons that have been unearthed, the frequent use of warrior and combat scenes in their art, and the huge defensive walls surrounding their cities. According to records found in the palace of Pylos, every rural community had to supply a certain number of men who had to serve in the army. The weapons used included spears, swords, daggers (Figure 2.12), maces, bows, axes,

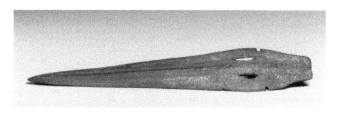

Figure 2.12. Mycenaean copper dagger (ca. 1450–1050 BCE)

(a) Drawing based on a fresco at Pylos, Greece, showing two helmeted warriors and a chariot (about 1350 BCE)

(b) Drawing based on a fresco of a Mycenaean woman (circa 1300 BCE)

Figure 2.13. Examples of frescoes found in Mycenaean palaces.

slings and javelins. Horse-drawn chariots were widely used in warfare.

Typically, soldiers wore a helmet made from the tusks of wild boar, bronze armour and a shield for protection.

The frescoes (Figure 2.13) that decorated the walls of the palaces were in a style similar to that found in Knossos and portrayed hunting, bull leaping, battle scenes, processions, etc. The frescos fall into several main categories: (a) scenes from everyday life, (b) scenes of religious activities, (c) battle scenes, (d). portrayals of animals in their natural surroundings and (e). purely decorative elements such as spirals, teeth etc.

Pottery was also heavily influenced by the Minoans, particularly during the early phase of the period i.e. 1600-1450 BCE, and was typically decorated with stylized representations of marine and plant life. However, it evolved continually throughout the period in terms of style and decoration. Pots were often light in colour and the designs were often painted with a red to black iron-based colour (Figure 2.14).

(a) Long-beaked jug (15th century BCE). This jug has a long beak-like spout showing a Minoan influence. The body of the vessel has simple designs based on the nautilus that are also common on Minoan pottery.

(b) Terracotta kylix (drinking cup) with flower (ca. 1300–1225 BCE).

Figure 2.14. Mycenaean pottery

Despite the war-like nature of the Mycenaeans, much time and effort was also put into the manufacture of luxury goods such as jewellery, carved gems, vases in precious metals and glass ornaments (Figure 2.15).

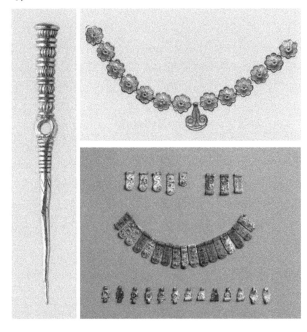

(a) Gold pin (ca. 14th century BCE).

(b) Gilt terracotta ornaments from a necklace (ca. 1400–1050 BCE).

(c). Glass ornaments (ca. 1370–1200 BCE). The presence of tiny holes through each of these indicates that they were strung together, and evidence from excavations shows that they were worn as diadems and as necklaces.

(d). Gold kantharos (drinking cup with two high vertical handles) ca. 1550–1500 BCE.

(e). Glass ornaments with gold leaf overlay (ca. 1370–1200 BCE).

Figure 2.15. Examples of Mycenaean luxury goods

Interestingly, a series of golden funerary masks were found on bodies within a burial site in Mycenae by Heinrich Schliemann during his 1876 excavation. A total of seven masks were found and one of these was claimed by Schliemann to be the death mask of Agamemnon (Figure 2.16). In a telegram, he said to the King of Greece: "I have gazed upon the face of Agamemnon." However, the mask was later dated to 1580-1550 BCE which is approximately three hundred years earlier than the Trojan war and the time of Agamemnon.

Little is known of the religious beliefs of the Mycenaeans during Daidalos' time in Athens. Most of the religious sites identified belong to the later LH III period (approximately 1450-1100 BCE). Some of these are located within the megaron where there are low steps against the wall opposite the entrance on which votive offerings were placed. Portable altars have also been found within the palaces. Separate buildings, referred to as "cult centres" have also been identified outside the palaces. Terracotta figurines have frequently been found in these centres as well as in ordinary houses (Figure 2.17).

Evidence of Mycenaean religious practices comes from their depiction in frescos in palaces as well as

Figure 2.16. Photograph of the gold "mask of Agamemnon"

on sealstones, rings, figurines (Figure 2.18) and vases. These, like their equivalents in Crete, portray processions, scenes of worship and offerings being made to goddesses in the open air.

The texts on Linear B clay tablets from the mid-15th century BCE shed little light on the Mycenaean's religious practices. These were found mainly in Pylos, Mycenae, Tiryns and Thebes but only record the expenses involved in specific sacrifices. Nevertheless, they do give us the names of the gods who received these sacrifices and these included Zeus, Hera, Poseidon, Artemis, Hermes and Dionysus. In addition to these well-known divinities, who re-surfaced after the dark ages in archaic Greece, mention is also made of the "Mistress of animals" (Potnia Theron) who, perhaps, is equated to Athena. Of particular interest are references to two female goddesses, Dinja and Posidaeja, whose names are connected etymologically with Zeus and Poseidon respectively. This hints at the conversion of female deities from the matriarchal "old religion" to the new patriarchal religion that dominated after the dark ages[2].

With regard to daily life in Athens during the early

Figure 2.17. Three Terracotta female figures (ca. 1400–1300 BCE).

These terracotta female figurines are referred to as phi, tau, or psi figurines, because of their resemblance to those Greek letters. They generally wear a long, enveloping garment, perhaps a kind of robe. Their long hair is usually drawn back in a plait or "ponytail," with some loose locks over the forehead. The two phi-type figurines (on the right) have circular bodies covered with painted wavy lines, perhaps indicating folds of drapery. Breasts are indicated, although the arms are little more than bulges hanging down at the sides. Their faces are typically pinched, with eyes applied as separate slips of clay. The tau-type figurine on the left has the usual hollow, columnar stem with the head somewhat larger in proportion to the body. Characteristically, the figure is high waisted with arms folded over the breasts. Like the other two figurines, this one wears a long garment, only here it is simply decorated with two vertical lines down the front and back.

LH period, we know very little. The staple diet for the common people would probably have been bread made from wheat or barley. This would have been supplemented with a wide range of vegetables, fruits and nuts including peas, beans, vetch, lentils, figs, pears, apples, plums, almonds, walnuts and hazelnuts. Other important items would have been olive oil, cheese, honey and wine. A wide range of meats and fish were available, although these were probably consumed mainly by the upper echelons of society. These included lamb, goat, pork, beef, venison, wild boar, hares, ducks, geese, partridges, fish, shellfish and octopi.

Figure 2.18. Terracotta female figure in three-legged chair (13th century BCE). Such representations are often interpreted as portraying a deity sitting on a throne.

We know about the clothing worn in these times from frescos and other works of art. Mycenaean women were dressed in a similar way to their Cretan counterparts – they wore a tight bodice with short sleeves, their breasts were left uncovered and they had a long, pleated skirt (see Figure 2.13b). Some of these clothes were richly decorated with gold sequins and the skirt hems were bordered with thin gold plate. Jewellery, including necklaces, rings and earrings, was worn.

Of course, we do not know whether the clothes portrayed were the clothes that women wore every day or whether they were reserved for special occasions or, perhaps, worn only by priestesses and/or members of the ruling classes.

Everyday clothing for men appeared to consist of a loincloth or short kilt. On formal occasions, they wore a short-sleeved tunic, a short skirt and leggings.

Following the decline of the Minoan civilization in the 15th century BCE, the Mycenaeans became the dominant culture in the Aegean and expanded their influence throughout the Mediterranean. One of their most important achievements was, of course, the invention of the Linear B writing system (Figure 2.19) which was used from approximately 1450 to 1100 BCE.

The script was used for the economic administration of the Mycenaean palaces, mainly those at Mycenae, Pylos, Thebes and Tiryns on mainland Greece as well as at Knossos in Crete. The Mycenaeans ruled Crete from about 1450 BCE and fought wars against cities in Asia Minor such as Troy. However, by the end of the 13th century BCE, most of the Mycenaean centres (with the important exception of Athens) had been destroyed and abandoned, this was due to a combination of factors including natural disaster and invasion by the Dorians and/or the mysterious "sea-peoples" who were raiding coastal towns throughout the Mediterranean at the time.

Although we have portrayed an advanced society

Figure 2.19. This linear letter sequence in linear B translates as "a-ta-na-po-ti-ni-ja". The inscription was found on a clay tablet in Knossos and is considered to refer to the name of the Greek goddess Athena.

that was highly organised and, for the ruling elite, quite luxurious, this was characteristic of Mycenaean cities during their most flourishing period i.e. the 14th and 13th centuries BCE. However, Daidalos would have been in Athens during the early Mycenaean period, which was two or three centuries before this golden age, and what life would have been like for him at that time is difficult to determine. It is unlikely that it would have been as luxurious as that described for the Mycenaeans at their peak. Nevertheless, as a renowned sculptor, and inventor, it is likely that he would have been a member of the elite and treated accordingly. We can imagine, however, that there would have been an edginess to daily life due to the overall bellicose nature of the culture. The defensive walls surrounding Athens were there to provide protection against neighbouring Mycenaean cities and, later, against invaders from the North and the "sea peoples" (Figure 2.20). It was Athens' proud boast that it was the only city that did not fall to the invaders that overwhelmed other Mycenaean cities around the beginning of the 12th century BCE.

Perhaps, as an ambitious young man, Daidalos would have been rather glad to leave Athens and

Figure 2.20. Migrations, invasions and destructions during the end of the Bronze Age (c. 1200 BCE). This was a time of great upheaval and resulted in the downfall or weakening of a number of Mediterranean empires.

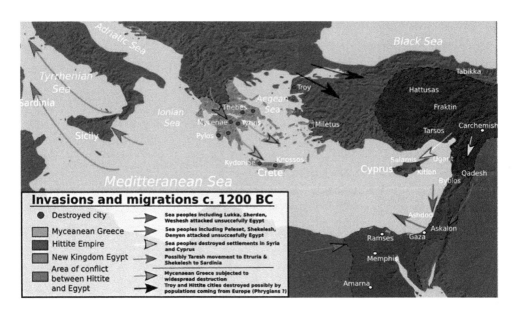

Invasions and migrations c. 1200 BC

- Destroyed city
- Myceanean Greece
- Hittite Empire
- New Kingdom Egypt
- Area of conflict between Hittite and Egypt

Sea peoples including Lukka, Sherden, Weshesh attacked unsuccefully Egypt
Sea peoples including Peleset, Shekelesh, Denyen attacked unsuccessfully Egypt
Sea peoples destroyed settlements in Syria and Cyprus
Possibly Taresh movement to Etruria & Shekelesh to Sardinia
Myceanean Greece subjected to widespread destruction
Troy and Hittite cities destroyed possibly by populations coming from Europe (Phrygians ?)

take his chances at making his way in Minoan society which was not only considerably more affluent but would have offered greater possibilities for such a multi-talented individual.

Daidalos in Knossos

All of the ancient writers describe how Daidalos was a guest/employee of king Minos and so we know exactly where he would have lived - in the palace of Knossos on the island of Crete (Figure 2.21).

The earliest mention of Knossos was by Homer[3] in *The Iliad*: "...on a dancing-floor like unto that which in wide Cnosus Daidalos fashioned..." Both Knossos and Crete are referred to in the famous "catalogue of ships" in *The Iliad*[4]: "And the Cretans had as leader Idomeneus, famed for his spear, even they that held Cnosus and Gortys, famed for its walls, Lyctus and Miletus and Lycastus, white with chalk, and Phaestus and Rhytium, well-peopled cities; and all they beside that dwelt in Crete of the hundred cities."

Figure 2.21. Map of Minoan Crete showing the location of the main palaces and other important sites.

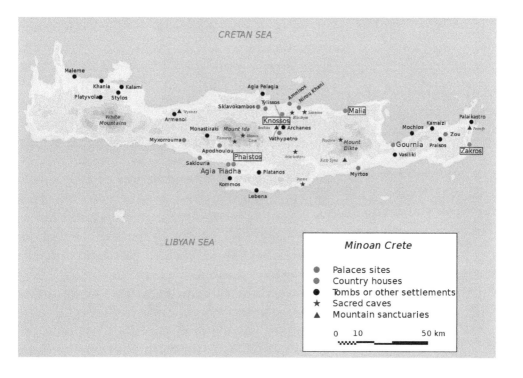

Figure 2.22. Sir Arthur J. Evans. Much of the material he excavated at Knossos is currently housed in the Ashmolean Museum, Oxford.

In *The Odyssey*, as well as referring to Knossos, Homer gives a short description of the island of Crete[5]: "There is a land called Crete, in the midst of the wine-dark sea, a fair, rich land, begirt with water, and therein are many men, past counting, and ninety cities. They have not all the same speech, but their tongues are mixed. There dwell Achaeans, there great-hearted native Cretans, there Cydonians, and Dorians of waving plumes, and goodly Pelasgians. Among their cities is the great city Cnosus, where Minos reigned when nine years old..." Crete, at the time, appears to have been a highly-urbanised and polyglot society. Interestingly, this excerpt also mentions King Minos. Hesiod, a Greek writer in the 8th century BCE, also talks about Mino in his *Catalogues of Women*[6]: "Minos, who was most kingly of mortal kings and reigned over very many people dwelling round about, holding the sceptre of Zeus wherewith he ruled many cities..." Unfortunately, only fragments of his *Catalogues of Women* remain. One of the things for which Crete was renowned was its law codes. These were among the earliest developed and were greatly admired in the Greek world and Aristotle, in his lost *Constitution of the Cretans*, wrote that Minos revised the laws of Crete every 10 years. These revisions occurred following consultation with Zeus on Mount Ida[7].

So what would life have been like for Daidalos in Knossos? Because of the absence of any decipherable contemporary texts (see the insert on Minoan writing), piecing together what Minoan history, culture and religion were like has proved to be a huge problem. All we have to go on is what has been uncovered by archaeological studies carried out by Sir Arthur Evans (Figure 2.22) and later investigators. The palace of Knossos has been the subject of intense investigation since its discovery in 1878 by Minos Kalokairinos and its first excavation by Sir Arthur Evans in 1900.

Knossos was the main prehistoric settlement on Crete and has been inhabited since approximately

7,000 BCE. It is situated on a hill (Kephala Hill) that lies between the confluence of two streams (the Vlychia Stream and the Kairatos River) and is located about 5 miles inland from the coast, south of the modern city of Heraklion. The first palace was built there during the period 1950-1800 BCE and, despite numerous destructive episodes (earthquakes, fire etc), it was never replaced by a new structure and was finally abandoned more than 500 years later in approximately 1370 BCE. However, during this long period it went through periods of expansion as well as extensive re-modelling following various disasters. During its final 75 years, it was occupied by the Myceneans rather than the Minoans.

On its west side there was a town consisting of mudbrick and wooden houses (Figure 2.23) which had a population of approximately 70,000 and this, together with the palace, constitutes the first truly urban centre in Europe.

Although we don't have an exact date for when Daidalos was in Knossos, we do know that, at the time of his sojourn there, the Minoan civilisation, under King Minos, was at the peak of its power and influence. It is reasonable, therefore, to give a depiction of life at Knossos as it would have been during this era - approximately the 16th century BCE. One small diver-

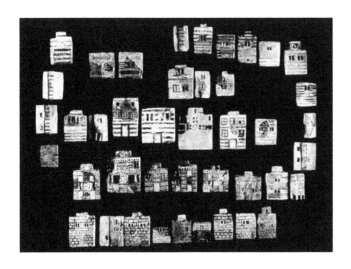

Figure 2.23. A group of small tablets each depicting the front of a house. These were found in the palace of Knossos.

sion. It was Sir Arthur Evans who coined the term "Minoan" (after King Minos) for the civilization he discovered in Crete in 1900. The Minoans certainly did not use such a term. Crete was known as Keftiu by the Egyptians (Figure 2.24), Kaptaru by the Syrians and is referred to in the bible as Kaphtor or Kaptor.

The palace of Knossos was, unquestionably, a magnificent and complex edifice and Figure 2.25 shows a plan of its overall structure in approximately 1500 BCE.

Its multitude of rooms, corridors and courtyards is truly labyrinthine. Surprisingly, there do not appear to be any defensive walls and this has been attributed to the superiority of the Cretan navy who "ruled the

Figure 2.24. Cretans (Keftiu) bringing gifts. Details from a wall painting in the tomb of Rekhmire the vizier, the highest official under the pharaohs Tuthmosis III and Amenophis II (1479–1425 BCE). The tomb was outside Thebes, Egypt. The fresco was labelled "gifts from the princes of the land of Keftiu and of the isles that are in the midst of the sea".

waves" and would have been the main means of defence for this island nation (Figure 2.26).

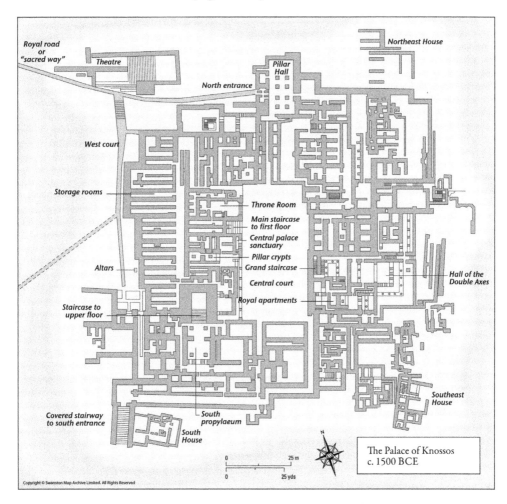

Figure 2.25. Plan of the palace of Knossos in approximately 1500 BCE showing the location of the main features discussed in the text.

Thucydides (an Athenian historian born in 460 BCE) tells us:[8] "And the first person known to us by tradition as having established a navy is Minos. He made himself master of what is now called the Hellenic sea, and ruled over the Cyclades, into most of which he sent the first colonies, expelling the Carians and appointing his own sons governors; and thus did his best to put down piracy in those waters." As we will see (Chapter 4), Daidalos was credited with the invention of sails and masts. If this was an exaggeration of his talents, perhaps his contribution was to improve on sail design and this might account for the superiority of the Minoan navy.

Figure 2.26 Replica of a Minoan ship.

Figure 2.27. Artist's impression of the Palace of Knossos as it may have looked in the 2nd millennium BCE.

The palace of Knossos was the largest Minoan building ever built. It covered approximately 20,000 square metres and would have housed approximately 12,000 people. Although what has been uncovered has revealed it to be a prosperous and highly-devel-

ΚΝΩΣΟΣ · KNOSSOS

oped centre, interpretation of its functions and organisation remain speculative due to the absence of descriptive records. It was roughly rectangular in shape with a huge gateway in each of the sides. In some places, it had up to five storeys and on the ground floor there were approximately 300 rooms – the whole palace may have had 1600 rooms in total. Figure 2.27 is an artist's impression of what it may have looked like.

Bull-leaping

Bull-leaping is represented on frescos, pottery and seals and appears to have been an important feature of Minoan religious practices. What we know of its practice is, of course, based on these representations as we have no written description of how it was enacted. Its objective seems to have been the domination of the bull without actually harming it, although the animal may have subsequently been ritually slaughtered. The performers appear to have worked in pairs consisting of a boy and a girl, although the girl was always dressed in male clothing.

The performance is likely to have involved the following sequence. First, the boy approached the head of the bull then grabbed its horns and swung himself up onto the back of the bull, turning in the air as he did so. This resulted in him standing on the bull's back facing its rear end. He then did a forward somersault, leaving the bull's back and landed on the ground where he was supported by the girl's outstretched arms.

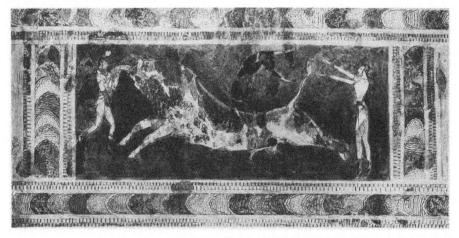

Bull-Leaping Fresco from Knossos Palace.

As can be seen from Figure 2.25, the palace consisted of four main wings arranged around a rectangular central courtyard approximately 45 x 23 m. In this courtyard, various procession and ceremonies were enacted and the sport of bull-leaping was practised (Figure 2.28).

Figure 2.28. Silhouette drawing of the famous Bull-leaping fresco in the palace of Knossos (see Box on previous page).

Limestone was the main material used for building the palace although gypsum was used for areas that were protected from the weather. The internal walls were faced with alabaster. Cypress wood was extensively used e.g. in columns (which were characteristically downward-tapering), as beams, on stairways, as window and door frames. Clay bricks were used for the upper stories.

(a) The Gypsum Throne in the "Throne Room" of the palace of Knossos.

(b) The Throne Room in the Palace of Knossos. The throne can be seen up against the far wall which is decorated with frescos.

Figure 2.29. The throne room in the palace of Knossos.

The west wing was probably the administrative centre and consisted of storage rooms as well as rooms for the enactment of rituals. It also housed one of the most important complexes of the palace which consisted of the Throne Room (Figure 2.29), the Lustral Basin and associated ancillary rooms.

The throne room was windowless and contained an alabaster seat up against a wall painted with griffons. The seat was flanked by altar benches and in front of it was a stone offering bowl. It was connected to the central court via an anteroom.

The lustral basin was for ritual washing of those participants partaking in whatever ceremonies were performed there. It is thought that the complex was used for rituals associated with Potnia ("The mistress"), a mother goddess.

Another site of ritual significance in the West Wing was the Snake Goddess Sanctuary in which were found large numbers of statuettes of the Snake Goddess (Figure 2.30).

(a) This statuette is typical of the many ceramic and faience examples found in the palace of Knossos. It is made of gold and ivory (15th century BCE).

(b) The goddess wears a tall headdress with a snake wound around it. Her hands are pierced to hold snakes (16th century BCE)

Figure 2.30. Statuettes of the snake goddess from the palace of Knossos. Many of these objects are identified as priestesses or goddesses and are associated with fertility.

Storerooms containing giant pithoi for storing oil, grains and wine were also present in the west wing (Figure 2.31). Each pithos could hold approximately 230 Litres and there was room for approximately 400 pithoi which means that the storage capacity in the west wing alone amounted to almost 100,000 Litres. On the upper floors there were banqueting halls.

In the East Wing were the Royal Apartments which were richly adorned with frescoes (Figure 2.32) and a grand staircase (Figure 2.33) consisting of 54 steps which descended through four stories to the hall of the Double Axes (Figure 2.34).

Figure 2.31. A restored Cretan pithos – 122 cm high (7th century BCE)

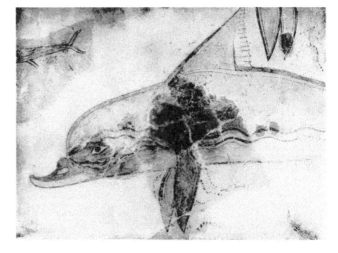

*Figure 2.32. Part of the dolphin fresco from the Queen's megaron. Colour photographs of this and other frescos in the palace can be seen at **https://isaw.nyu.edu/exhibitions/minoans/objects***

Figure 2.33. Photograph showing part of the grand staircase and the Hall of Colonnades.

Figure 2.34. Central and eastern sections of the Hall of the Double Axes. The bases of two rows of columns can be seen (right and foreground) as well as the remains of the upper door jambs (to the left)

Storage rooms and craft workshops were also present and it is here, perhaps, that Daidalos made his sculptures and developed his inventions. The North Wing had storerooms and also many chambers, one of which was decorated with the famous bull-leaping fresco.

In the South Wing is a corridor in which one of the walls is decorated with the famous "Prince of the Lillies" fresco (this can be seen at *https://isaw.nyu.edu/exhibitions/minoans/objects*) and the south gateway was once topped by the emblematic "Horns of Consecration", a phrase introduced by Arthur Evans. The bull was a sacred animal in ancient Crete and played a large role in religious rituals. The horns of consecration (see Figures 2.35 and 2.43) were placed on the roofs of buildings as well as on tombs and shrines and were thought to represent the horns of a sacrificial bull. They were also depicted in frescoes (Figure 2.35) and on seals.

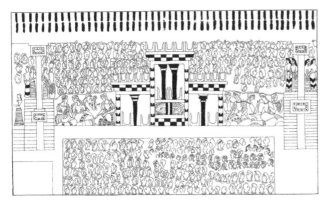

Figure 2.35. Reconstruction drawing of the Grandstand Fresco from the Palace of Knossos. This was found in the central court and probably depicts a crowd viewing some event taking place there. Note the tripartite shrine and horns of consecration.

Satisfying the basic needs of the palace's inhabitants would have been an immense task. Food would have been plentiful and the vast storage capacity provided by the large numbers of pithoi in the palace would have ensured supplies during times of drought or crop failure. The main foods were grains (wheat and barley), legumes (peas, lentils, chickpeas), fruits (figs, apples, pears, grapes, quince), nuts (almonds, pistachios, chestnuts), seeds (poppy, sesame, castor) and olives. Cattle, goats, sheep, pigs, geese, deer wild boar, partridges and fish were the main sources of meat, but chickens and ducks were not available. A variety of herbs were used in cooking and these included coriander, cumin, fennel, celery, mint, safflower and cress.

Large quantities of water would have been needed by the many inhabitants of the palace for a variety of purposes including cooking, cleaning, rituals and personal hygiene. It would also have been needed for a variety of crafts such as dyeing, pottery, winemaking etc. Water was delivered to Knossos via aqueducts from springs at Archanes which is about 10 km away. Rainwater was also collected on rooftops and diverted to large cisterns. It was distributed throughout the

Figure 2.36. Terracotta pipes were used in the water delivery system at Knossos. The end of each section was tapered so that it would fit tightly into the next section.

Figure 2.37. Part of the stone drain uncovered below the North entrance of the palace.

palace by an elaborate and sophisticated system of clay pipes (Figure 2.36).

The palace had flushing toilets which were connected to an elaborate sewage disposal system (Figure 2.37). The Minoans were the first civilisation to use underground clay pipes for sanitation and water supply – 1500 years before the Romans. Individual bathtubs (Figure 2.38) have been found in the palace but it is not known how widely available they would have been.

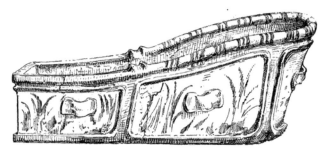

Figure 2.38. Drawing of a bathtub from the palace of Knossos

Heating was supplied to some of the rooms by means of a hypocaust system. This involved producing hot air in a furnace and circulating this through under-floor ducting.

As for entertainment, there was feasting, music, singing, story-telling, dancing, boxing, wrestling, running, jumping, bull-leaping and board games (Figure 2.39).

Crete had extensive trade links with other parts of the Mediterranean and its wealth was derived from the export of a variety of goods. This was aided by the dominance of the Cretan navy[9] "...as soon as Minos had formed his navy, communication by sea became easier, as he colonized most of the islands..."

Figure 2.39. Left-hand upper corner of a gaming board inlaid with ivory, blue glass paste and rock crystal, plated with gold and silver from the palace at Knossos (1700-1450 BCE). The rules of the game remain unknown. The drawing illustrates a restoration of part of the board. The complete restoration can be seen at https://www.artefactsalive.com/tzax/ ancient

One of its most important exports was decorative, painted and distinctively-shaped pottery. This was regarded as the finest pottery in the world at the time (Figure 2.40) and was exported all over the Aegean. The Minoans were superb craftsmen and sophisticated works were produced in a variety of materials. Other important exports therefore included; lead figurines, bronze figurines, vessels made of gold, silver and bronze and even decorative ostrich eggs. Minoan goods have been found as far west as the Lipari Islands (off the Italian coast), Troy in the north, Egypt in the south and Syria in the east. Egyptian tomb paintings in Thebes show Cretans bearing gifts of silver and gold cups as well as pottery, jewellery and metal ingots (Figure 2.24).

Examples of a variety of objects showing the range of Minoan craftsmanship are shown in Figure 2.40.

Other important exports were olive oil, wine,

Figure 2.40. Examples of Minoan craftsmanship

(a) Minoan gold ornaments (2300-2100 BCE)

(b) Minoan Terracotta jar with three handles (1600-1500 BCE).

(c) Terracotta conical rhyton (vase for liquid offerings) ca. 1600–1500 BCE

(d) Minoan cup (1600-1450 BCE)

(e) Group of 6 serpentine bowls (1600-1450 BCE)

(f) Terracotta vase in the form of a bull's head (1450-1400 BCE). This vase is a type of rhyton, or libation vase. The offering was poured through the hole in the animal's muzzle.

(g) Decorated clay jug (ca. 1575-1500 BCE). This is one of the most famous works of Minoan pottery. It shows five molluscs (nautili) floating above the sea floor and demonstrates the Minoans' love of bold, sweeping designs.

Minoan writing

Examination of seals, clay tablets and other objects at Knossos has revealed that three types of writing were in use – hieroglyphic, Linear A and Linear B. Of these, Linear B is the most recent and was deciphered by Michael Ventris in 1952. Unfortunately, only 300 words in Cretan hieroglyphic and 800 words in Linear A have been found and such small numbers have prevented them from being fully deciphered. Cretan hieroglyphics are pictographic i.e. they convey their meaning through their resemblance to physical objects. Sir Arthur Evans used the term "Linear" to describe the other scripts he found in Knossos because the characters used were mainly composed of lines rather than pictograms.

Hieroglyphics (Figure a) were probably in use prior to Linear A (Figure b) but both of these scripts then appear to have been in use concurrently for some time although the latter continued to be used for much longer. Hieroglyphics were used during the period 2100 to 1675 BCE but were then abandoned. Linear A was used from 1925 to 1470 BCE but was then replaced by Linear B which was introduced by the Mycenaeans. Although neither the Cretan hieroglyphics nor Linear A script have been deciphered, some understanding of both has been achieved. They appear to have been used mainly for administrative purposes. It is generally thought that Linear A represents a pre-Hellenic language that is not related to Greek.

Figure a. The Phaistos Disc. This is a clay disc discovered in the palace at Phaistos, Crete. It is covered with Cretan hieroglyphs and symbols and is believed to have been made sometime between 1850 and 1600 BCE.

Linear B (Figure 2.19) emerged around 1500 BCE and is an adaptation of Linear A that enabled the writing down of Mycenaean Greek – an archaic form of the Greek language. It is, therefore, the oldest written form of Greek. With the ascendancy of the Mycenaeans in Crete, Linear A was abandoned and all writing in Crete and Greece was subsequently in Linear B.

Linear B was deciphered by Michael Ventris in 1952. Many of the clay tablets found in Crete are concerned with dealings relating to sheep and it has been estimated that there were approximately 100,000 sheep on the island. Other examples of the type of information on the tablets include:

(i) Dynios owes the palace 2,220 litres of barley, 526 litres of olives, 468 litres of wine, 15 ams, 8 yearlings, one ewe, 13 he-goats, 12 pigs, one fat hog, one cow and 2 bulls

(ii) The names of 4 oxen – dusky, dapple, whitefoot and noisy
(iii) The wheat and fig rations for 37 bath attendants and 28 children in Pylos

Figure b. Copy of inscriptions in Linear A
written round the inner surface of a cup (1750-1650 BCE)

Minoan seals

These are small semi-precious or common stones that have been polished, pierced and engraved with images, patterns or inscriptions (Figures a and b). When pressed into wax or clay they left an impression that identified the seal owner. They could therefore be used as a signature on clay tablets or to denote ownership of goods or objects. As well as denoting ownership, their use also facilitated business transactions and could be used as evidence of the existence of contracts and agreements between individuals. They were usually worn on a cord around the neck or as a bracelet or pendant and so also functioned as jewellery. Sometimes they were attached to metal rings so they could be worn on a finger. A wide range of materials was used in their construction including marble, quartz, jasper, agate, amethyst, bone, ivory, steatite, carnelian, haematite, chalcedony, lapis lazuli, obsidian, rock crystal and gold. The final shape of the seal also varied considerably and could be in the form of a button, lens, almond, cylinder, cone, prism, crescent or an animal. For many centuries, up to modern times, Cretan women wore these seals, which they found on the Kephala Hill, in the belief that they ensured that nursing mothers would have a plentiful supply of milk they were known as "milk stones". The designs were sometimes exquisite and intricate, demonstrating the great skills of the carvers – they commonly featured animals, dancing, goddesses, altars and bull-leaping. In Phaistos, a total of 327 different seals were found and most of these had geometric designs but 22% had more complex images of plants, animals and humans.

(a) Minoan sealstone depicting a Bull (15th century BCE)

(b) A Minoan cylinder seal made from haematite and a modern impression taken from it (14th century BCE). It depicts the "Master of Animals" between lions and griffins.

currants, timber (particularly cypress wood), herbs, cloth and woollen goods. Crete also functioned as a distribution centre for metals that were shipped in from Central Europe. Recent research has suggested that Crete is likely to have been the major centre of production of one of the most highly-prized dyes of the ancient world known as Royal Purple or Tyrian Purple (Figure 2.41).

This dye is extracted from a tiny gland (the hypo-branchial gland) of two types of sea snail - *Murex trunculus* and *Murex branda* (Figure 2.42).

Figure 2.41. A small sample Royal Purple and an example of cloth dyed with it.

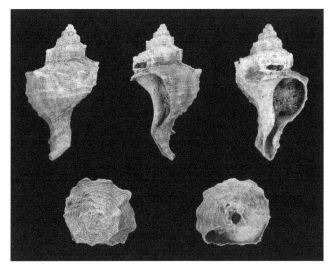

Figure 2.42. Fossilised shells of Murex trunculus *found in Kos, Greece*

Thousands of such shells have been found at excavations at a number of Cretan sites and recently a workshop for the production of the dye was found at Pefka on the south coast. A Linear B tablet from Knossos (KN X976) has the words "wa-na-ka-te-ro po-pu-re" inscribed on it and these mean "royal purple". It is likely that Crete was the main centre of Royal Purple production and export in the Aegean and Mediterranean regions from as early as 2,500 BCE. Tyrian purple was expensive and Theopompus (a 4th century BCE Greek historian) tells us that[10] "Purple for dyes fetched its weight in silver..."

As for imports, these would have included silver and lead (from the Cyclades), ivory and lapis lazuli (from Syria), gold, alabaster and semi-precious stones from Egypt and copper from Cyprus. Tin, for bronze making, probably came from Spain and Italy but Portugal, Brittany and England (Cornwall) were also known to be major sources of this crucial metal in ancient times.

We know little about the Minoan religion and what we do know is based largely on the interpretation of images from frescos, pottery, seals and from figurines and votive offerings. Religious practices were carried out at three types of site on Crete – peak sanctuaries, cave sanctuaries and in palaces. Peak sanctuaries, as the name implies, were located on, or near to, mountain tops. The finds at such sites include figurines, stone vessels, double axes, "horns of consecration", seals, linear A inscriptions and jewellery. The peak sanctuary nearest to Knossos was located on Mount Jouktas which is 13 kilometres away and clearly visible from the palace. The buildings at these sites were often decorated with horns of consecration and contained a tripartite shrine (Figure 2.43). Such shrines had a middle section that was higher than the two flanking wings and invariably the roofs of all three sections were adorned with horns of consecration. We know little of who was worshipped at such sanctuaries but one possibility is that it was a goddess known as the "Mother of the Mountains".

Cave sanctuaries were very common and stalagmites were often used to mark out the most important areas of the cave. There is evidence that feasting and drinking rituals were carried out there.

During the time of Daidalos, the most important religious sites were within the palaces. In fact, it has been suggested that the term "palace" is a misnomer and that the main purpose of such buildings was to act as a religious centre although they also had important administrative and economic functions. At Knossos, the Throne Room was an important site for religious ceremonies. Originally it was thought that the throne belonged to the king, but nowadays many scholars think that it was occupied by the high priest-

Figure 2.43. Drawing of a tripartite shrine decorated with horns of consecration. From a fresco at Knossos.

ess when she played the role of a goddess during an epiphany ritual i.e. a ceremony that involved the summoning of the goddess and her resulting appearance. The tripartite shrine in the West Wing of the palace was also important in religious ceremonies. It has been suggested that the high priestess, representing a goddess, would have appeared to the crowds from between the columns of the shrine during an epiphany ritual. The West Court, which is above the underground granaries, may have been the site of a harvest festival or could have been where the bull was sacrificed after it had been used in the bull-leaping ceremony. Also in the West wing is the Snake Goddess sanctuary.

On the basis of the frequent representation of female goddesses in frescoes, statues (Figure 2.30) and on seals, it is likely that a female deity was the main focus of the Minoan religion. One school of thought suggests that one "Great Goddess" was worshipped although she appeared in a number of aspects including the "Mother Goddess", the "Mistress of the Animals", the "Guardian of Cities", the "Mistress of the Mountains" and the "Snake Goddess" (Figure 2.30). However, others have suggested that the Minoan pantheon included a large number of goddesses as well as gods. A very important religious ceremony appears to have been the summoning of a goddess and her resulting appearance. Often a high priestess would represent the goddess in such rituals but Minoan art also has representations of people worshipping a baetyl (a sacred rock), a tree or the dress of a goddess. Important objects associated with religious practices include horns of consecration (Figure 2.43), double-headed axes (Figures 2.44), bulls head rhyta (Figure 2.45) and images of bull-leaping and sacrifice.

As well as being supplied with all of his bodily needs, Daidalos would have had access to fine clothes and jewellery and would have been surrounded by beautiful works of art. He would have had a flushing

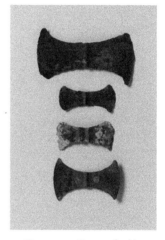

Figure 2.44. Bronze double-headed votive axes from the Diktean cave on Crete (1700-1450 BCE). Many others have been found and these were sometimes made of gold.

toilet, centrally-heated living quarters and his own bathtub. Furthermore, a wide variety of entertainments were available to him. Life would have been extremely pleasant for him while he lived in the palace. Also, we can imagine that Minos would have ensured that he was supplied with everything necessary for his many projects. Would he have engaged in the religious rituals that were regularly practised in the palace? We can imagine that Knossos would have been very much like an ancient version of *Gormenghast* with complex, probably bizarre, rituals being undertaken that might have bemused, or even amused, Daidalos. After all, he had been brought up in Athens with its different religious practices. I think he would have regarded such rituals as being ridiculous but would probably have kept his opinions to himself so as not to offend Minos who played an important role in the religious life of the city. However, as we shall see in the next chapter, he may have sought comfort from the gods following the death of his son.

Figure 2.45. Black steatite bulls-head rhyton (16th century BCE). This vessel also had a double axe on the brow. Liquid would have been poured into the circular opening at the top of the head and then would have dripped out of the small hole at the muzzle, suggesting that this object was intended to be used to make ritual libations.

Life in Sicily

Daidalos' stay in Sicily was at the court of King Cocalus, who ruled the Sicanians, at Kamikos. The Sicanians were the oldest of the three main groups of peoples indigenous to Sicily and occupied the central zone of the island while the Eastern and Western regions were occupied by the Siculi (Sicels) and Elymi (Elymians) respectively (Figure 2.46).

The Uluburun ship-wreck

In 1982 a sponge-diver discovered the remains of a bronze-age ship off the coast of Uluburun near the town of Kas in south-west Turkey. Excavation of the wreck revealed the largest and richest collection of bronze age trade goods ever found – 17 tons of artefacts have been recovered so far. The ship was dated to the late 14th century BCE and has given us enormous insight into Mediterranean trade of that time[11]. The cargo it carried consisted of raw materials and manufactured goods but personal effects and ship's equipment were also recovered. Most of the cargo came from Cyprus and the Syrian region and it was probably destined for somewhere in the Aegean. The raw materials consisted of: 10 tons of copper ingots, one ton of tin ingots, glass ingots, terebinth resin and oil, teeth of elephants and hippopotami, African blackwood (ebony) logs, spices, murex shell opercula and orpiment. A total of 348 copper ingots were recovered, each weighing approximately 24 kilograms. These were mainly in the form of oxhide-shaped slabs which is typical for that time (Figure a).

Figure a. Copper ingots from the Uluburun shipwreck.

Terebinth oil and resin are obtained from *Pistacia* trees and were used mainly in the manufacture of perfume and incense although they may also have been used medicinally. The operculum of the murex sea snail is a protective "trap-door" that protects the animal when it retracts inside its shell. It was used as an ingredient of incense. Orpiment is an orange-yellow arsenic mineral and was an important pigment used in painting (Figure b).

The manufactured goods included: Cypriot pottery, copper-alloy vessels, glass and faience beads, seashell rings, ivory and boxwood containers, gold and silver jewellery and vases made from ostrich eggshells.

Personal and shipboard goods included tools, balances, seals, weapons, galley-ware, lamps and jewellery. Analysis of these has revealed that the crew were Canaanite (i.e. from the region of modern Israel, Palestine, Lebanon, Jordan and Syria) merchants and sailors and these were accompanied by two Mycenaeans of elite status and another individual from somewhere North of Greece.

Figure b. A lump of the mineral orpiment showing the mark it can make on paper

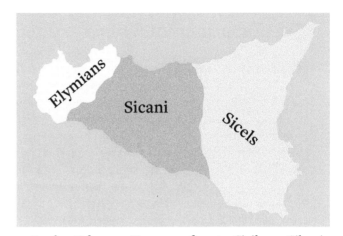

Figure 2.46. The approximate locations of the Elymians, Sicani and Sicels in Sicily during the bronze age prior to the arrival of the Phoenicians and the Greeks.

In the Odyssey, Homer refers to Sicily as Sikania and mentions the Sikanian Mountains which are located in the south-central region of the island. The main settlements were at Hyccara, Omphake and Kamikos. The exact location of Kamikos (Camicus), where Cocalus had his court, is not known but Sant'Angelo Muxaro (Figure 2.47) is currently regarded as being a likely possibility. This is spectacularly located on top of a hill approximately 35 Km from present-day Agrigento. The town has numerous bronze-age graves (circular rooms or rock-cut chambers with a domed roof known as Tholoi) and in these have been found grave goods such as cups and gold rings dated to 1200-1300 BCE. One of these, known as the "Tomb of the Prince" is 3.5 m high and has a diameter of 8.8 m.

Figure 2.47. Panoramic view of Sant'Angelo Muxaro which was possibly the location of Kamikos.

There is evidence that the Sicani had contact with the Minoans and Mycenaeans and in approximately 1500 BCE the Mycenaeans started establishing trading posts in Sicily. Little is known of their culture except that they were active traders and an important link on the trade route of copper from Spain to the eastern Mediterranean. Strabo, in his *Geography* written in the 1st century CE, states that:[12] "Many of the barbarian cities, also, have been wiped out; for example, Camici [i.e. Camicus], the royal residence of Cocalus, at which Minos is said to have been murdered by treachery."

Excavations at Thapsos (located on a peninsula known as Magnisi near present-day Priolo Gargallo, approximately 8 miles north-west of Syracuse – Figure 2.48) have revealed a little about the culture of the times and this is regarded as typical of the middle bronze age (1700-1350 BCE) throughout Sicily. During this period settlements were becoming more permanent and more populous.

The residential quarter of the settlement occupied an area that is approximately 1000 m long and 300 m

Figure 2.48. Aerial photograph of the Thapsos peninsula.

wide and this was located on the higher, western, side of the peninsular (Figure 2.49).

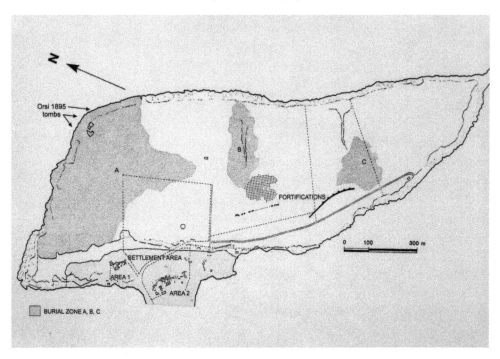

Figure 2.49. Map of the settlement at Thapsos showing the residential areas (area 1 and area 2), the burial zones (A, B and C) and the remains of fortifications.

Adjacent to this were the burial grounds. The houses at Thapsos generally consisted of small, circular or rectangular stone huts with stone foundations and their thatched roofs were supported by internal wooden poles (Figure 2.50). The floor and internal walls were plastered and a low stone bench flanked the inside walls. The door usually faced south. A hearth and cooking platform were usually near the centre of the house. These simple buildings were located in area I in Figure 2.49.

There is evidence of a defensive wall around the settlement and the remains of a 300 m long section of this have been found on the scarp on the western side of the settlement (Figure 2.49). Such walls have even been found around settlements dating from the preceding early bronze age, Castelluccian, culture.

In the 15th century BCE, a different building style emerged. This was characterised by long rectangular structures up to 20 m in length grouped around a paved courtyard (area 2 on Figure 2.49). The doors of

Figure 2.50. Partial reconstruction of a circular house at Thapsos

the buildings opened mainly onto the central court-yard. These groups of buildings were joined by paved roads.

The economy was based on farming, herding, hunting and fishing. Agricultural practices were greatly developed during the middle bronze age and the simple plough was introduced during this era. Furthermore, animals were kept not just as sources of meat but also to produce milk and wool. Dark-coloured (generally grey or brown) pots were produced often decorated with incised motifs. Characteristically, the pots were large bowls with high horn-shaped feet as well as jugs and cups with bifurcated handles (these can be viewed at https://commons.wikimedia.org/wiki/File:Pithoi_di_Thapsos.JPG). Small items of gold jewellery, glass-paste beads and amber beads have also been found during excavations of these settlements as well as middle bronze-age pottery from Malta. The Thapsos culture was not restricted to south-east Sicily as evidence of its presence has also been found at a number of other coastal and inland sites including Milena, Ribera (east of Sciacca), Ognina (near Catania), S. Angelo Muxaro, the Belice Valley and at Gaffe, Licata.

They buried their dead in rock-cut chambered tombs (Figure 2.51) and approximately three hundred such tombs have been found in three distinct areas at Thapsos (labelled A, B and C in Figure 2.49) although some of these are from the late bronze age. Some of the tombs are approached by ramps cut into the rock and so resemble Mycenaean tombs. Inside these tombs, Mycenaean and Cypriote pottery has been found – evidence of trade with mainland Greece and as far away as Cyprus.

Thapsos had a good harbour and was strategically placed for trade with Africa, the western and eastern Mediterranean and the Aegean. It would have also been an important stopping point on longer trade

Figure 2.51. Remains of a chamber tomb at Thapsos.

routes between east-west and north-south trade routes. Sicily was rich in a number of important materials including amber, pumice, rock-salt and sulphur but was not an important source of metals or their ores.

Although we have little to go on, life in Sicily in the 16th and 15th centuries BCE would appear to have been far less sophisticated than at Knossos or Athens. We have no archaeological evidence to help us picture what kind of buildings King Cocalus occupied at Camicus or in the new city that Daidalos' built for him at Acragas (see Chapter 4). However, the excavations at Thapsos would suggest that they would not have been particularly impressive. There is no evidence of grand palaces or other significant buildings and little indication of large quantities of luxury goods during the time Daidalos would have been in Sicily. It was not until the 13th century BCE (long after the time of Daidalos) that there is evidence of the formation of an aristocratic society. Palaces then started to be erected, usually inside defensive walls, similar to those in Mycenaean Greece.

References

1. Homer, *The Iliad*, 11.45

2. *Myth, Religion, and Mother Right: Selected Writings of J.J. Bachofen.* Johann Jakob Bachofen, Joseph Campbell. Princeton University Press, 1992.

3. Homer, *The Iliad*, 18.587

4. Homer, *The Iliad*, 2.645

5. Homer, *The Odyssey*, 19.177

6. Hesiod, *Catalogues of Women*, Fragment 74 – referred to by Plato

7. Strabo, *Geography*, 10.4.8

8. Thucydides, *History of the Peloponnesian War*. 1.4

9. Thucydides, *History of the Peloponnesian War*. 1.8

10. Theopompus, *Athenaeus*, 12.526c

11. Uluburun Shipwreck by Cemal Pulak. In: *The Oxford handbook of the Bronze Age Aegean*. Eric Cline (editor) Oxford University Press. Oxford, 2012, pages 862-876.

12. Strabo, *Geography*, 6.2.6.

Other useful reference works

Mainland Greece: Late Bronze Age. Kim Shelton. In: *The Oxford handbook of the Bronze Age Aegean*. Eric Cline (editor) Oxford University Press. Oxford, 2012, pages 139-148

Crete: Late Bronze Age. Erik Hallager. In: *The Oxford handbook of the Bronze Age Aegean*. Eric Cline (editor) Oxford University Press. Oxford, 2012, pages 149-159

Knossos. Colin Macdonald. In: *The Oxford handbook of the Bronze Age Aegean*. Eric Cline (editor) Oxford University Press. Oxford, 2012, pages 529-542

The Archaeology of Ancient Sicily. R. Ross Holloway. Routledge, London. 2000

Architecture of Minoan Crete: Constructing Identity in the Aegean Bronze Age John C. McEnroe. University of Texas Press, 2014

Cultural Identity in Minoan Crete. Social Dynamics in the Neopalatial Period. Ellen Adams. Cambridge University Press, 2017

The Archaeology of Athens. John M Camp. Yale University Press, 2004

Sicily: culture and conquest. Dirk Booms and Peter Higgs, British Museum Press, 2016

Knossos. Renzo Rossi. David and Charles, 2007

Minoan and Mycenaean Art. Reynold Higgins. Thames & Hudson, 1997

The Bronze Age in Sicily. Anna Maria Bietti Sestieri. In: *The Oxford Handbook of the European Bronze Age* (Harry Fokkens and Anthony Harding, Editors). Oxford University Press, 2015

Building the Labyrinth: Arthur Evans and the Construction of Minoan Civilization. Ilse Schoep. *American Journal of Archaeology*, 2018; Vol. 122, pp. 5-32

Everyday Life in Ancient Crete. R. F. Willetts. B. T. Batsford Ltd., London, 1969

Chapter 3

DAIDALOS' STORY

IN THIS CHAPTER WE will summarise what is known of the life of Daidalos. It will become obvious that we know very little of his early or his later years, but his middle years were action-packed with many highs and lows. Direct quotations from ancient texts will be used frequently so that the we can get a sense of "looking over the shoulders" of those writers of long ago and share with them what they knew and felt about Daidalos' story.

Apart from brief mentions of Daidalos in earlier texts (described in Chapter 1), the main literary sources from which we derive Daidalos' story were written during the period 2nd century BCE to 2nd century CE. These are *Bibliotheca* (*Library*) by Pseudo-Apollodorus, *Bibliotheca* by Diodorus Siculus, *Aeneid* by Virgil, *Ars Amatoria* by Ovid, *Metamorphoses* by Ovid, *Theseus* by Plutarch, *Description of Greece* by Pausanias and *Fabulae* by Hyginus. Most of the many 5th and 4th century BCE plays written about Daidalos and his associates have been lost apart from a few fragments.

Family life

Where Daidalos was born is not specified in the earliest mentions of him and, although Homer's passage in the *Iliad* refers to him working in Crete, this does not necessarily mean that he was born there. This vagueness enabled subsequent writers (mainly Athenian) to claim that he was born in Athens. Who Daidalos' parents were is not clear and ancient Greek writers mention a number of possible fathers - Metion, Eupalamus and Palamaon.

Metion was considered to be the father of Daidalos by Diodorus Siculus[1]. However, there is some confusion as to the lineage of Metion, who was either the son or grandson of King Erechtheus of Athens. As well as fathering Daidalos, Metion had two other sons – Sicyon and Eupalamus. Metion's three sons were said to have overthrown Pandion, the eighth King of Athens, in order to put their father on the throne. Hyginus states that Daidalos was the son of Eupalamus who was a demi-god, being the offspring of Metion and Athena[2]. Apollodorus also says that Daidalos' father was Eupalamus[3]. But Eupalamus, as we have seen, was also said to have been the brother of Daidalos – it's all very confusing. Palamaon was considered to be the father of Daidalos by Pausanias although he says nothing more about him other than that he was an Athenian[4]. The two people most-frequently stipulated as being the father of Daidalos are certainly Metion and Eupalamus. In both cases, the name is appropriate for the father of such a skilled son. Metion is derived from the Greek word metis which means "wisdom, skill, craft" while Eupalamus means "skilful hand".

Although there are conflicting accounts of his lineage, the general consensus is that Daidalos was a descendant of one or other of the ancient kings of Athens. It has been suggested that the confusion over his ancestry has arisen because the Greek writers of the 5th century BCE were keen to claim Daidalos as a Greek (because of his fame) and so they invented a Greek lineage for him, portraying him as a member of the aristocracy (see Chapter 1). This goes to show that the concept of "fake news" is not a recent phenomenon and extends back thousands of years.

In contrast to his Athenian origins, there are a

Figure 3.1. Ausonius of Bordeaux.

Figure 3.2. Bust of Pherecydes of Syros, a 6th century BCE philosopher who was said to have been a teacher of Pythagoras and was one of the first Greeks to write in prose.

few reports of him being from Crete, although these appear in much later writings. Ausonius, a 4th century Latin poet from Bordeaux (Figure 3.1) wrote[5]: "On soaring wings above the air was borne the man of Crete [i.e. Daidalos]."

Eustathius, a Greek scholar and Archbishop of Thessalonica who was famous for his commentaries on Homer, also suggests that Daidalos was from Crete[6]. However, we have no idea as to who his parents were if he had been born there.

There is even less certainty about Daidalos' Athenian mother who has been reported to have been Alcippe, Iphinoe, Merope, Metiadousa or Phrasimede. Alcippe is named as the mother of Daidalos (and fathered by Eupalamus) in the *Bibliotheca* of Pseudo-Apollodorus, Unfortunately, the book says nothing more about her. Pherecydes of Syros (Figure 3.2), a 6th century BCE Greek thinker, stated that the mother of Daidalos (fathered by Metion) was Iphinoe but does not elaborate on who she was.

Merope (a daughter of King Erechtheus), Metiadousa (daughter of King Eupalamus) and Phrasimede (about who nothing is known) are also mentioned as the possible mother of Daidalos. If, as suggested by Cleidemus, Daidalos' mother was Merope, then this would make him a cousin of Theseus. If Daidalos' father was Metion then he would have had two brothers, Eupalamus and Sicyon, but these do not feature in any of the subsequent stories told about Daidalos. In contrast, his sister Perdix (or Polycaste), whose father was Eupalamus, plays an important part in his life. There is, however, confusion with regard to her name as she has a son who is also referred to as Perdix. But more about this unfortunate nephew later.

There is less confusion in the ancient texts with regard to his wife because so few mention her. According to the *Bibliotheca* of Pseudo-Apollodorus, Daidalos' wife was Naucrate[7], a slave of King Minos. However, nothing more is known about her other than she was the mother of Ikaros. Pausanias mentions that Daidalos may also have had another wife who came from Gortyn[8], a city in Crete, and had two more sons by her, Scyllis and Dipoenus, who were skilled artists and were famous for their work in marble, wood, ebony and ivory. According to Pliny, they appeared to have worked mainly in Sicyon on the Greek mainland around 580 BCE and established there a famous school of sculpture[9]. If this dating is correct then it means that they could not possibly have been the genetic sons of Daidalos but were "sons" in the sense that they were Daidaladai i.e. trained by those who had themselves been taught the skills of Daidalos. Strabo, in his *Geographica* (written between approximately 7 BCE and 23 CE) also stated that Daidalos had a son, Japyx (or Iapyx), by an unnamed Cretan woman and that this son was the founder of Iapygia a region that constitutes the "heel" of Italy[10]. The Iapygian Point (present-day Capo di Santa Maria di Leuca) and a river near modern Brindisi were also named after him. Japyx cannot have been a very loyal son as Strabo relates that he accompanied Minos on his journey to Sicily to capture Daidalos. Following the death of Minos, the leaderless Cretans tried to return home but were blown off course and founded a number of cities in Southern Italy, one of which was Iapygia.

Daidalos in Athens

Nothing is known of Daidalos' early years which, presumably, were spent in Athens. Homer's mention of him in the *Iliad* while describing the design of Achille's shield has been the basis for him being known as an architect, sculptor or choreographer depending on how the passage is translated. The main problem is with the translation of the word "choros" in the passage - Homer could have been referring to a dancing floor, the dance itself or a representation of the dance. The prevailing view is that the correct translation of the passage[11] is "...on a dancing-floor like unto that which in wide Cnosus Daidalos fashioned of old for fair-tressed Ariadne." This has encouraged the view of Daidalos achieving fame primarily as an architect. Later writers considered him also to be a sculptor and an inventor (see Chapter 4). However, as well as these positive attributes, he also gained a reputation for being a murderer. His nephew Talos (also known as Calos, Callus, Tantalus, Circinus, Attalus or Perdix) had been apprenticed to him by his sister Perdix (or Polycaste). However, Talos proved to be an exceptionally clever student which apparently made Daidalos very jealous. He was said to have invented the compass and potter's wheel and things came to a head when he was inspired by either the rows of teeth in a snake's jawbone or (according to some sources) a fish's backbone, to invent the saw. Daidalos also suspected Talos of having an incestuous relationship with his own mother and so he threw him either from the Acropolis[12] or (in a different version) from the roof of Athena's temple on the Acropolis[13] (Figure 3.3).

Figure 3.3. Athena turns Talos (Perdix) into a bird. Crispijn van de Passe (1564-1637 CE). Rijksmuseum, Amsterdam. The drawing shows Daidalos throwing Talos from the roof of the temple of Athena on the Acropolis but he is turned into a partridge by Athena.

Dædale, qui natum docuisti flectere pennas,   Circinus et fera. Puerum tu culmine turbas
  Te docuit Perdix testis, utrumq, fuit   Præcipitem! Tanti muneris idq, loco!

So, what was behind all this? As a research scientist, I know of the intense competition to obtain funding for one's research. There is a finite pot of money and bitter rivalries can arise among scientists who are working in the same field and are competing for these limited funds. Perhaps this was the case with Daidalos and Talos. Not that it justified murder. But also, perhaps Talos claimed an invention that wasn't his e.g. the saw. Different authors attribute this invention to Daidalos[14] as well as to Talos[15]. In the present day, similar problems can arise between a PhD student and their supervisor over important discoveries. Should the discovery be attributed to the PhD student or to their supervisor who, perhaps, came up with the idea and suggested appropriate experiments even though these were actually carried out by the student? Not that such disagreements or rivalries ever justify, or often result in, murder. But there could be a lot more to this incident than meets the eye.

This terrible act meant that Daidalos was guilty not only of murder but also of blaspheming against Athena. However, Athena is said to have taken pity on Talos and before he hit the ground turned him into a partridge (which in Greek is "Perdix"). This is said to explain why partridges are, apparently, afraid of heights and build their nests on the ground rather than in trees: "But Athena, goddess of ingenious men, saving the pupil changed him to a bird, and in the middle of the air he flew on feathered wings; and so his active mind — and vigour of his genius were absorbed into his wings and feet; although the name of Perdix was retained. The Partridge hides in shaded places by the leafy trees its nested eggs among the bush's twigs; nor does it seek to rise in lofty flight, for it is mindful of its former fall"[16]. Diodorus Siculus has a lot to say about this incident and relates how Daidalos was caught in the act of burying Talos. Apparently, when asked what he was doing, Daidalos replied: "I am inhuming a snake." Diodorus is intrigued by this response and comments "Here a man may well

Figure 3.4. First page (AA-AB) from an early printed edition of the Suda.

wonder at the strange happening, that the same animal that led to the thought of devising the saw should also have been the means through which the murder came to be discovered"[17]. Talos was buried at a site that lay between the theatre and the acropolis[18]. Perdix hanged herself when she heard of her son's death and, according to the *Suda* (a 10th century CE Byzantine encyclopaedia of the Mediterranean world: Figure 3.4), the Athenians built a sanctuary in her honour beside the Acropolis[19].

It's interesting to note that Diodorus says that Talos was inspired to produce an iron saw after looking at the row of teeth in a snake's jaw[20]: "......... when once he had come by chance upon a jawbone of a snake and with it had sawn through a small piece of wood, he tried to imitate the jaggedness of the serpent's teeth. Consequently, he fashioned a saw out of iron, by means of which he would saw the lumber which he used in his work." Although Diodorus lived in the iron age, it has been estimated that the earliest use of iron in Greece and the Aegean was not until approximately 1100 BCE which is long after the demise of the era of King Minos and Daidalos who lived in the bronze age.

For his crimes, Daidalos was brought before a judicial council (the Areopagus) and sentenced to banishment. However, according to Diodorus Siculus, he escaped from Athens to Alopece (present-day Ampelokipoi) a small village which was then outside the city walls and a few kilometres north-east of Athens. How long he remained there is uncertain but it could have been for a considerable length of time as it has been recorded that his descendants from his stay there were named after him[21]: "And Daidalos, having been accused and adjudged guilty of murder by the court of the Areopagites, at first fled to one of the demes of Attica, the inhabitants of which, we are told, were named Daedalidae after him." However, there is uncertainty as to whether the term "Daedalidae" (or Daidalidai) refers to the actual genetic descendants of

Daidalos or is simply a formulaic name ("the sons of Daidalos") for a guild of craftsmen.

Evidence supporting Daidalos' presence in Athens is provided by a stele (an upright stone with inscriptions; Figure 3.5) found there in 1938 that records the transactions of the Poletai for the year 367/6 BCE. The Poletai are the officials responsible for selling public contracts (e.g. for collecting taxes, for working on sacred land and in the silver mines) and confiscated property. In that year the Poletai dealt with the sale of one confiscated house and the leasing of seventeen mining concessions. The sale of the house is particularly interesting because it is in Alopece and the inscription on the stele describes its exact location22: "Kichonides son of Diogeiton of Gargettos and the association of the brothers of the Medontidai claimed that 100 drachmai were due him and the

Figure 3.5. A marble stele with a Greek inscription found in the city of Kyme in Asia Minor (1st century BCE). The inscription honours Kleanax, an illustrious citizen and patron of the city.

brothers on the house in Alopeke which Theomnestos of Ionidai registered as (the property) of Theosebes of Xypete, the house of which the boundaries are on the north the road leading to the Daidaleion and the Daidaleion, on the south (the property of) Philip of Agryl. (the property had become public) because Theosebes was convicted of sacrilege and did not await the trial." The "Daidaleion" mentioned on the inscription is a sanctuary sacred to Daidalos and demonstrates that he was venerated in Athens until at least the 4th century BCE.

Daidalos then left the Greek mainland and went to Knossos in Crete but there is nothing in the ancient texts to suggest why he decided to go to Crete in particular or how he got there. Crete was one of the dominant powers in the Mediterranean at that time so perhaps it was a combination of ambition and a desire to escape his past mistakes.

Daidalos in Crete

The ruler of Crete at that time was King Minos who lived in Knossos. Minos would have been delighted to have such an eminent inventor and sculptor in his court and Daidalos also endeared himself to Pasiphae, Minos' wife, and her daughters (Ariadne and Phaedra) by making them life-like wooden dolls[23]. His first recorded accomplishment was to build the labyrinthine palace of Knossos (described in Chapter 2), although there are no details as to how he did this. In doing so he gained a reputation as a great architect. His next project was carried out at the behest of Pasiphae. But, before describing this, we need to fill in some background as well as explain the importance of bulls in the overall story.

Crete was the birthplace of Zeus (Figure 3.6), the main Greek god.

Figure 3.6. Marble head of Zeus. Greece (1st century BCE)

Zeus was brought up in a cave not far from the village of Psychro on the Lasithi plateau. This cave, known as the Diktean (or Psychro) cave, is on Mount

Dikte and was one of the most important sacred sites
for both the Minoans and the Greeks. It is an impressive, atmospheric cave (Figure 3.7) and can still be
visited today.

*Figure 3.7. Photograph of the
Diktean cave near Psychro a
village on the Lasithi plateau in
eastern Crete.*

Zeus, who had a great interest in human women,
was said to have lusted after Europa, a Phoenician
princess, and appeared to her in the form of a white
bull while she was gathering flowers in a meadow in
Tyre. After climbing onto the bull's back, Europa was
carried off to Crete where Zeus revealed himself to be
a god[27]: "Zeus saw Europa the daughter of Phoenix
gathering flowers in a meadow with some nymphs
and fell in love with her. So he came down and
changed himself into a bull and breathed from his
mouth a crocus. In this way, he deceived Europa,
carried her off and crossed the sea to Crete where he

had intercourse with her." According to Pliny, intercourse took place under a plane tree near the city of Gortyn[28]: "There is a single plane-tree at the side of a spring at Gortyn in the island of Crete which is celebrated in records written both in Greek and Latin, as never shedding its leaves; and a typical Greek story about it has come down from early times, to the effect that underneath it Jupiter [i.e. Zeus] lay with

Zeus

Zeus was the chief deity of the Greek pantheon. He was a sky and weather god who was responsible for thunder, lightning, rain and wind. His traditional weapon was the thunderbolt. He was considered to be the father of both gods and men. A Cretan myth that was adopted by the Greeks says that Cronus, king of the Titans (the generation of gods that preceded the Olympian gods) found out that one of his children would ultimately dethrone him. He therefore swallowed each of his children as soon as they were born (Figure).

However, when Zeus was born, his mother, Rhea, gave Cronus a stone wrapped in swaddling clothes, pretending that this was the baby. Rhea then hid the baby in the Diktean cave where he was nursed by Amalthea (who was either a goat or a nymph) and guarded by a group of 5 brothers (the Curetes) who danced and clashed their weapons together in order to drown out the baby's cries. The Curetes were the first inhabitants

Saturn (i.e. Cronos) devouring his son. An engraving by Giovanni Jacopo Caraglio (1526 CE)

of Crete. Zeus later led a revolt against the titans and dethroned Cronus, thereby fulfilling the prophecy. Zeus ruled over the 11 other deities of the Greek pantheon and lived on Mount Olympus, the highest mountain in Greece.

Europa..." Interestingly, coins have been found in Gortyn, that are thought to depict Europa in a plane tree and these have a bull on the other side (Figure 3.8).

Figure 3.8. Coin from Gortyn (4th – 3rd century BCE). On one side is a semi-naked Europa sitting in a plane tree, raising her veil with her right hand and, with her left, holding an eagle with spread wings in her lap. On the other side of the coin is a bull with its head turned back to ward off a fly from his left rear hoof.

Although the earliest mention of Europa (by Hesiod) states that her father was Phoenix, king of Phoenecia, there is considerable uncertainty about her mother who has been named by different writers as being Telephe, Telephae, Perimede, Tyro, Telephaassa, Kassiepeia, and Argiope.

How long Zeus stayed with Europa in Crete is not known, but it must have been a considerable time because their liaison resulted in the birth of three sons - Minos, Rhadamanthys, and Sarpedon[29]. Possibly the earliest portrayal of her is on a 14th century BCE blue glass plaque found in a tomb in Dendra, Greece. This depicts a female figure with both arms raised high, sitting side-saddle on an animal. She was a popular subject in both Greek and Roman art, with Greek images being common from as early as the 7th century BCE (Figure 3.9).

Following the departure of Zeus, Europa married the King of Crete, Asterion (or Asterius/Asterios) who raised her three boys as his sons. Minos married Pasiphae who was the daughter of the sun god (Helios) and a nymph. Her sister was the sorceress Circe, who was famous for turning Odysseus' companions into pigs. Pasiphae, like her sister, had magical powers.

When Asterion died, Minos considered himself to be his rightful successor and Apollodorus describes how he managed to achieve the throne[30]: "Minos wished to reign over Crete, but his claim was opposed. So he alleged that he had received the kingdom from the gods, and in proof of it he said that whatever he prayed for would be done. And in sacrificing to Poseidon he prayed that a bull might appear from the depths, promising to sacrifice it when it appeared. Poseidon did send him up a fine bull, and Minos obtained the kingdom, but he sent the bull to the

(a) Europa on the bull. Ivory and bone. Roman (2nd-3rd century CE). Zeus in the form of a bull carries off Europa who rides on his back with her left hand on his head and her legs turned towards the rear. Her cloak, held over her head, flies in the breeze.

(b) Black-figure trefoil oinochoe (wine jug) showing Europa on a bull. Greek (530 BCE)

(c) Earthenware plate with tin glaze (maiolica) and lustre decoration by Giulio da Urbino (1533 CE). In the foreground, Europa, who hasn't realised that the amiable bull with which she and her friends have been playing is a god, mounts the back of the bull. In the background, the bull is shown carrying her across the sea to Crete.

(d) The Abduction of Europa by Rembrandt Harmensz. van Rijn (1632 CE). Bewildered, Europa grasps the bull's horn and turns back to look at her companions. One young woman falls to the ground and raises her arms in alarm, while her friend clasps her hands in consternation and watches helplessly. The carriage driver rises to his feet and stares at the departing princess in horror.

Figure 3.9. Depictions of Europa over the ages.

herds and sacrificed another." Poseidon was furious that Minos had tried to deceive him and retaliated by making Pasiphae fall in love with the bull (Figure 3.10).

Despite her advances, the bull, not surprisingly, showed no interest in her[31]: "She [Pasiphae] who suffered the disdain of a Cretan bull...." Ovid, in his *Art of Love*, tells of how Pasiphae hated the rival cows in the herd, cut fresh leaves for the bull and beautified herself for her bull lover[32]:

"The heifers of Cnossos and Cydon longed
 to have him mount up on their backs.
Pasiphae joyed in adultery with the bull:
 she hated the handsome heifers with jealousy.

I sing what is well-known: not even Crete, the
    hundred-citied,
can deny it, however much Cretans lie.
They say that, with unpractised hands, she
    plucked
fresh leaves and tenderest grasses for the bull.
She went as one of the herd, unhindered by any
    care
for that husband of hers: Minos was ousted by a
    bull.
Why put on your finest clothes, Pasiphae?
Your lover can appreciate none of your wealth.
Why have a mirror with you, when you seek
    highland cattle?
Why continually smooth your hair, you foolish
    woman?
But believe the mirror that denies you're a heifer.
How you wish that brow of yours could bear
    horns!"

Figure 3.10. Pasiphaë adorning the bull with Flowers. By César-Isidore-Henry Cros (1840–1907)

However, unlike most writers, Hesiod suggested that the attraction was mutual and tells us:[33] "... the bull seeing Pasiphae, with its eyes, was seized by desire for her." This is unlikely as, if it were true, Pasiphae would have had no need to seek the help of Daidalos.

Bacchylides a Greek poet of the 5th century BCE, tells us[34]: "... to Eupalamos' son Daidalos, most skilled

King Minos

Minos was one of three sons born to Europa and fathered by Zeus. He became King of Crete and established one of the most powerful navies in the Mediterranean which he used to rid the seas of pirates. Pliny states that "Minos was the first who waged war by means of ships"[24]. Every nine years he was said to have conversed with Zeus and received advice and instructions from him[25] ("Among their cities is the great city of Cnosus, where Minos reigned when nine years old,

Minos, Judge of the Damned by Gustave Doré (1890)

he that held converse with great Zeus". On the basis of this advice, he established the first Cretan constitution. He was so respected by the gods that, after his death, he was made one of the three "judges of the dead" (Figure). This description of a just and wise king contrasts starkly with other stories about him – a notorious womaniser, torturer and war-monger who demanded the regular sacrifice of 14 Athenian youths to the Minotaur. To rationalise this, some ancient writers suggested that "Minos" is simply the Cretan term for a king and there were, therefore, a number of individuals who bore that name. Others say that there were only two kings of Crete who used that name – Minos I (the "good' king) and Minos II (the "bad" king).

According to Apollodorus, he had many children[26]: "He begat sons, to wit, Catreus, Deucalion, Glaucus, and Androgeus: and daughters, to wit, Acalle, Xenodice, Ariadne, Phaedra; and by a nymph Paria he had Eurymedon, Nephalion, Chryses, and Philolaus; and by Dexithea he had Euxanthius"

In addition to his involvement with Daidalos, two other stories are widely known about him. The first concerns Scylla, the daughter of King Nisos (Nisus) of Megaria. Minos attacked Megaria during his war with Athens following the death of his son, Androgeus. However, Nisos had a lock of purple hair which made him invulnerable. Scylla fell in love with Minos who persuaded her to cut off her father's purple lock. However, when presented with the purple hair, Minos was so disgusted at Scylla's disloyalty that he abandoned her. When she tried to get on board his ship, she was attacked by Nisos, who had turned into a sea eagle, and she herself was then transformed into a bird.

The second concerns his son, Glaucus who fell into a jar of honey and drowned. The famous seer, Polyidus, found the child but admitted that he couldn't revive him so Minos locked him away with his son's corpse. One day a snake came into the cell and Polyidus killed it. Later, he saw the snake's mate revive the dead snake with a herb so Polyidus used the same herb to bring back Glaucus to life. Minos refused to let Polyides leave Crete until he had taught

Glaucus the art of divination, which he did. However, as he was leaving Crete, Polyides told Glaucus to spit into his mouth and, on doing so, he immediately forgot all he had been taught.

Pasiphae

Some of the earliest known references to Pasiphae (which means "wide-shining") are by Isokrates (4th century BCE)[38]: "At about the same time appeared the monster reared in Crete, the offspring of Pasipha, daughter of Helius" and by Apollonius of Rhodes (3rd century BCE)[39]: "In days past the maiden Ariadne, daughter of Minos, with kindly intent rescued Theseus from grim contests -- the maiden whom Pasiphae, daughter of Helios, bore." Both of these writers also identify her as being a daughter of the sun god, Helios. It is not until much later, in the first century BCE, that we learn that her mother was Perseis[40]: ". ... because she is the daughter of Cadmus, are Circe and Pasiphae and Aeetes, the children of Perseis the daughter of Oceanus by Sol [Helios], to be not counted in the list of gods?". Perseis was one of the Oceanic nymphs i.e. the 3000 daughters of Oceanus, one of the Titans. Other sources say that her mother was a different nymph, Crete, after whom the island was named.

Detail of a miniature of queen Pasiphae embracing the bull, in 'L'Épître Othéa'. France (1410 CE).

She had a sister, Circe, and two brothers Aeetes and Perses. Like her sister, Pasiphae was a sorceress and both were known for their skills with potions and herbs. An example of her powers is described by Pseudo-Apollodorus[41]: "Prokris fled to Minos, who wanted her and tried to persuade her to have sex with him. But if a woman had sex with Minos, she could not be saved; for after he had slept with many women, Pasiphae put him under a spell whereby, whenever he went to bed with another woman, he would ejaculate wild creatures into her vagina, thus killing her.". The "wild creatures" were listed by Antoninus Liberalis, a 2nd century CE Greek writer, as being "snakes, scorpions and millipedes"[42].

Pasiphae rarely appears in Greek art, but was a popular figure in both Etruscan and Roman art. She was also the subject of a number of plays and other literary works including: *Pasiphae* by Alceus the son of Miccus (active in 388 BCE), *Cretan Women* by Euripides (480 – c. 406 BCE) and *Pasiphae* by Alcaeus of Mytilene (620 – 580 BCE).

of carpenters, she [Pasiphae] told her unspeakable sickness..." (Figure 3.11).

Figure 3.11. Pasiphae soliciting the assistance of Daidalos. From a neo-classical intaglio (late 18th/ early 19th century) belonging to Prince Poniatowski.

The ever-resourceful Daidalos came up with the idea of building a cow-like wooden framework on wheels which would be large enough for Pasiphae to enter and covered this with the skin of a cow (Figure 3.12). It was constructed in such a way that it would allow Pasiphae to be impregnated when the bull mated with the artificial cow – which it duly did[35]: "... and [Daidalos] set it in the meadow in which the bull used to graze. Then he introduced Pasiphae into it; and the bull came and coupled with it, as if it were a real cow." Bacchylides gives a more graphic description of the copulation[36]:

> "And, splayed down its hollows,
>   Took the lurch
>   Of the hulking bull."

Figure 3.12. Pasiphae. An etching by Léonard Gaultier (1600) after Antoine Caron (1521–1599 CE). This shows Daidalos making the wooden cow for Pasiphae

Another early reference to this interesting contraption was by Palaiphatos in the 4th century BCE[37]: "It is said of Pasiphae that she fell in love with a grazing bull, that Daidalos built a wooden cow, and shut up Pasiphae there. In this way, the bull mounted her and joined the young woman; the latter gave birth to a baby with a human body and a horned bovine head." However, he argued that this could not have happened because[37]: "First, it is impossible for one animal to fall in love with another of a different species if its sexual organs do not correspond to its own. It is not possible for a dog to unite with a monkey; a wolf with a hyena; not even a buffalo with a deer: the species are indeed different."

Pasiphae became pregnant and gave birth to the minotaur, named as Asterion (or Asterios), "the starry one" in some versions of the story[43]. The first mention of the birth of the Minotaur was by Hesiod:[44] "She became pregnant, bore to Minos a strong son. A wonder to see for it resembled a man in its body down to its feet, but up above grew a bull's head." Minotaur is a compound word derived from "Minos" and "Tauros" (bull) and therefore means "the bull of Minos". Interestingly, the word first appears in literature in the 4th century BCE and was used by Palaiphatos[45]. The minotaur is usually represented in Classical art with the body of a man and the head and tail

Figure 3.13. A terracotta aryballos (oil flask) in the shape of the head of the minotaur who is wearing a tunic with a patterned collar and appears quite docile. Found in eastern Greece (580-560 BCE)

Palaiphatos

Palaiphatos (Palaephatus) was an Athenian writer who lived in the 4th century BCE - a time when the Greek myths were being scrutinised by scientists and sceptics. In approximately 320 BCE he wrote a book called *Peri apiston* (*Concerning Incredible Tales*) in which he attempted to provide rationalisations of the Greek myths. The book consists of an introduction followed by 52 chapters (Figure). Each chapter consists of a brief version of one particular myth followed by a rational explanation of it. The

Contents page from Palaiphatos' book On incredible things. *German edition produced by Johann Heinrich Friedrich Meineke in 1774.*

last seven chapters are Byzantine additions written in a different style and appear in only one version of the surviving manuscripts and, consequently, are not considered to have been part of the original book. In his introduction to the book he wrote: "And in my travels through many countries I inquired of old men what they had heard about each of these stories and I write here what I learned from them. And I personally visited as many countries as I could, and I have written these things down not as they were told to me, but as I myself have learned by travel and research." He was a contemporary of Aristotle and was widely known - at least 10 ancient writers refer to his book. He included in his book chapters devoted to the following individuals who are relevant to this book: Daidalos, Ikaros, Pasiphae and Europa.

Palaiphatos is not a common name and it may have been a pseudonym for one or several writers. The literal meaning of the name is "of ancient fame" or "speaker of old tales". Attempting to rationalise Greek myths was a dangerous thing to do in the 4th century BCE – Anaxagoras, a pre-Socratic philosopher, had been sent into exile in the previous century for doing just that.

Heracles and the Cretan Bull

As well as making Pasiphae fall in love with the bull, Poseidon also made the bull mad so that he rampaged around Crete destroying crops and terrifying the population. One of the twelve labours assigned to Hercules by King Eurystheus of Tiryns and Mycenae was to capture this bull. Hercules therefore sailed to Crete and Minos was all too happy to let him subdue the beast. Hercules captured the bull (Figure a) and sent it to Eurystheus who was very afraid of it and hid in a wine storage jar (Figure b). He decided to sacrifice the bull to Hera but, unfortunately, she refused to accept this as it would have enhanced the standing of Heracles, who she hated. The king therefore released the bull in Marathon where it again caused problems. It became known as the Marathonian bull and eventually Theseus killed it and sacrificed it to Athena.

The capture of the bull by Hercules became a popular subject for display on pottery around the 6th century BCE. More than 200 examples of pottery depicting the episode have survived and most of these are from around 510-500 BCE.

Figure a. Terracotta neck-amphora with Herakles and the Cretan bull (520-510 BCE). From Vulci, Italy. Herakles, having forced the Cretan bull down on one knee, tightens a rope that binds the animal around its horns, left hind leg, and testicles.

Figure b. Terracotta vase depicting Heracles delivering the Erymanthian boar to King Eurystheus who, being a notorious coward, hides in a storage jar. 525 BCE.

of a bull. Although depictions of Minotaur-like creatures are found as early as the 18th century BCE, the first time the word Minotaur appears anywhere in art is on a 6th century cup made by Archikles and Glaukytes. An early example of a representation of the minotaur is shown in Figure 3.13.

The minotaur rarely appears alone on ancient vases, etc. (Figure 3.14), but is usually shown fighting with Theseus.

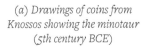

(a) Drawings of coins from Knossos showing the minotaur (5th century BCE)

(b) The minotaur on a terracotta skyphos (drinking cup) ca. 470–460 BCE.

Figure 3.14. Examples of representations of the minotaur on his own.

Apart from having the head of a bull and a human body, classical writers tell us little else about the creature. However, Euripides, in his play *The Cretans*, gives slightly more information in a dialogue between Minos, who has asked about the minotaur, and the creature's nurse[46]:

> "**Nurse:** It is mixed, with a two-fold nature, of bull and human.
> **Minos:** I have (heard) that before too; but how...?
> **Nurse:** It bears a bull's head set above its breast.
> **Minos:** So does it go on four legs or walk on two?
> **Nurse:** On two...dark with black...
> **Minos:** And is there anything further...?
> **Nurse:** ...a tail... against the maddening cattle-fly"

Elsewhere in the play we are also told[47]: "... an infant of mixed appearance, born to sterility..."

What is frequently overlooked is the fact that the minotaur was partly divine given that he was the son of Pasiphae who herself was the daughter of Helios, the sun god. Not that this appears to have helped him in any way.

Pasiphae's interaction with a bull is worth contrasting with that of her mother-in-law, Europa. Europa is fooled by a bull, which is really Zeus in disguise, and this results in her impregnation and the birth of Minos and two other sons. In contrast, Pasiphae fools a bull into thinking she is a cow and the subsequent impregnation produced the Minotaur.

Naturally, King Minos was both surprised and furious at the birth of the minotaur – his wife had not only shown herself to have been unfaithful but had copulated with a bull. In *The Cretans* by Euripides, Minos says to Daidalos[48]: "You are a carpenter, but what you practised is not woodwork." This is very much an understatement. Daidalos' actions had resulted in not only the cuckolding of Minos but also the performance of an unnatural sexual act and the birth of a monster. Not surprisingly, Minos' reacted by imprisoning Daidalos[49]: "When Minos found out the affair he cast Daidalos into prison..." However, he did not have the Minotaur killed, which might have been the expected response of such a cruel individual. Why he did not do so remains a mystery. Perhaps he had some sympathy with the Minotaur because, after all, he himself was the offspring of a bull (Zeus) and Europa and therefore could have been born a bull-man. Perhaps he also felt guilty as he may have come to realise that this may have been Poseidon's revenge for not having sacrificed the white bull he had been sent. Finally, the fact that he possessed such a monstrous creature would have made him appear a formidable foe to his enemies and enabled him to dominate Athens. Because he was uncertain as to what to do, he decided to consult the oracle at Delphi for advice (Figure 3.15).

On the basis of what the oracle told him, he ordered Daidalos to construct something in which the minotaur could be hidden. Daidalos therefore built the labyrinth (see Chapter 4)[50]: "Now the Minotaur was confined in a labyrinth, in which he who entered could not find his way out; for many a winding turn shut off the secret outward way. The labyrinth was constructed by Daidalos...." As pointed out in Chapter 1, there is confusion about the term "labyrinth" as it may refer to a number of Daidalos' constructions. In this case, the term refers to some form of prison for the Minotaur and this may have been located beneath the palace of Knossos or may have been in a

Figure 3.15. The Temple of Apollo at Delphi. The Delphic oracle was consulted in the inner chamber of the temple.

cave system (known as the Labyrinthos Caves) some distance away near the city of Gortyn (see Chapter 4).

We know very little about the life of the poor Minotaur who seems to have been fed periodically with Athenian boys and girls (Figure 3.16). However, this

Figure 3.16. "The tribute to the minotaur" by Ernest Augustin Gendron (1876 CE). This portrays the arrival at the labyrinth of a batch of seven female sacrificial victims.

was Minos' idea and nothing in the ancient texts say that this is something that the minotaur wanted. Given that he had a bull's brain (presumably) and desires, he would probably have been happier with grass. What it fed upon between these human sacrifices is not known. No mention is made of whether or not his mother, sisters or step-father visited him.

Daidalos' next major accomplishment in Crete was, again, at the request of a woman who was having problems with her love life. This time it came from Pasiphae's daughter Ariadne (which means the "utterly pure"). Ariadne had fallen in love with Theseus who, as mentioned previously, may have been a cousin of Daidalos. Theseus, the son of King Aegeus of Athens, was determined to put an end to the tribute of 7 young men and 7 young women that Athens had to pay to Minos every 1, 7, 8 or 9 years (according to different versions). As related by Isokrates (436–338 BCE), an ancient Greek rhetorician and educator[51]: "At about the same time appeared the monster reared in Crete, the offspring of Pasipha, daughter of Helius, to whom our city was sending, in accordance with an oracle's command, tribute of twice seven children. When Theseus saw these being led away, and the entire populace escorting them, to a death savage and foreseen, and being mourned as dead while yet living, he was so incensed that he thought it better to die than to live as ruler of a city that was compelled to pay to the enemy a tribute so lamentable." Consequently, on the third sacrificial occasion, he took the place of one of the youths so that he could get access to the Minotaur and kill him. On arriving at Knossos, he immediately quarrelled with Minos who, true to form, lusted after one of the 7 Athenian maidens. Theseus prevented him from taking things further by stating that it was his duty, as a son of Poseidon (Figure 3.17), to protect virgins from tyrants. Minos demanded that Theseus prove his divine parentage by retrieving his golden ring which he promptly threw into the sea. Theseus dived into the water and was escorted by a school of dolphins to the palace of the Nereids - 50 sea-nymphs who lived with their father Nereus. The Nereids (Figure 3.18) searched for, and found, the ring and

Figure 3.17. Terracotta neck-amphora (jar) ca. 470–465 BCE. On one side is Poseidon while on the reverse is his son, Theseus, shown as a youth.

gave it to Theseus who returned it to Minos[52,53]. While searching for the ring, Theseus was given a gem-studded crown by either Thetis (the leader of the Nereids) or by another of the Nereids, Amphitrite[54].

All of this had a huge impact on Ariadne who immediately fell in love with him (Figure 3.19) as described by Catullus (a 2nd century BCE Roman consul, poet and orator)[55]: "As soon as the royal maiden had caught sight of him with desiring eyes (the girl whom her chaste little bed used to rear in her mother's soft embrace, breathing sweet scents like the myrtle trees which fringe the river Eurotas or when the spring breeze coaxes forth bright colours), she did not lower her love-enflamed gaze from him before she had conceived a fire deep down all over her body and was utterly ablaze from the very marrow of her bones." Interestingly, this poem is regarded as Catullus' masterpiece and it has been said that it is one of the greatest literary works ever written. Ariadne therefore decided to help Theseus and, of course, turned to Daidalos for help[56]: ".........Ariadne, daughter of Minos, being amorously disposed to him, offered to help him

Figure 3.18. Terracotta hydria (water jar) ca. 450–440 BCE. This shows heroic Peleus (king of Phthia) and Thetis who was a sea goddess and leader of the Nereids. Their child was the Greek hero Achilles.

if he would agree to carry her away to Athens and have her to wife. Theseus having agreed on oath to do so, she besought Daidalos to disclose the way out of the Labyrinth."

Ariadne asked Daidalos to help Theseus to kill the minotaur and to find his way back out of the labyrinth. Daidalos told Ariadne to give Theseus a ball of thread and to tie one end to the door of the labyrinth and unwind it as he went along "forwards, always down and never left or right" until he reached the centre and there he was to grab hold of the minotaur by his hair and sacrifice him to Poseidon[58]. After killing the minotaur he would then be able to re-trace his path by following the thread (Figure 3.20). Interestingly a ball of thread is known in English as a "clew" which is an old form of the word "clue" which means something that points the way or is a guide. In one version of the story, the ball of thread appeared to have an in-built motor and homing device of some sort as we are told that it went on ahead of Theseus of

(a) Terracotta red-figured skyphos (ca. 470 BCE) depicting Ariadne.

(b) Theseus and Ariadne by Antonio Canova (late 18th-early 19th century CE). Theseus is holding in his left hand the ball of thread that Ariadne has given to him.

(c) Ariadne by George Frederic Watts (1894 CE)

Figure 3.19. Images of Ariadne.

its own accord and guided him to the centre of the labyrinth where the Minotaur lurked.

Ariadne also gave Theseus a sword to kill the Minotaur and a luminous crown to light his way through the labyrinth. This crown had been a gift from Dionysus who, according to Hyginus, had come to Crete because he wanted Ariadne[59]: "...........at the time when Liber [i.e. Dionysus] came to Minos with the hope of lying with Ariadne, he gave her this crown as a present. Delighted with it, she did not refuse the terms. It is said, too, to have been made of gold and Indian gems, and by its aid Theseus is thought to have

Minos' feud with Athens

The Oracle by Camillo Miola (1880 CE). The Pythia (the high priestess at the temple of the Delphic oracle) sits on the sacred tripod ready to give advice.

One of Minos' sons, Androgeos, was very athletic and went to compete in the Panathenaic games held by King Aegeus in Athens. According to Diodorus Siculus[57]: "...and defeating all the contestants in the games he became a close friend of the sons of Pallas. Thereupon Aegeus, viewing with suspicion the friendship which Androgeos had formed, since he feared that Minos might lend his aid to the sons of Pallas and take from him the supreme power, plotted against the life of Androgeos. Consequently, when the latter was on his way to Thebes in order to attend a festival there, Aegeus caused him to be treacherously slain by certain natives of the region in the neighbourhood of Oinoe in Attica"

On hearing of the death of his son, Minos besieged Athens but did not manage to overcome the city's defences. He therefore prayed to Zeus for help and Zeus responded by afflicting the city with plaque and famine. The Athenians consulted an oracle for advice (Figure) and were told to sacrifice the four daughters (Hyacinthides) of Hyacinthus the Lacedaemonian at the tomb of the Geraistos the cyclops. This, however, did not stop either the plague or the famine so the oracle then advised the Athenians to give to Minos whatever he wanted. Minos demanded that every 1, 7, 8 or 9 years (according to different versions) the 7 most courageous young men and the 7 most beautiful maidens were to be sent to Crete and fed to the Minotaur.

Figure 3.20. Ariadne and Theseus by Pietro da Cortona, Italian (1597-1669). Ariadne is holding the ball of string that will help Theseus to find his way back out of the labyrinth

come from the gloom of the labyrinth to the day, for the gold and gems made a glow of light in the darkness." This shows that, prior to meeting Theseus, Ariadne appears to have been quite happy to share her favours with others in exchange for gifts.

The first literary reference to the liberation of the hostages and, by inference, the killing of the Minotaur was by Sappho (630-570 BCE)[60]. As to how the minotaur was actually killed, Apollodorus tells us[61]: "...and having found the Minotaur in the last part of the Labyrinth, he killed him by smiting him with his fists." The only other description of the actual encounter between Theseus and the minotaur is in a fragment of a Euripides play *The Cretans*. Unfortunately, the fragment is incomplete and damaged and all we have are parts of a speech made by an unidentified messenger who relates[62]: "... (before or behind?) the pillars...I had...(top-most or distant) and...a spectator...(taking a safe position?). And (I caught sight of) the (bull, bull-formed, bull-horned?)... curved, (tossing his horns in anger), sweeping (with his tail?)... ...full of courage...of his thighs...(But) Theseus (who is called the son of Aegeus) in name, but (in reality is sprung from) Poseidon, threw off (his garments and approached?) the beast, (armed) with his...club in his right hand...." Interestingly, the minotaur is described as being courageous and so is being endowed with a human, or even heroic, quality. Portrayals of the minotaur's death on pottery and in mosaics and frescos also show Theseus using a sword or a club while the Minotaur is generally shown defending himself with rocks (Figure 3.21). In the 6th century BCE, depictions of the fight became very popular on pottery and in these Theseus is usually shown using a sword while the Minotaur uses a stone.

What can we say about the death of the minotaur? Shut up in a prison for many years for no fault of his own, innocent of any crime. Shunned by his family, isolated from humans and from cattle. Encouraged to behave monstrously by being fed periodically with terrified young men and women. He didn't ask for the poor youths – they were the outcome of Minos' demands on Athens, the unfortunate victims of a power game. He harmed no one. His death was simply one step on the road for an ambitious young man trying to establish a name for himself so that he could claim the throne of Athens. Catullus is one poet who managed to instil some sympathy for the poor creature in his description of its slaughter[63]: "For as an unconquered whirlwind twisting the trunk with its blast downs an oak tree shaking its arms on the top of the Taurus mountains, or a cone-bearing pine tree with its sweating bark (it falls prone afar, thrown out from the roots, and smashes everything in its way far and wide), so Theseus laid the beast low, its body

(a) Terracotta kylix (drinking cup) from Attica, Greece (ca. 530 BCE). Theseus fights the minotaur while Ariadne (to the left) and another person (to the right) look on.

(b) Terracotta neck-amphora (jar) from Attica, Greece. ca. 500 BCE. Theseus and the minotaur fight while Ariadne looks on.

(c) Terracotta amphora (jar) from Attica, Greece. ca. 540 BCE. Theseus fights the minotaur watched by some of the intended sacrificial victims and, possibly, Ariadne. The minotaur has a stone in his hand – this is the weapon of adversaries considered by the Greeks to be less civilized.

(d) Black-Figure terracotta amphora from Athens (550-540 BCE). Theseus is plunging his sword through the monster's neck while the freed youths and maidens watch. The artist stressed the Minotaur's bestial nature by showing that his weapon is a rock, seen clutched in his hoof-like hand, whereas civilized Theseus fights with a sword.

Figure 3.21. The slaying of the minotaur by Theseus

tamed, as it tossed its horns in vain at the empty air." In its death throes, the Minotaur is portrayed as resembling a huge tree falling – this is an image that recalls the death of a Homeric hero. For example, in *The Iliad*, the death of Asius at the hand of Idomeneus is described as: "And he fell as an oak falls, or a poplar, or a tall pine that among the mountains shipwrights fell with whetted axes to be a ship's timber."[64] Catullus is, therefore, conveying a sense of regret at the destruction of such a mighty creature.

Theseus, the 14 youths and Ariadne then escaped from Crete in a boat but not before Theseus had knocked holes in Minos' boats to prevent him from pursuing them. We are told that Theseus had promised Ariadne that he would take her away with him to Athens when he left Crete and marry her. Although he kept his promise to take her away, she never made it to Athens. A variety of explanations are given with regard to what actually happened to Ariadne and the involvement of Theseus and Dionysus in her fate:

(i) Theseus fell in love with another woman, Aegle, and so abandoned Ariadne on Naxos where she hung herself[65]. The Roman poet Catullus (84-54 BCE) captures something of the despair Ariadne must have felt having been abandoned by her lover and having betrayed both her father and brother: "To be sure, I pulled you out as you twisted in the midst of death's whirlwind, and I decided rather to lose a brother than to desert you, false one, in your hour of need"[66] "...Or should I hope for help from my father? When I myself left him and followed a young man spattered with my brother's blood?"[67]

(ii) Theseus abandoned Ariadne on Dia (an island just off the coast of Crete, near Heraklion) because he thought that the Athenians would not accept someone who had betrayed her country. Ariadne was then killed by Artemis but not before she had given birth to twin sons (by

Theseus) called Oenopion and Staphylus[68].
Ariadne was killed by Artemis because she had
been unfaithful – she was already in a
relationship with Dionysus (as mentioned
previously) prior to meeting Theseus.

(iii) a storm drove their ship to Cyprus and Ariadne,
who was pregnant, was sea-sick so Theseus let
her disembark but he was blown back out to sea
and when he eventually returned she had died
during child-birth[69].

(iv) on arriving at Naxos, Dionysus fell in love
with Ariadne (Figure 3.22) and took her away
to Lemnos and they had four sons; Thoas,
Staphylus, Oenopion, and Peparethus[70]

(v) "Ariadne was taken away from Theseus by
Dionysus, who sailed against him with superior
forces......"[71]

(vi) " ... Dionysus showed himself on the island,
and because of the beauty of Ariadne he took
the maiden away from Theseus and kept her
as his lawful wife, loving her exceedingly"[72].

*Figure 3.22. Attic Black-Figure
Column Krater showing profiles
of Dionysus and Ariadne. From
Athens (530 BCE).*

As a wedding present, Dionysus gave Ariadne a crown which he placed in the heavens as the constellation known as the Corona Borealis. Other versions say that the crown was the one given to her by Theseus – Dionysus took this from her and threw it into the heavens where it became the constellation: "He set in the dark heavens the bright crown that rested on her brows. Through the soft air it whirled, while all the sparkling jewels changed to flashing fires, assuming in the sky between the Serpent-holder and the Kneeler the well-known shape of Ariadne's Crown"[73]. According to Hesiod[74], she was also made immortal: "And golden-haired Dionysus made brown-haired Ariadne, the daughter of Minos, his buxom wife: and the son of Cronos made her deathless and unageing for him."

Theseus' abandonment of Ariadne on Naxos has given rise to many paintings (Figure 3.23) and to the famous opera by Strauss, *Ariadne auf Naxos*.

Daidalos' interactions with the two main women (Pasiphae and Ariadne) that feature in his life are similar in that in both cases he is asked by them for help with their love-lives. In both cases, he obliges but each ultimately has tragic consequences. In the case of Pasiphae, a monster is born while Ariadne is abandoned by Theseus on Naxos (or Dia). Although, in at least one version of her story, Ariadne ends up married to Dionysus. Fortunately for Daidalos, he did not get involved in helping another female member of the Minos family – Phaedra, Ariadne's sister. But he had a lucky escape there because Phaedra would certainly have asked for his help if he had been around in Athens because she had fallen in love with Hippolytus, her stepson. Seneca has her saying[79]: "But as for me, what god, what Daidalos could ease my wretched passion? Though he himself should return, mighty in Attic cunning, who shut our monster [the Minotaur] in the dark labyrinth, he could afford no help to my calamity......"

Minos eventually found out about Daidalos' involvement with his wife and his daughter and was obviously none too pleased. He therefore locked up Daidalos and his son Ikaros in a tower or, in other versions, in the labyrinth itself or in a cave in Soulia (present-day Agia Galini). However, Pasiphae released them from imprisonment. There are three main versions as to what happened next.

In one of these, Daidalos says to Ikaros[80] "Although Minos obstructs the land and waves, the sky at least lies open; we will fly there. Minos may possess

(a) *Ariadne* by Asher Brown Durand (ca. 1831–35 CE). Ariadne lies abandoned on Naxos. In most depictions of this event, she is shown lying down and often asleep.

(b) *Terracotta Red-Figure Chous* from Lucania, South Italy (early 4th century BCE). At the left, Ariadne sits on a rocky outcrop. A bearded, wreathed Dionysos, holding a kantharos in his right hand and a thyrsos in his left, stands at the right looking toward her. The discovery of Ariadne by Dionysos was a popular subject in ancient art. This vessel shows the moment Ariadne realizes Theseus has abandoned her on the island of Naxos. She sits with her head bent and eyes downcast, distracted and still unaware of Dionysos' presence and her imminent rescue.

(c) *Bacchus and Ariadne* by Henry Bone (1811 CE). Bacchus (i.e. Dionysus) and his followers find Ariadne as she was gazing out to sea looking at Theseus' ship (just visible by her left shoulder) sailing away.

Figure 3.23. The abandonment of Ariadne by Theseus and her rescue by Dionysus.

Theseus

Theseus (Figure a) was a great Athenian hero who engaged in a large number of heroic deeds (the "six labours") in addition to killing the minotaur.

He had two fathers because his mother, Aethra, had sex on the same night with both her husband Aegeus, the king of Athens, as well as Poseidon. After his adventures in Crete, he returned to Athens but forgot that he had promised Aegeus to hoist a white sail if his mission to kill the Minotaur had been successful. The ship that carried away the 14 sacrificial youths to

Figure a. Plaster relief of the head of Theseus.

Crete always used a black sail. Consequently, on seeing a black sail, Aegeus assumed that his son had been killed and drowned himself – the sea bordering Athens then became known as the Aegean.

The ship in which Theseus returned from Crete was kept in the Athenian harbour as a memorial for several centuries. As each old plank decayed, it was replaced by a new one. This gave rise to the "Ship of Theseus paradox" because eventually it wasn't clear how much of the old ship remained and this raised the philosophical question as to whether or not it should be considered to be "the same" ship or not[75].

On his return from Crete, the victorious Theseus united the people of Athens into a single city-complex, put a democratic government in place, built a town-hall and council chamber and introduced festivals[76,77]. Although a great hero, his attitude to women left a lot to be desired. He abducted the nine-year-old Helen of Troy (who was later rescued) as well as Antigone, the sister of the Queen of the Amazons, who became his first wife. Having abandoned Ariadne, he eventually married her sister Phaedra after Antigone had died in battle. Unfortunately, Phaedra fell in love with Hippolytus, Theseus' son from a previous marriage. Hippolytus did not reciprocate Phaedra's love and so she told Theseus that she had been raped by Hippolytus (Figure b). There are various versions of what happened next, but they all end up with the death of Phaedra and Hippolytus.

Figure b. Phaedra Rejecting the Embraces of Theseus by Anne-Louis Girodet de Roucy-Trioson (about 1800). The drawing depicts a scene in act III of Racine's play Phaedra. On his return home, Theseus reaches out to greet Phaedra, who shies away from him. Surprised at this reception, Theseus looks at his son Hippolytus for an explanation.

The death of Theseus is rather an anti-climax. All that is said is that he became unpopular and fled to Lycos where he was thrown to his death from a cliff by the king of the island, Lycomedes[78].

everything, but he does not possess the air." He then "turns his mind to unknown arts; changing the laws of nature"[81]. What he did was to construct two sets of wings (Figure 3.24) and use these to fly away from Crete. In Chapter 4 we will describe how he might have achieved this – he may have built a hang-glider. The earliest version of this story is by Palaiphatos[82].

Daidalos was obviously worried about the dangers involved in flying and instructed his son[83]: "Fly behind me with the wings I give you: I'll go in front: your job's to follow: you'll be safe where I lead. For if we go near the sun through the airy aether, the wax will not endure the heat: if our humble wings glide close to ocean, the breaking salt waves will drench our feathers. Fly between the two: and fear the breeze as well, spread your wings and follow, as the winds allow." As

Figure 3.24. Ikaros and Daidalos by Frederic Leighton (1830-1896). This is a black and white reproduction of the original colour painting which can be viewed at https://www.frederic-leighton.org/Daedalus-And-Icarus.html. In this painting father and son are shown preparing for their flight. On the edge of some precipice, Daidalos is making the final adjustment to the straps that hold the wings to his son's body. They are silhouetted against a bright sky and blue waters below. The wind is blowing Daidalos' dark cloak. Behind the pair is a bronze statue of Athena. Both Daidalos and Ikaros are gazing into the sky where they will soon be flying. There is a dramatic contrast between father and son with the former looking darkly tanned, with aged flesh and bald. Ikaros seems barely aware of the presence of his father and is pale, looks very young and is standing in the classical pose of a kouros.

he warns, he fits the wings to his child, shows how they move, as a bird teaches her young nestlings." All went well for a while and they flew to the right of Delos and Paros and then to the left of Lebynthos and Calymne (Figure 3.25).

But then, despite his father's warning about not flying too high, Ikaros did just that and the sun melted the wax and he fell into the sea (Figure 3.26) where he drowned[84]: "Proud of his success, the foolish Ikaros forsook his guide, and, bold in vanity, began to soar, rising upon his wings to touch the skies; but as he neared the scorching sun, its heat softened the fragrant wax that held his plumes; and heat increasing melted the soft wax — he waved his naked arms

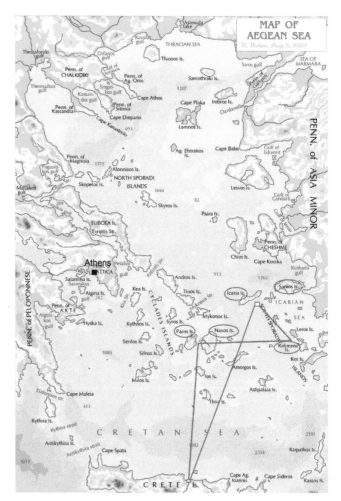

Figure 3.25. Map of the Aegean Sea showing the flight path of Daidalos and Ikaros from Crete (bottom) to Icaria (halfway up on right). The red line shows the flight path based on Ovid's description. The islands mentioned by Ovid are circled in red. The blue line shows a more direct path that is also in keeping with what Ovid describes. The location of Athens is indicated by a black square.

instead of wings, with no more feathers to sustain his flight."

Siet hier Voorsightigheyd, en Deraasheyd voor uw Oogen;
Want met een Jaager Vlucht raackt DÆDALUS aan 't Land.
Door Vleugel-maakings Kunst: maar ICAR t'hoog gevloogen,
Valt Vleugelloos in Zee: en komt nooyt weer aan Strand.
J. Lysma.

(a) The fall of Icarus by Jan Luyken (1686 CE). Daedalus glances up and is shocked to see Icarus tumbling out of the sky.

(b) Terracotta, red-figure vase attributed to the "Ikaros painter" (470 BCE). The vase shows the winged figure of Ikaros with most of his legs immersed in the sea. The downward-plunging bird indicates that he has just plummeted from the sky.

Figure 3.26. The fall of Ikaros

Why Ikaros failed to follow his father's advice has been the subject of endless debate over the centuries. Was he so exhilarated by the experience of flying that he forgot the warning? Did he, like many a rebellious youth, deliberately ignore his father's advice? Or did he display disdain for the idea of choosing a cautious "middle way" and decide to "live life to the full" and so experience the joy of soaring way up into the sky? Andre Gide's view is that "Ikaros was, before his birth, and remains after his death, the image of man's disquiet, of the impulse to discovery, the soaring flight of poetry – the things of which, during his short life, he was the incarnation. He played out his hand, as he owed it to himself to do; but he didn't end there. What happens, in the case of a hero, is this; his mark endures. Poetry and the arts re-animates it, and it becomes an enduring symbol"[85].

This tragedy happened near a small island close to Samos. The name of both the island (Icaria) and the surrounding sea (Icarian Sea) commemorate his death. This version of events is also related by Strabo[86], by Pseudo-Apollodorus[87] and by Hyginus[88]. Pseudo-Apollodorus tells us that Heracles happened to be passing by and buried Ikaros' body[89]: "And having put in to the island of Doliche, he saw the body of Ikaros washed ashore and buried it, and he called the island Icaria instead of Doliche."

Two aspects of the story immediately invite comment. First of all, it is nonsense that flying high would lead to the melting of the wax on Ikaros wings because he was getting closer to the sun. In fact the greater the altitude the colder it gets. However, as we shall see in Chapter 4, there were good reasons for Daidalos to warn Ikaros against flying too high or too low. Secondly, the flight path described by Ovid is puzzling. The direct route from Knossos to Athens would have been in a north-westerly direction passing over the islands of Milos, Serifos and Kythnos. Examination of the map in Figure 3.25 shows that, according to Ovid, Daidalos and Ikaros flew directly North and then, turned east towards Calymne (present-day Kalimnos). This eastward turn does not make sense if their ultimate destination was Athens. Even if we trace a path that does not go directly to each of the islands mentioned, which is probably the case as Ovid talks about the islands being to the left or the right of their path, the overall direction is north-east rather than north-west. There is also a tradition in present-day Gocek (on the south-west coast of Turkey) that Ikaros fell into the sea near this city (see the "endgame" section later in this Chapter) which is

The flight-path of Daidalos and Ikaros

A number of commentators have suggested alternative explanations for the puzzling flight-path described by Ovid. The most plausible of these is based on the idea that there was a mistake in identifying the place where Ikaros died. It has been proposed that this was near Icaria on the Greek mainland rather than the island of Icaria in the Aegean (The flight-plan of Daedalus. Peter Green. In: *From Ikaria to the Stars: Classical Mythification, Ancient and Modern*. Green P. University of Texas Press, 2004, pages 40-46). Stephanus Byzantius says that Icaria is an Attic deme of the Aegeid tribe and is located about 3 miles southwest of Marathon. The sanctuary of Dionysus of Icaria was discovered there in 1888. Geographically, it makes far more sense that Daidalos and Ikaros would have been heading in this direction which is only 14miles northeast of Athens, as the crow flies. Furthermore, the scholiast on Euripides reported that Ikaros fell into "the sea by the Paralia" i.e. the coastal waters of Attica between Marathon and Euboea (Schol. Eur. *Hipp.* 887).

How then did the island of Icaria come to be so-named? One possibility is that the settlers who originally colonised Icaria in the 10th or 11th century BCE were from Attica and simply used the name of their place of origin. Later writers then simply confused the two Icarias when relating the fall of Ikaros.

The perils of flying

It is interesting to compare Daidalos' interactions with the two young men (Talos and Ikaros) with whom he is associated. Both resulted in death attributable to a failure to fly. In the case of his nephew, Talos, Daidalos throws him into the air from the Acropolis (or the top of Athena's temple) and his inability to fly results in his death. However, one version of the story has Talos being turned into a partridge by Athena which, of course, can fly and he thereby avoids death – but at the expense of being transformed into a bird. A partridge (Perdix in Greek) is said to have watched the burial of Ikaros on Icaria from a nearby tree and made a chattering, joyful sound – this has been interpreted as representing the soul of the murdered nephew rejoicing in its revenge. In contrast, with regard to his son, Daidalos tried to convert Ikaros into a bird by giving him wings but, because of his inability to use these properly (flying too close to the sun), Ikaros falls from the sky and is killed. So, Daidalos' involvement with each of these two young men resulted in them falling to their death.

approximately 100 miles southeast of Calymne. The ancient name for Gocek was Kalimche which is very similar to Calymne and, therefore, could have been confused with it. Regardless of where Ikaros drowned, he and his father were a long way off the direct route to Athens. Only Strabo appears to have commented on this discrepancy and attributes it to them "having lost control of their course"[90]. The prevailing winds in this part of the Aegean tend to be from the north-west throughout most of the year and could be the reason for them being so far east. The direction of prevailing winds, as well as their strength, is a well-known hazard for modern human-powered aircraft, gliders, hang-gliders and parachutists. That two such inexperienced flyers as Daidalos and Ikaros would have been blown of course should not come as a surprise to us.

According to Diodorus Siculus, however, Daidalos and Ikaros escaped from Crete in a boat supplied by Pasiphae and, on reaching a small island, Ikaros fell into the sea and drowned while disembarking[91]. Pausanias also supports this version of events[92]: "For when he was fleeing from Crete in small vessels which he had made for himself and his son Ikaros, he devised for the ships' sails, an invention as yet unknown to the men of those times, so as to take advantage of a favourable wind and outsail the oared fleet of Minos. Daidalos himself was saved, but the ship of Ikaros is said to have overturned, as he was a clumsy helmsman."

A third, earlier, version of the story of Daidalos' escape from Crete has him going to Athens rather than Sicily or Italy[93,94,95]. Cleidemus[93] (a 5th century BCE Greek historian) says that Daidalos fled from Crete to Athens in a merchant ship and was pursued by Minos with his battle fleet. However, a storm blew Minos off course and he was driven to Sicily where he died, although details of his death are not revealed. Deucalion, the son of Minos, demanded that Theseus give up Daidalos or else he would kill the Athenian hostages. Theseus refused this on the grounds that

Daidalos was his cousin and started to secretly build a fleet. When his fleet was ready, he sailed to Crete, guided by Daidalos, and stealthily brought his troops to Knossos. There he slew Deucalion and made a truce with Ariadne who was now in charge of things. Cleidemus was considered by Pausanias to be the earliest Athenian historian and wrote a book, *Atthis*, about the history of the city. Unfortunately, none of the works of Cleidemus, other than a few fragments, have survived and the above version of events is credited to him but related by Plutarch in his *Theseus*. Unfortunately, Plutarch does not tell us what Cleidemus had to say about the fate of Ikaros or Ariadne.

This alternative version of events in which Daidalos goes to Athens rather than to Sicily may simply be an attempt by Athenian writers to "bring home" Daidalos to Athens, reclaim him as an Athenian (see Chapter 5 for a further discussion of this theme) and incorporate him into their history.

The two contrasting means of escape, using wings or sails, possibly stemmed from the confusing interchangeable use by the Greeks' of the words "wings" and "sails", particularly in poetry. For example, Hesiod talking about the origins of seafaring says[96]: "They were the first to build ships, curved on both ends, and they first put up sails, the wings of a seagoing ship."

Minos was furious when he learned of Daidalos' escape from Crete[97]: "...... and king Minos, desiring to wreak vengeance upon him and yet being unable to find him, caused all the boats which were on the island to be searched and announced that he would give a great sum of money to the man who should discover Daidalos."

Daidalos' journey from Crete to Sicily

It is a long way from Crete to Sicily – more than 600 miles. Although the ancient writers tell us little about the route that Daidalos took, two incidents are described that are said to have occurred on the way.

In the *Aeneid*, Virgil relates that Daidalos does not go directly to Sicily but instead flew first to Cumae and built a temple to Apollo there[98] (Figure 3.27). This is also mentioned by Silius Italicus.[99]

Figure 3.27. Ruins of the Temple of Apollo at Cumae

Cumae is near Naples and has a huge cave (Figure 3.28) which was the home of one of the most important oracles of the ancient world – the Cumaean Sybil (Figure 3.29) – as well as being an opening to the underworld.

It is this oracle that Aeneas visited and, after praying to Apollo in the temple built by Daidalos, descended into the underworld guided by the Sybil. As well as offering his wings to Apollo, Daidalos also embarked on a complex work of art and decorated the golden doors of the temple with scenes from his life and the lives of those he had known. These scenes included: the killing of Androgeus (one of Minos' sons), the drawing of lots for selecting the Athenian victims to be sent to the Minotaur, the love of Pasiphae for Poseidon's bull, the Minotaur in the labyrinth and himself showing Ariadne how to get out of the labyrinth using a ball of thread. But what was missing was his flight from Crete with Ikaros. Daidalos was too grief-stricken to be able to portray this scene and, after several attempts, abandoned trying to carve it. Virgil makes no further reference to Daidalos. This little story is really the only time that Daidalos speaks to us across the millennia. Here we see him expressing emotions for the first time, he is human after all! Although he was willing to help Pasiphae and Ariadne with their problems, we don't know why he did so. Was it because he felt sorry for them? Was he getting something from them in return? Was it because he just loved solving difficult problems? We simply don't know. But here, at the temple of Apollo in Cumae, we see a broken man, an artist who cannot portray the story of his son's death because he is so

Figure 3.28. Entrance to the Sybil's cave at Cumae

overcome with grief. From what I have seen of ancient pottery, the people portrayed on them very rarely show any recognisable expression. However, one important and very moving exception appears on a fragment of a red-figure calyx krater (Figure 3.30). This shows a winged, bearded man who is gently carrying a child in his hands. The child was originally painted white and the drooping head and hanging limbs clearly show that s/he is dead. The man has a tragic expression on his face and the furrows on his brow and between his eyebrows show that he is in pain. His unfocused eyes and the protruding lower lip emphasise his sadness. The clothes he wears are appropriate for a craftsman which, together with the wings, indicate that this is a portrait of Daidalos carrying his dead son off for burial[100]. The artist shows amazing empathy with his subject matter, perhaps he also had experienced the loss of a child?

Once again I can empathise with Daidalos for I too have lost a son. Andrew lived for 8 months in a

Figure 3.30. Fragment of an Apulian calyx-krater (390-380 BCE). British Museum.

membrane-bound world having started, like all of us, as a single cell and having passed through a series of wondrous transformations into a complex, highly-differentiated, advanced life form. But he never made it through that final transition from the enclosed, highly-constricted aquatic realm of his mother's womb into our gaseous, open world. The death of Ikaros was a reverse of this progression as it involved the devastatingly rapid passage from the boundless sky to a relatively unyielding sea. My tragedy happened 30 years ago and at that time I didn't know how I would ever manage to cope. How could I possibly go on? How would I be able to continue with my life and the day-to-day trivia after such a horror? And now, as I look back, I'm simply astonished at how I managed to survive through all the intervening years. An astonishment tinged with guilt. Why wasn't I totally over-

Flight-related death

A premonition of flight-related death is beautifully portrayed in a poem written by Yeats in 1918 - "An Irish Airman foresees his Death"

> I know that I shall meet my fate
> Somewhere among the clouds above;
> Those that I fight I do not hate,
> Those that I guard I do not love;
> My country is Kiltartan Cross,
> My countrymen Kiltartan's poor,
> No likely end could bring them loss
> Or leave them happier than before.
> Nor law, nor duty bade me fight,
> Nor public men, nor cheering crowds,
> A lonely impulse of delight
> Drove to this tumult in the clouds;
> I balanced all, brought all to mind,
> The years to come seemed waste of breath,
> A waste of breath the years behind
> In balance with this life, this death.

whelmed by the pain? I don't have the answers to these questions and never will. Somehow you just get on with life. Everything is duller. No joy is ever felt with quite the same intensity as before.

Prior to launching off on their flight from Crete, Ovid conveys Daidalos' anxiety (or perhaps his premonition) and tells us[101]: "Now, about to fly, he gave the small boy a kiss, and the tears ran down the father's cheeks." Likewise, I kissed my tiny child, in the smart, spotless baby clothes kindly provided by

As we will see in Chapter 5, the death of Ikaros has inspired great art throughout the ages. The death of my son, Andrew, may have indirectly resulted in a few minor inventions but has not inspired any great art – just a simple poem written on his 29th birthday:

For Andrew on his 29th birthday

Lying in the cold dark earth
A cradle hungry for your birth.
From the still and silent ground
Escapes no gentle breath or sound.
We buried you so long ago
That now you're of the soil below.
You will not walk upon this land
Or hold your mother's guiding hand.
Nor will you hear my words of praise
Or be the focus of our gaze.
Oh what wonders would you have seen
If alive you could have been?
Our little one, our darling boy
You would have filled our lives with joy.
But now our remaining days are few
And soon we will be joining you.
Could there be a hereafter
Where we might catch your childish laughter?
We dare not wish for such delight
And fear instead an endless night
From which there will be no returning
Or respite from our endless yearning

the hospital – the first and last kiss I would ever give him. But, unlike Daidalos' kiss, mine was planted on cold, unresponsive flesh.

Fortunately, unlike Daidalos, I never had to deal with the guilt of having been the agency of my son's death. Nevertheless, Daidalos did carry on and managed to undertake a succession of amazing projects. Perhaps labour is the answer to such tragedies. I also threw myself into my work – the rigours of scientific research were certainly a great distraction and enabled me to come up with a few inventions. Does this mean I can consider myself to be a Daidalian? I hope so. Is tragedy a spur to scientific creativity?

In another event said to have occurred on Daidalos' journey from Crete to Sicily, Charax of Pergamon (a Greek historian active in the 2nd century CE) relates that Daidalos stayed for a while as the guest of King Augeas in Elis[102]. Augeas is famous for having had vast herds of cattle and one of Hercules' tasks was to clean out his stables of the dung that had accumulated there for 30 years (Figure 3.31).

During Daidalos' visit, Augeas discovered that his treasury was being robbed and asked Daidalos for help to find out who was behind this. What had happened was that the builders of the treasury, Agamedes and his illegitimate son Trophonios, had left a loose stone in the wall which was carefully disguised so as to make it undetectable. At night they, together with Kerkyon, the legitimate son of Agamedes, would loosen this stone, remove some treasure and then carefully replace the stone. Augeas was puzzled because the lock and seal on the door of the treasury had not been tampered with so he couldn't understand how the treasure was being removed. Daidalos decided that the best way to solve the problem was not to try to work out how they were getting in but simply to set a trap for the thieves inside the treasury. Agamedes was caught in this trap (its nature was not disclosed) and died. The story then tells us, rather strangely, that Trophonios cut off and removed the head of his dead father. He did this so that people wouldn't associate him and his half-brother with the robbery and they then both fled to Orchomenos. The story was well known in the 6th century BCE because it was also told by a poet of that time, Eugammon of Kyrene, in his *Telegonia*. The *Telegonia* was the life story of Odysseus and in this was related that he visited Augeas and received a gift of a bowl on which the above tale was depicted.

Daidalos in Sicily

Figure 3.31. Labours of Hercules (3rd, 5th, 7th), (1500-1525 CE). The left part of the tapestry shows Hercules cleaning the stables of Augeas by diverting the rivers Alpheus and Peneus. In the centre, he is shown capturing the Cretan bull.

According to Diodorus Siculus[103]: "Daedalus...... landed in Sicily near the territory over which Cocalus reigned as king, who courteously received Daedalus and because of his genius and his renown made him his close friend." This is supported by other writers – Herodotus[104] and Apollodorus[105]. King Cocalus

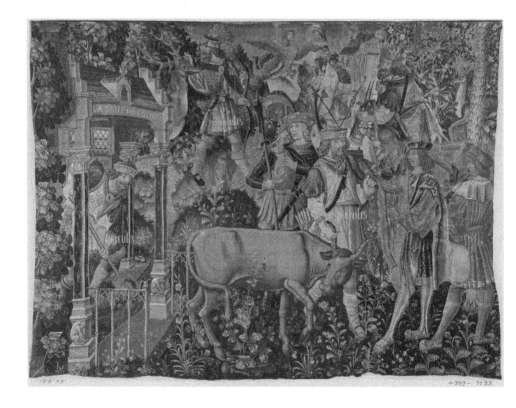

(Kokalos) was the ruler of the Sicani, in Camicus (Kamikos) on the south of the island. The location of Camicus is uncertain but current opinion is that it may have been present-day Sant'Angelo Muxaro which is about 12 miles north of present-day Agrigento (see Figure 2.47 in Chapter 2). In contrast to most writers, however, Pausanias says that King Cocalus was based at Inycus, a city on the South West coast of Sicily[106].

After arriving there, Daidalos built a temple to Apollo and hung up his wings in it as an offering. This relinquishment of his wings (mentioned also by Virgil) could be highly symbolic. Had Daidalos resolved to be more "down to earth" and to stop dabbling in futuristic enterprises? This may have been the case as reports of his achievements in Sicily are of a more engineering nature rather than being inventive or artistic. But what compelled him to abandon further experimentation with one of his most sensational inventions? He had demonstrated the enormous potential of an exciting new mode of transport. Why not develop this further? An obvious explanation is that, following the death of Ikaros, he wanted nothing more to do with flying – further flights would only have been painful reminders of what had happened. Another possibility is that Ikaros' death may have brought home to him just how dangerous flying was. Perhaps he thought it would be irresponsible of him to reveal to the general public such a hazardous activity. The ethics of scientific research and the responsibility of scientists for their discoveries are discussed further in Chapter 5. But what a sacrifice. It can't have been easy for Daidalos to give up the thrill of soaring high up into the sky and swooping down low over the land and sea. The exhilaration, the joy, the sights, the excitement, the freedom.

During his stay in Camicus, Daidalos was very popular with Cocalus and his daughters. Although he delighted the girls by making dolls for them he, fortunately, did not get involved in their love-lives. Nevertheless, Pausanias says that[106] "He was so much admired by the daughters of Cocalus for his artistic skill that to please him these women actually plotted against Minos to put him to death." In the meantime, Minos frantically searched for Daidalos and came up with a cunning plan to track him down. He informed all of the kings of the known world that he would give a prize to whoever could devise a way of stringing a linen thread through a conch shell. Minos was convinced that only Daidalos would be able to solve this difficult puzzle. Daidalos, of course, came up with the ingenious solution of piercing a hole in the tip of the conch shell (which is, in effect, a miniature labyrinth), smearing this with honey, and tying a gossamer thread to an ant, which, attracted by the honey, would wind its way through the spirals of the shell taking the thread with it. He then tied a linen thread to the gossamer and so pulled that through the hole as well[107]. But why did he do this? He knew that Minos was after him and that by solving the puzzle Minos would know that he was in Cocalus' court. The answer has to be that he simply could not resist the challenge, he loved problem-solving. Cocalus informed Minos of this solution to the puzzle and Minos immediately knew that Daidalos must be there. He sailed for Sicily with a large fleet and, according to Diodorus Siculus[108], he landed at a place in the territory of Acragas which was subsequently named Minoa after him. After disembarking his troops, he sent messengers to King Cocalus demanding that Daidalos be turned over to him. This put Cocalus in a very difficult position as he did not want to oppose such a powerful king but neither did he want to hand over Daidalos. Together with his daughters, he decided to murder Minos but to make it look like an accident. First of all, he invited Minos to a conference at his palace. There are a number of versions of what happened next. Some say that Daidalos had built a plumbing system that delivered hot water for bathing.

Cocalus' daughters persuaded Minos, as an honoured guest, to have a bath and he was then scalded to death. Others say that Minos was scalded to death by hot oil, hot water or boiling pitch poured over him in the bath by either Cocalus, his daughters or by Daidalos himself. Herodotus merely says that Minos died violently[109]. Cocalus then gave Minos' body to the Cretan troops, explaining that he had slipped in the bath and fell into the hot water and had been scalded to death. The Cretans who had sailed with Minos were now devoid of a leader. Some of them decided to sail back to Crete while others opted to settle in Sicily and they established two towns, one at Minoa (Figure 3.32) and the other at Engyum[110].

Minos' men also constructed a two-storey building – the upper storey was made into a shrine to Aphrodite while the body of Minos was placed in the lower storey. Herodotus tells us that later on Crete decided to avenge the death of Minos[111]: "...after a time the Cretans, urged thereto by a god, all except the men of Polichne and Praisos, came with a great armament

Figure 3.32. Ruins of a residential quarter at Heraclea Minoa (formerly known as Minoa)

to Sicania and besieged for seven years the city of Camicos, which in my time was occupied by the Agrigentines; and at last not being able either to capture it or to remain before it, because they were hard-pressed by famine, they departed and went away." In the 5th century BCE, Theron (the tyrant of Acragas between 489 and 472 BCE) dismantled Minos' tomb and sent his bones back to Crete for burial at Knossos.

Daidalos then settled down in Camicus and designed many interesting buildings and public works (described in Chapter 4). According to Pausanias[112] "It is plain that the renown of Daidalos spread over all Sicily and even over the greater part of Italy." However, one can't help but feel a little sorry for him and the words of a song come to mind in which the singer (Leonard Cohen) reflects on a fall from fame and glory that is both a long and a strange way down. From the luxury of Knossos with its stunning frescoes, beautiful clothes and jewellery, gorgeous pottery and ornaments, exquisitely carved sealstones, fine foods and wines to this relatively primitive backwater on the edge of the civilized world. And, of course, the shadow of the death of his son hanging over him. Cocalus' daughters may have been there to interest and amuse him but they were surely just pale shadows compared to the full-blooded royal women he had known in Knossos. However, he may have taken some consolation that he was, like the frontiersmen in the USA, one of the pioneers of the wild west. Although Sicily was a long way west of Crete and Greece, we have already seen that the Minoans had begun to establish a few colonies on the island. From the time of the Trojan war (approximately 1200 BCE), and particularly during the 8th century BCE, the island was to be extensively colonised by the Greeks (Figure 3.33). In fact, there were so many colonies there that Sicily and the coastal regions of Southern Italy were to become known as "Magna Graecia"[113].

Endgame

For many of the ancient writers, that was the end of
Daidalos' story. However, there are a few fragmentary
reports of Daidalos leaving Sicily. In one he is said
to have gone to Sardinia at the request of Iolaus, the
charioteer and nephew of Hercules[114]. There he is said
to have executed a number of major works and these
are described in Chapter 4.

Another account also had Daidalos sailing to
Sardinia, this time to escape from Minos who had
arrived in Sicily[115]. There he is said to have joined Aristaeus who was the son of Apollo and Cyrene and the

*Figure 3.33. Map of Magna
Graecia showing the main
colonies and also the dialects of
the Greek colonisers (500 BCE).*

god of bee-keeping, cheese-making and olive growing (Figure 3.34).

However, Pausanias pours scorn on this suggestion[116]: "...it is nonsense to think that Daidalos, a contemporary of Oedipus, king of Thebes, had a part in a colony or anything else along with Aristaeus." In a book entitled *On Marvellous Things Heard*, yet another possibility is suggested. This book, which is a collection of anecdotes, was traditionally attributed to Aristotle but is now regarded as having been written by another, as yet unknown, author who is referred to as Pseudo-Aristotle. In this, we are told that, after leaving Sicily, Daidalos went to the Elektrides Islands, erected statues there (see Chapter 4) and then went on to the island of Icarus[117]: "They say that Daedalus came to these islands [i.e. the Elektrides], and putting in there set up in one of them his own image, and in the other that of his son Icarus. Later on, when the Pelasgians, who were expelled from Argos, sailed there, Daedalus fled, and sailed to the island of Icarus."

It's interesting at this stage to reflect on the enormous impact Daidalos had on the Mediterranean world at that time. Firstly, by helping Theseus (via Ariadne), he ended Crete's domination of Athens and so encouraged the rise of Athens as a major power in the region. Secondly, the death of Minos (in pursuit of Daidalos in Sicily) contributed to the downfall of the Minoans. Finally, the help he gave to King Cocalus in Sicily would have contributed significantly to the development and influence of Magna Graecia.

The classical writers tell us what happened to all the major protagonists in Daidalos' story – Minos (murdered), Theseus (murdered), Ariadne (either married to Dionysus or committed suicide), Ikaros (drowned) but leave us guessing with regard to Pasiphae and Daidalos.

Neglecting to tell us what happened to Pasiphae is a great disappointment. All we really know of her is that she was the daughter of Helios, was a sorceress, had an unnatural passion for a bull and gave birth to a bull-man hybrid. What were her feelings about being the mother of a creature that everyone considered to be a monster? There is a curiously touching portrayal of her holding the baby minotaur on her lap on a 4th century BCE drinking cup which can be seen at *https://commons.wikimedia.org/wiki/File:Pasiphae_Minotauros_Cdm_Paris_DeRidder1066.jpg*

Not surprisingly, she has an apprehensive look on her face ("what on earth have I done? What is going to happen to my baby?"), but there is also tenderness there. The baby has what appear to be bootees on his feet, so he's being well cared for – either by Pasiphae or her servants. She is wearing a loose-fitting, transparent gown and her breasts can clearly be seen. Has she just suckled him? In one of the few fragments that remain of a play written by Euripides, entitled *The Cretans*, a conversation held between Minos and a nurse tells us that Pasiphae did suckle the baby mino-taur[118]:

Minos: "...a mother's breast, or a cow's...?"
Nurse: "Its parent feeds it..."

A more recent portrayal of the baby minotaur is shown in Figure 3.35.

Figure 3.35. Pasiphae with the little minotaur. By Nicolai Abildgaard (1743-1809 CE). Here the baby minotaur appears to be happy sitting on his mother's lap next to his very docile father.

As the infant grew older she must have puzzled over what to feed him. What does a minotaur eat? Bulls, of course, eat grass and other vegetation. Perhaps the human milk he was given generated a taste for something other than grass? When did he develop a taste for human flesh? I can't help but feel that she loved her little hybrid. There is an interesting portrayal of the minotaur in the centre of a 6th-century kylix which can be viewed at: *https://commons.wikimedia.org/wiki/File:Tondo_Minotaur_London_E4_MAN.jpg*. The minotaur is shown running and clutching stones (his preferred weapon) but around the image is an inscription which reads "the boy is beautiful". Perhaps the artist is conveying what Pasiphae felt for her son? Or else it could have been meant as a cruel joke to amuse any drinker who used the cup.

How did Pasiphae feel about her son being locked away in the labyrinth? Maybe he became unmanageable when he reached puberty – human teenagers are difficult enough, so imagine a teenage minotaur. So, perhaps she resigned herself to the inevitable and

consented to have him locked away in the labyrinth
- but imagine the guilt she must have felt. The Greek
and Roman historical authors say very little about
her. The poets and playwrights, however, found her
intriguing. In the few fragments that remain of Euripides' play *The Cretans*, Pasiphae receives some attention but she gets far more coverage by the Roman
poets Ovid and Virgil. In *The Cretans*, Pasiphae argues
before Minos that obviously she could not possibly
have loved a bull and so she must have been under the
malign influence of a god[119]: "There is nothing to gain
now by deceiving you; what has happened is already
too well known. But consider: if I had sold the gifts
of Kypris, given my body in secret to some man, you
would have every right to condemn me as a whore.
But this was no act of the will; I am suffering from
some madness brought on by a god. It's not plausible!
What could I have seen in a bull to assault my heart
with this shameful passion? Did he look too handsome in his robe? Did a sea of fire smolder in his eyes?
Was it the red tint of his hair, his dark beard? His
body, so [different] from my husband's? [...] Are these
the things that drew me to lie in his bed, in my cow
skin [...]? I did not imagine that my lover could give
me children [...] What diseased my mind?" She then
turns the tables on Minos and says that it is all his
fault - she had been cursed by a god because Minos
had failed to sacrifice Poseidon's bull[120]: "Why then
was I (maddened) by this affliction? It was this man's
destiny that (brought) me too (my fill) of trouble, and
he especially... since he did not slaughter (that) bull
(which) he vowed to sacrifice to the sea god when
it was manifested. This is the reason, I tell you, why
Poseidon undermined you and exacted punishment,
but launched (the affliction) upon me." This makes
us return to the age-old question of why Minos failed
to sacrifice the bull to Poseidon. How could he have
been so stupid as to defy the commands of a god?

As to how Pasiphae ended her days, in another fragment from *The Cretans*, Minos condemns Pasiphae

and her nurse to death[121]: "...seize this evil woman so she may get a fine death, and her accomplice here, and take them inside the palace and shut them in a hidden prison, so they will no longer see the orb (of the sun)."

But the above extracts are taken from a play by Euripides and not from an historical account so we don't know how much weight should be given to them.

The ancients are also peculiarly silent about the death of Daidalos. Was this in Sicily or, possibly, in Sardinia? There is mention of a temple built for him near Memphis in Egypt[122], but that doesn't necessarily imply that he died there. Ovid says that Daidalos was very anxious to return to Athens and, before his escape from Crete, he told Minos that he wanted to die there[123]: "He spoke to Minos saying, "O thou who art so just, set a term to my exile; let my native land receive my ashes. If the Fates forbid that I should live in my own country, grant at least that I may die there." Life in Sicily certainly lacked the luxury of Knossos and Athens but perhaps such a Spartan existence served as a form of penance to ease the guilt over the death of Ikaros? Perhaps he was tired of trying to shake off the hold that mighty kings, determined to make use of his talents, had over him? Socrates suggests that Daidalos was more of a slave than a guest in Sicily. In the *Memorabilia*, a set of

Figure 3.36. Statue of the Ancient Greek historian and philosopher Xenophon in front of the Austrian Parliament Building in Vienna.

Socratic dialogues written by Xenophon (Figure 3.36) in 361 BCE, Socrates comments[124]: "Indeed! Have you not heard how Daidalos was seized by Minos because of his wisdom, and was forced to be his slave, and was robbed of his country and his liberty, and essaying to escape with his son, lost the boy and could not save himself, but was carried off to the barbarians and again lived as a slave there?"

After much investigation, I have found only one reference to the death of Daidalos and I wish I hadn't. I had imagined Daidalos as someone who would not just fade away and "go quietly into that dark night" but would "fight against the dying of the light". I thought he would continue with his work right up to the end and would invent a whole range of mechanical aids and devices to help him cope with old age. Unfortunately, I can't allow you, dear reader, to be comforted by the thought of such an ending to what had been an amazing life. The reality is far worse. The only mention of the death of Daidalos is contained in a reference by Stephanus Byzantius[125,126] to a passage in *Lyciaca*, a work of Alexander Polyhistor. Lucius Cornelius Alexander Polyhistor (ca 50 BCE) was a Greek writer and native of Ephesus who was given the surname Polyhistor on account of his great learning. He wrote 42 books on the history and geography of all the countries of the ancient world and these included Crete and Lycia. Only fragments of his work

Figure 3.37. Map of Anatolia in the 2nd century BCE showing the Rhodian Peraea in red.

have survived but he is quoted innumerable times by Stephanus Byzantius and Pliny. In the *Lyciaca* it says that Daidalos died in the Rhodian Peraea which is a coastal region in the southwest of Turkey that had been colonised by the nearby island of Rhodes. The region comprised two districts - Caria and Lycia (Figure 3.37).

On the eastern limit of the Peraea, the River Ninus/ Ninos (later known as Iniji Chai or Ineje) flows into the Gulf of Glaucus (present-day Gulf of Fethiye) and probably formed the boundary between Caria and Lycia. According to Stephanus Byzantius[125]: "And there is the city named after Daedalus the father of Icarus, which is in Lykia. For he was walking through a marsh along the river Ninos, and Alexandros says that, after being bitten by an amphibious serpent, he died and was buried there and a city was founded among the Lykians." The city was known as Daidala or Daedala. A nearby mountain on the west side of the river valley was also named Daidala[127] but is now called Kizildag. Two islands in the gulf at the mouth of the river were said by Pliny to belong to the city[128]. Daidala is situated on a hill between the modern towns of Inlice and Gocek, but nearer the former. On the top of the hill is a ring wall and inside this are the remains of a small fort, a circular cistern, house foundations and rock-cuttings. On a ridge lower down are the remnants of a cyclopean wall. In the vicinity are numerous rock tombs which are in the characteristic Lycian style (Figure 3.38). According to Arkwright[129], Daidala appears to have been a small place because Pliny[130] called it an "oppidum" (i.e. a town rather than a city) and Ptolemy[131] referred to it as a "topos" (i.e. a place) rather than a city.

Daidala appears to have been well known in ancient times, probably because it was a frontier town of Lycia and Caria, and is mentioned in a number of books. Livy (Titus Livius Patavinus), a 1st century BCE Roman historian talks about the city having been besieged during the 2nd century BCE Seleucid war[132]:

"Two days before Eudamus arrived with the fleet from Samos, a squadron of thirteen ships, together with four which had been guarding the coast of Caria, had been despatched from Rhodes under the command of Pamphilidas to meet this same Syrian fleet, and had raised the siege of Daedala and other fortified places belonging to Peraea which the king's troops were investing." It is also mentioned by

Figure 3.38. Lycian rock tombs.

Strabo[133], Pliny[134] and Ptolemaeus[135]. Daidala is also mentioned in *The Stadiasmus Maris Magni* which is an ancient periplus i.e. a manuscript that lists the ports and coastal landmarks that a ship could expect to find along the coast. It covered only the Mediterranean Sea and has been dated to the 3rd century CE but its author is unknown. The distances are given using the ancient Greek unit of measurement – the stade i.e. 600 feet. This was the distance covered in the standard footrace during the Olympic games and from it the word stadium is derived. According to this periplus, the distance from Daidala to Telmessos (present-day Fethiye) was 50 stades i.e. approximately 5.7 miles.

Figure 3.39. Map showing the location of the city of Daedala (arrowed). Note the location of Cujek (present-day Gocek) to the west of the city and the River Iniji Chai (to the east) on the banks of which stands the modern town of Inlice.

In 1842 CE, a British naval survey conducted by Hoskyn (Master of the ship H.M.S. Beacon) described the region around Daidala (Figure 3.39) as follows[136] "The village of Coujek [present day Gocek] is at the foot of the hills at the head of the plain; fresh provisions may be occasionally procured here. Two miles and a half S.E. of this is a rugged cape, near which a small stream, Iniji Chai (probably the ancient Ninus), empties itself; the valley through which it flows is highly picturesque and well cultivated. On the mountains on the W. side of the valley is an ancient site, probably Daedala: here are numerous tombs hewn in the rocks in the usual Lycian style; some are well finished. The acropolis stood on a detached hill; on its summit are remains of wells and a large cistern. We did not find any inscriptions."

So, what can we make of all this? My first reaction was to dismiss the possibility of this ignominious fate for such an eminent person. After all, it was just one obscure reference that had never been incorporated into the usual stories about his life. And why on earth would he have ended up in what at first sight appeared to be such an unlikely spot? So far from his usual haunts of Crete, Athens and Sicily. However, as I probed deeper, the feasibility of the story increased.

First of all Lycia was a kingdom founded and ruled by Sarpedon, the brother of Minos. As mentioned in Chapter 1, the sons of Europa argued about who was to succeed their step-father, Asterius, as ruler of Crete. Minos won and the other two brothers were banished. According to Herodotus[137]: "The Lykians however have sprung originally from Crete ....: and when the sons of Europa, Sarpedon and Minos, came to be at variance in Crete about the kingdom, Minos having got the better in the strife of parties drove out both Sarpedon himself and those of his party: and they having been expelled came to the land of Milyas in Asia, for the land which now the Lykians inhabit was anciently called Milyas." Apollodorus relates a slightly different story and says that the brothers fell out because they all loved the same young boy, Miletus[138]: "Now Asterius, prince of the Cretans, married Europa and brought up her children. But when they were grown up, they quarrelled with each other; for they loved a boy called Miletus, son of Apollo by Aria, daughter of Cleochus. As the boy was more friendly to Sarpedon, Minos went to war and had the better of it, and the others fled." Interestingly, Apollodorus then goes on to say that: "Miletus landed in Caria and there founded a city which he called Miletus after himself; and Sarpedon allied himself with Cilix, who was at war with the Lycians, and having stipulated for a share of the country, he became king of Lycia."

Consequently, both of the two main territories of Rhodian Peraea, Caria and Lycia, were colonised by Cretans. Another possible reason for Daidalos wishing to live there is because Lycian legends relate that Gocek, whose ancient name was Kalimche (or Callimache), is where Ikaros landed in the sea on his flight from Crete. This differs from the more widely-accepted version of the flight which has him falling into the Icarian sea. But perhaps this is the real version of events and Daidalos simply wanted to be close to where he had lost his son. Furthermore, as mentioned previously, Pseudo-Aristotle tells us that Daidalos went to the island of Icarus after leaving Sicily[117].

The idea of Daidalos travelling to this region therefore does not seem so unlikely. If, as has been suggested by Socrates[139], Daidalos was not really a free-man in the alien land of Sicily we can imagine him wanting to return to a more familiar and hospitable environment. He would have been aware of the Cretan settlements in Lycia and might have expected a warm reception from Sarpedon who, like him, had fallen out with Minos. The journey, even for a relatively old man, would not have been that difficult. The distance from Sicily to Daidala is approximately 700 nautical miles and Pliny estimates that in his day the average speed of a sailing ship with a favourable wind was approximately 5 knots[140]. This means the journey would have taken approximately 6 days by ship. It is, therefore, not unreasonable for Daidalos to have ended his days there. As for the way he died, what is there to say? Dreadful. It's not a death I would have wanted for such a hero and reinforces my strong dislike, and fear, of snakes – particularly the collared adder, the species that bit poor Daidalos.

Figure 3.40. Sign supposedly marking the site of the city of Deadala (Daidala, Daedala) near Gocek, Turkey.

What I find additionally upsetting and disturbing is that here we have the final resting place of one of the greatest human beings who ever lived and it is virtually unknown. The local tourist information office hadn't heard of it and couldn't point us in the right direction. All there is to mark the possible burial place of this illustrious individual is a small, faded signpost in the middle of nowhere (Figure 3.40).

Interestingly, the sign has been mounted outside a rock-tomb which is in the typical Lycian style (Figure 3.41). Unfortunately, this is certainly not the tomb of Daidalos as it was built in the 5th or 4th century BCE. Furthermore, the sign does not even denote the correct site of the city of Daidala which is located on a hill approximately 1.5 Km to the North-east of this tomb (Figure 3.42).

Figure 3.41. Tomb close to the sign denoting "Deadala". Paavo Roos describes the site, commenting that most of the remains of the city are to be found on the acropolis hill[141].

Figure 3.42. The hill on which the acropolis of Daidala is situated.

On this hill are the ruins of a small fort and on three sides this is protected by a wall – the western side of the hill is so steep that no wall was necessary. The remains of a cistern and house foundations are also present and further protective walls, and possibly a gate or tower, can be seen on the North-east of the hill (Figure 3.43).

Figure 3.43. Remains of the walls surrounding Daidala.

Some pottery was found at the site (Figure 3.44)

That there is so little to denote the grave of this famous person, or the city that grew up around it in his honour, is very disappointing. However, on the positive side, there are no hoards of tourists shuffling along in the heat trying to catch a glimpse of where our naissance man died. No stalls selling plastic replicas of his wings, no seedy "adult" shops selling life-size replicas of Pasiphae's cow, no "find your way out of the labyrinth" competitions and no "try your strength against the minotaur" booths. So, it's best that it remains a quiet and forgotten site where Daidalos can rest in peace. Although the circumstances and whereabouts of his death may have been forgotten, his life story has not and, as we shall see in Chapter 5, his name lives on in innumerable, significant ways.

Figure 3.44. Pottery found at Daidala. These consisted of a red-glazed skyphos and jug and two black-glazed bowls.

References

1. Diodorus Siculus, *Bibliotheca Historica*, 4.76.1

2. Hyginus, *Fabulae*, 39

3. Pseudo-Apollodorus, *Library*, 3.15.8

4. Pausanias, *Description of Greece*, 9.3.2

5. Ausonius. *Idylls*, 12

6. Eustathius on Homer's *Iliad* 18.590

7. Pseudo-Apollodorus, *Library*, 3.15.9

8. Pausanias, *Description of Greece*, 2.15.1

9. Pliny, *Naturalis Historia*, 36.4

10. Strabo, *Geographica*, 6.3.2

11. Homer, *The Iliad*, 18.587

12. Pseudo-Apollodorus, *Library*, 3.15.8

13. Hyginus, *Fabulae*, 39

14. Pliny, *Naturalis Historia* 7.57

15. Diodorus Siculus, *Bibliotheca Historica*, 4.76.5

16. Ovid, *Metamorphoses*, 8.236

17. Diodorus Siculus, *Bibliotheca Historica*, 4.76.5

18. Pausanias, *Description of Greece*, 1.21.4

19. Suda, *Encyclopedia*, p. 1042.

20. Pseudo-Apollodorus, *Library*, 4, 76.5

21. Diodorus Siculus, *Bibliotheca Historica*, 4.76.7

22. Margaret Crosby and John Young. Greek inscriptions: a poletai record of the year 367/6 BCE. *Hesperia: The Journal of the American School of Classical Studies at Athens*, 1941: 10; 14-27

23. Pausanias, *Description of Greece*, 7.4.5

24. Pliny, *Naturalis Historia*, 7.57

25. Homer, *The Odyssey*, 19.164

26. Pseudo-Apollodorus, *Library*, 3.1.2

27. Hesiod, Fragments, CW.F19

28. Pliny, *Naturalis Historia*, 12.5.4

29. Diodorus Siculus, *Bibliotheca Historica*, 4.60.1

30. Pseudo-Apollodorus, *Library*, 3.1.3

31. Propertius, *Elegies*, 3. 19.

32. Ovid, *Art of Love*, 1.293-1.308

33. Hesiod, *Catalogue of Women*, 93.14-17

34. Bacchylides, Ode 26.

35. Pseudo-Apollodorus, *Library*, 3.1.4

36. Bacchylides, Ode 26

37. Palaiphatos, *Concerning Incredible Tales*, 2

38. Isokrates, *Helen*, 27

39. Apollonius of Rhodes, *Argonautica* 3.999

40. Cicero, *De Natura Deorum* 3.19

41. Pseudo-Apollodorus, *Library*, 3.197

42. Antoninus Liberalis, *Metamorphoseon Synagoge*, 41

43. Pseudo-Apollodorus, *Library*, 3.1.3.

44. Hesiod, *Catalogue of Women*, Fragment 93

45. Palaiphatos, *Concerning Incredible Tales*, 2

46. Euripides, *The Cretans*, fragment f472b

47. Euripides, *The Cretans*, fragment f472a

48. Euripides, *The Cretans*, fragment f988

49. Hyginus, *Fabulae*, 40

50. Pseudo-Apollodorus, *Library*, 3.15.8

51. Isokrates *Helen*, 27.

52. Hyginus, *Astronomica* 2.5.3

53. Pausanias, *Description of Greece*, 1.17.3

54. Hyginus, *Astronomica* 2.5.3

55. Catullus, Poem 64, 86–93.

56. Pseudo-Apollodorus, *Library*, e.1.8).

57. Diodorus Siculus, *Bibliotheca Historica*, 4.60.3-60.5.

58. Pherecydes 3F148.

59. Hyginus, *Astronomica* 2.5.1.

60. Sappho, Fragment 206.

61. Pseudo-Apollodorus, *Library*, e 1.9.

62. Euripides, *The Cretans*, Fragment 386b.

63. Catullus, Poem 64, 105–11).

64. Homer, *The Iliad*, 13.389–91).

65. Hesiod, Fragments, CW.F76.

66. Catullus 64.149–51

67. Catullus 64.180–1

68. Homer, *Odyssey*, 11.225

69. Plutarch, *Life of Theseus*, 20

70. Pseudo-Apollodorus, *Library*, e 1.9

71. Pausanias, *Description of Greece*, 10.29.4

72. Diodorus Siculus, *Bibliotheca Historica*, 4.61.5

73. Ovid, *Metamorphoses*, 8.174.

74. Hesiod, *Theogony* 947–9

75. Plutarch, *Life of Theseus*, 23

76. Plutarch, *Life of Theseus*. 24

77. Thucydides, *History of the Peloponnesian War*, 2.15

78. Plutarch, *Life of Theseus*, 35

79. Seneca, *Phaedra*, 112

80. Ovid, *Metamorphoses*, 8.185-87

81. Ovid, *Metamorphoses*, 8.188-90

82. Palaiphatos, *Concerning Incredible Tales*, 12

83. Ovid, *The Art of Love*, 2.57-2.67

84. Ovid, *Metamorphoses*, 8.220

85. Gide, A. *Theseus*, page 29

86. Strabo, *Geography*, 14.1.19

87. Pseudo-Apollodorus, *Library*, e 1.12-1.13

88. Hyginus, *Fabulae*, 40

89. Pseudo-Apollodorus, *Library*, 2.6.3

90. Strabo, *Geography*, 14.1.19

91. Diodorus Siculus, *Bibliotheca Historica*, 4.77.5

92. Pausanias, *Description of Greece*, 9.11.4

93. Cleidemus, FGrH 323 frag 17

94. Plutarch, *Theseus*, 19.8;

95. Hyginus, *Fabulae*, 40

96. Hesiod, Fragment 205

97. Diodorus Siculus, *Bibliotheca Historica*, 4.77.5

98. Virgil, *Aeneid* 6.14

99. Silus Italicus, *Punica*, 12.88

100. Daidalos and Ikaros on an Apulian fragment newly acquired by the British Museum. Susan Woodford. *Bulletin of the Institute of Classical Studies*, 2009; 52: 93-101

101. Ovid, *Art Of Love*, 2.69-2.70.

102. Charax, Fragment 103 F 5; Schol. Aristophanes *Clouds* 508

103. Diodorus Siculus, *Bibliotheca Historica*, 77.5

104. Herodotus, *Histories*, VII, I70

105. Apollodorus, *Epitome* I. I4-15

106. Pausanias, *Description of Greece*, 7.4.6

107. Pseudo-Apollodorus, *Library*, e.1.14-1.15

108. Diodorus Siculus, *Bibliotheca Historica*, 4.79.1

109. Herodotus, *Histories*, VII, 170

110. Diodorus Siculus, *Bibliotheca Historica*, 4.79.3

111. Herodotus, *Histories*, VII, 170).

112. Pausanias, *Description of Greece*, 7.4.7

113. Strabo, *Geography*, 6.1

114. Diodorus Siculus, *Bibliotheca Historica*, 4.30.1

115. Sallustius Crispus, *Histories*, 2.9

116. Pausanias, *Description of Greece*, 10.17.4

117. Pseudo-Aristotle, *On Marvellous Things Heard*, 81

118. Euripides, *The Cretans* f472b.38-9

119. Euripides, *The Cretans*, Fragment 472e, 5-20

120. Euripides, The Cretans, Fragment 472e, 21-26

121. Euripides, *The Cretans*, f472e.45-9,

122. Diodorus Siculus, *Bibliotheca Historica*, 1.97.1

123. Ovid, *Artis Amatoriae*, Book II, 23-30

124. Xenophon, *Memorabilia* 4.2.33

125. Stephanus of Byzantium, *Ethnica*, D216.6-216.8, M437.15

126. Crammer JA. *Geographical and Historical Description of Asia Minor; With a map*. Oxford University Press, Oxford. 1832. Volume II, page 197-198

127. Strabo, *Geography*, 14.3.2

128. Pliny, *Naturalis Historia*, 5.35.2

129. Arkwright, W. The Frontier of Lycia and Caria. *The Journal of Hellenic Studies* 1895; 15; 93-99

130. Pliny, *Naturalis Historia*, 5.29.1

131. Ptolemaeus, *Geography*, 5.3

132. Titus Livius, *History of Rome*, 37.22

133. Strabo, *Geography*, 14.3.1-4

134. Pliny, *Naturalis Historia*, 5.29.1 and 5.35.2

135. Ptolemaeus, *Geography*, 5.3.2

136. Hoskyn, R. Narrative of a Survey of Part of the South Coast of Asia Minor; And of a Tour into the Interior of Lycia in 1840-1; Accompanied by a Map., *The Journal of the Royal Geographical Society of London*, 1842; 12; 143-161.

137. Herodotus, *Histories*, 1.173

138. Pseudo-Apollodorus, *Library*, 3.1.2

139. Xenophon, *Memorabilia* 4.2.33

140. Pliny, *Naturalis Historia*, 19.1.1

141. Paavo Roos. Topographical and other notes on South-eastern Caria. *Opuscula Atheniensia* IX, 1969, 59-93.

Additional Sources of Information

Cretan Women. Pasiphae, Ariadne, and Phaedra in Latin Poetry. Rebecca Armstrong. Oxford University Press, 2006

Daedalus' myth and its occurrences in Ovid: A three-term comparison and some considerations on Ars 2, 21-98. Simona Martorana. *Myrtia*, 2016, n° 31, pages 167-195

The Daedalus of History and Myth: The Meaning of Creation in Literature from Homer to Joyce. Kristopher James Ide. University of California, Davis, 2011

What Daedalus told Ariadne, or, how to escape the labyrinth: the minotaur. Paul G. Kuntz. *The Monist*, 1966; Vol. 50, No. 4, pp. 488-504

Daedalus, Virgil and the End of Art. Michael C. J. Putnam. *The American Journal of Philology*, 1987; Vol. 108, No. 2, pp. 173-198

The Myth of Ariadne from Homer to Catullus. T. B. L. Webster. *Greece & Rome*, 1996; Vol. 13, No. 1, pp. 22-31

The unifying theme of Daedalus' sculptures on the temple of Apollo Cumanus

(AEN. 6.20-33). Michael Paschalis. *Vergilius* 1986; Vol. 32, pp. 33-41

Myth into Reality: The Metamorphosis of Daedalus and Icarus (Ovid, Metamorphoses, VIII,183-235). Marjorie Hoefmans. *L'Antiquité Classique*, 1994; T. 63, pp. 137-160

Phaedra and Pasiphae: The Pull Backward. Kenneth J. Reckford. *Transactions of the American Philological Association.* 1974; Vol. 104, pp. 307-328

Daedalus in the Labyrinth of Ovid's "Metamorphoses". Barbara Pavlock. *The Classical World*, 1998; Vol. 92, No. 2, pp. 141-157

Aspects of the Myth of Daedalus and Icarus in Propertius and Virgil. Tony Ullyatt. *US-China Foreign Language*, 2011; Vol. 9, pp. 602-610

Minos and Daidalos in Sicily. T. J. Dunbabin. *Papers of the British School at Rome*, 1948; Volume 16, pp. 1-18

The Greek Myths: The Complete and Definitive Edition. Robert Graves. Penguin Books, 2011

The Cambridge Companion to Greek Mythology. Roger D. Woodard. Cambridge University Press, 2007.

Chapter 4

THE WORKS OF DAIDALOS

THE SKILLS OF DAIDALOS were wide-ranging and greatly-praised by many ancient writers. The following passage of Diodorus Siculus[1] shows their extent and the regard in which he was held: "In natural ability he towered far above all other men and cultivated the building art, the making of statues, and the working of stone. He was also the inventor of many devices which contributed to the advancement of his art and built works in many regions of the inhabited world which arouse the wonder of men." Hyginus simply states that the talents of Daidalos were so great that he "is said to have received the art of craftsmanship from Athena"[2]. Furthermore, Athenaeus of Naucratis (a 3rd-century Greek rhetorician and grammarian) comments "All beautiful works of art, be it noted, are ascribed to Daidalos"[3].

Ancient writers tell of many great works that have been attributed to Daidalos but, after nearly 4,000 years, we shouldn't be surprised that little remains of any of them. In this chapter, we will describe the various buildings and works of art that he produced and will provide a list of the inventions that have been attributed to him.

The labyrinth/palace of Knossos

In Chapter 1 we have already discussed the confusion that exists over what is meant by the word

Figure 4.1. Photograph of a drawing of William James Stillman by Dante Gabriel Rossetti (1828-1882 CE). dated 1870.

(a) Minoan bronze double-headed axe (ca. 2200 BCE).

(b) Pillar with incised double-axes in the palace of Knossos.

Figure 4.2. The Minoan double-axe.

"labyrinth". The labyrinth, referring to the palace of Knossos, is one of the most famous of Daidalos' many constructions and is the only one that has survived to the present day after being revealed by the excavations of Sir Arthur Evans. The idea that the labyrinth referred to the palace was first suggested by William James Stillman (Figure 4.1), the U.S. consul in Crete after he had visited the site which had been partially excavated by Minos Kalokairinos in 1878.

He commented "Looking at the character of the fragments so far uncovered, the extreme narrowness of the passages ... the indication of a labyrinthine plan shown in the walls still remaining ... the extreme antiquity of the walls .... I am at a loss to attribute this work to any other period or any other use than that which would belong to the Daedalian Labyrinth"[4]. It was suggested that the word had been derived from the word "labrys" which, in Carian, means a double-headed axe and is associated with the ancient mother goddess of Crete. This was found to be a recurring motif in the palace of Knossos (Figure 4.2). Labyrinthos is a compound word formed from labrys and the suffix "–inthos" which denotes a place, hence it means "the place of the double-headed axe". Labyrinth is the anglicised version of labyrinthos.

This all seems quite convincing. However, critics of this word derivation have asked why the Minoans would have used a foreign word for the double-headed axe when they had their own word for this – "wao". The Greek word for such an axe is "pelekys". Both of these words are very different from the Carian word "labrys". Nevertheless, Arthur Evans, the original excavator of Knossos decided that the palace itself was the original labyrinth constructed by Daidalos for two reasons: firstly because of the frequent occurrence of images of the labrys on its walls and secondly because of its astonishing complexity. On 29th August 1894, Evans published an article in *The Times* in which he called the building "perhaps a Palace, perhaps the actual Labyrinth". The labyrinthine nature of the palace can immediately be appreciated by looking at a plan of it (Figure 2.25 in Chapter 2). Furthermore, a clay tablet found at Knossos has an inscription in Linear B which has been translated as being an offering of an amphora of honey to "the mistress of the labyrinth". The main features of the palace have been described in Chapter 2.

Another suggestion as to why the word labyrinth was used to refer to the palace of Knossos was because of its similarity to a vast necropolis at Hawara which was near Arsinoë, the city of Crocodiles, on the eastern bank of Lake Moeris in Egypt (Figure 4.3).

This was built for the Pharaoh Amenemhet III, also known as King Mendes by the Greeks. The prenomen (throne-name) of this pharaoh was Nemari, which was transliterated into Greek as "Labaris". Consequently, the building became known as the labyrinth[5].

Figure 4.3. Diagram showing the labyrinthine nature of the partially-excavated necropolis at Hawara – this is visible to the southwest of the pyramid. Diagram from the report "Monuments from Egypt and Ethiopia after the drawings of the scientific expedition sent by His Majesty to the King of Prussia, Frederick William IV, to these countries, and carried out in the years 1842-1845 by order of His Majesty".

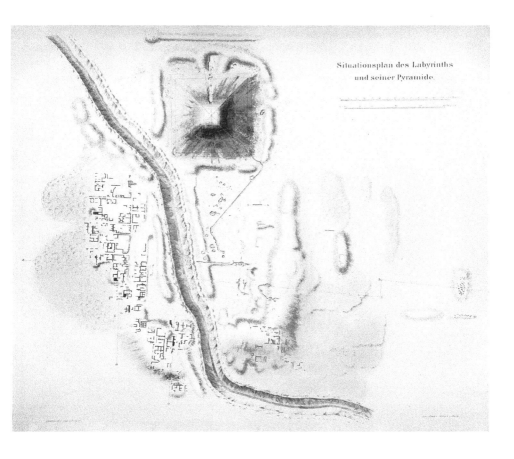

Situationsplan des Labyrinths und seiner Pyramide.

Yet another theory of the origin of the word is again associated with the building at Hawara. The Egyptian word for this "palace, or temple, by the lake" (i.e. Lake Moeris) is "loperohunt" and this would have been borrowed into Greek and adapted to Greek pronunciation as the word "labyrinth"[6]. Interestingly, the first ancient writer to use the term "labyrinth" was Herodotus in the 5th century BCE who used it to refer to the necropolis at Hawara. Furthermore, there is no mention of the appearance of images of the double-headed axe in descriptions of the Egyptian labyrinth.

There is some support for the suggestion that the idea for the Cretan labyrinth came from the labyrinth at Hawara. Pliny the Elder, writing about the Egyptian necropolis, states: "That Daidalos took this for the model of the labyrinth which he constructed in Crete, there can be no doubt; though he only reproduced the hundredth part of it, that portion, namely, which encloses circuitous passages, windings and inextricable galleries which lead to and fro... we must picture to ourselves a building filled with numerous doors, and galleries which continually mislead the visitor, bringing him back, after all his wanderings, to the spot from which he first set out"[7]. This suggestion was also made by Diodorus Siculus[8]. Herodotus and Strabo also described this Egyptian labyrinth and it was actually visited by Herodotus, Pliny and Diodorus Siculus. It was said to consist of 3,000 apartments, of which half were below ground, and was surrounded by a wall. Herodotus stated that it was built by Ammenemes III (Figure 4.4) in approximately 2300 BCE as a burial place for kings and so certainly pre-dates the palace of Knossos by at least 300 years.

He also described the upper apartments as consisting of a series of chambers, courts and collonades and had white marble walls adorned with carved figures. Interestingly, he says that he wasn't allowed to visit the apartments below ground but was told that they housed the sepulchres of kings and sacred crocodiles[9]. Pliny also mentioned that the labyrinth contained

Figure 4.4. Head of King Amenemhat III 1859–1813 BCE. He is wearing the double crown of Upper and Lower Egypt. The head has a distinctly youthful character.

images of the gods, statues of kings and representations of monsters. Interestingly, the renowned English Egyptologist, Flinders Petri (Figure 4.5), while excavating at Hawara found a Roman necropolis there that contained 81 "Mummy portraits".

These are naturalistic portraits painted on the canvas wrapping of the mummy or on a wooden board attached to it and they are dated between the 1st century BCE and the 3rd century CE. Examples of these are shown in Figure 4.6.

If Daidalos did model the Cretan labyrinth on this older Egyptian version, is there any evidence that he actually visited Egypt? Only Diodorus Siculus refers to the possibility that he did: "For the priests of Egypt recount from the records of their sacred books that they were visited in early times by Orpheus, Musaeus, Melampus and Daidalos....."[10]. He also mentions that Daidalos built a propylaeum (porch or gatehouse) for the temple of Hephaestus (Ptah) at Memphis and that a statue of him was placed in this temple: "The very beautiful propylon of the temple of Hephaestus

Figure 4.5. Photograph of Sir William Matthew Flinders Petrie.

(a) Portrait of a youth on wood (80-100 CE).

(b) Portrait of a young woman in red (90-120 CE)

Figure 4.6. Examples of mummy portraits of the type excavated by Flinders Petrie at Hawara.

in Memphis was also built by Daedalus, who became an object of admiration and was granted a statue of himself in wood, which was made by his own hands and set up in this temple......"[11]. Diodorus Siculus tells us that Daidalos was highly regarded in Egypt and that he was so revered that a temple was built in his honour: "....furthermore, he was accorded great fame because of his genius and, after making many discoveries, was granted divine honours; for on one of the islands off Memphis there stands even to this day a temple of Daidalos, which is honoured by the people of that region."[11].

The labyrinth/minotaur's prison

As discussed in Chapter 1, the word labyrinth is also used by many ancient writers to refer to some form of prison in which the minotaur was kept (Figure 4.7).

The earliest mention of such a place was by the 3rd century BCE poet Kallimachus: "....Theseus with the youths established when he was sailing back from Crete. Having escaped the cruel bellowing and the

Figure 4.7. Photograph of the Roman floor mosaic excavated at Cormerod, Switzerland, in 1830 showing the minotaur and Theseus at the centre of a labyrinth (200-225 CE).

wild son of Pasiphae and the coiled habitation of the crooked labyrinth...."[12]. Ovid gives a vivid description of the construction: "Daidalos, most famous for the genius of the craftsman's art built the work and confused the signs and drew the eye into a twisting trick by the windings of different paths. Just as the watery Maeander plays among the Welds of Phrygia and twists forward and back in confusing flow and meeting itself it sees its own waters coming up, and now turned towards its source, now towards the open sea it busies its confused waters: so Daidalos filled countless paths with wandering and scarcely himself managed to get back to the threshold: so great was the building's trickery"[13]

The idea that the labyrinth was a prison for the minotaur is supported by the finding of the word (on a Linear A tablet) in the Knossos palace and this refers to labyrinthine underground grottoes. Pliny the Elder gives four examples of labyrinths and these are all complex underground structures and this seems to have been the Classical understanding of the word[14]. Apollodorus also implies that the prison constructed for the minotaur was an underground structure: "Now the Labyrinth which Daidalos constructed was a chamber that with its tangled windings perplexed the outward way."[15]. A likely candidate for the location of the labyrinth as a subterranean prison is a series of underground tunnels at Gortyn known as the "Labyrinthos Caves" (Figure 4.8). These comprise two and a half miles of tunnels and caves some of which have smooth walls and columns and therefore appear to have been at least partially man-made. The site also corresponds to an unusual labyrinth symbol on a 16th-century map of Crete. Prior to Evans' excavations at Knossos, these caves were regarded as the site of the labyrinth. In his work of 1415, *Description of the Island of Crete*, Cristoforo Buondelmonti identified the caves at Gortyn as the site of the labyrinth. The belief that Gortyn was the site of Daidalos' labyrinth was promoted by the Venetian governors of the island who regularly organised journeys to the "Gortyn Labyrinth" for important visitors from Venice.

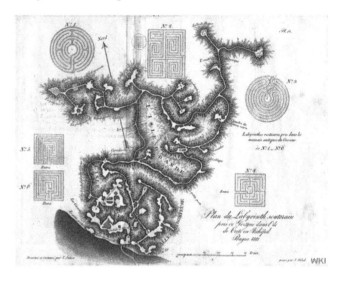

Figure 4.8. Map of the Gortyn caves. Franz Wilhelm Sieber explored the caves in 1817 and produced this map at his home in Prague in 1821. From then on, his map was known to be the best one and was widely used by visitors to the caves.

An interesting account of these caves is given by Charles Cockerell[16]. He and his friends entered the labyrinth via a small hole in a steep part of Mount Ida and found themselves in an intricately winding passage. They had equipped themselves with some string wound on a stick so they could retrace their path: "At first one enters a vestibule out of which lead several openings. Two of the three, perhaps four, dark entrances are blocked up but one remains open. This we followed and for three mortal hours and more we groped about intricate passages and in spacious halls. The windings bewildered us at once and, my compass being broken, I was quite ignorant as to where I was. The clearly intentional intricacy and apparently endless number of galleries impressed me with a sense of horror and fascination I cannot describe. Every few steps one was arrested, and had to turn to right or left, sometimes to choose one of three or four roads. What if one should lose the clue!"

It may be the case, of course, that the labyrinthine palace of Minos and the labyrinthine subterranean prison were both located at Knossos and this could account for the ancient writers using the term to refer to both constructions. The Minotaur's prison may have been carved out of the rock underlying the palace. The Egyptian labyrinth at Hawara consisted of a section above ground and one below. This idea of a two-tiered construction, with the upper section being devoted to the living while the underground section was for the dead, could well have been seized upon by Daidalos as an excellent model for the combined palace/prison at Knossos.

The original Cretan labyrinth (whether referring to the palace or the prison) was a complex network of paths (i.e. multicursal) with multiple branching and several entrances and exits. However, nowadays this type of structure is usually referred to as a maze while the term labyrinth is reserved for a structure consisting of a single, winding path (unicursal) without any dead-ends or false openings but with a single entrance which is also the only exit. Some early Cretan coins show multicursal patterns, but as early as 430 BCE the unicursal seven-course "Classical" design (Figure 4.9) became associated with the labyrinth on coins and became widely used to represent the labyrinth. However, both logic and literary descriptions make it clear that the Minotaur was trapped in a complex branching maze, otherwise Theseus would have had little need of a thread to re-trace his steps and find the exit.

Figure 4.9. Drawings of coins from Knossos showing the labyrinth (5th century BCE)

Andre Gide, in his book *Theseus*, had an altogether different take on the labyrinth as a place of imprisonment for the Minotaur. He suggested that Daidalos' construction was not designed to prevent the minotaur from escaping but was a place from which he did not want to escape. This was achieved by having constantly burning stoves that produced intoxicating vapours. This produced an inebriated state in anyone who inhaled them so that each became lost "in his own private labyrinth". The fumes were addictive and so produced a life-long dependence. So, perhaps, the palace and the prison were one and the same thing and the minotaur lived in one of the luxurious palatial suites in a drug-induced state of happy tranquillity?

The labyrinth/Ariadne's dancing floor

The word "labyrinth" has been used to refer to a roofless dancing ground at Knossos[17,18]. Consequently, as mentioned in Chapter 1, this may be a reference to Ariadne's dancing floor which would probably have consisted of a complex, winding path marked out in stone of a contrasting colour to guide the dancers. Pausanias reported that it was made of white marble[19]. Pausanias also praises the workmanship involved: "Homer naturally was bound to admire it, ... just as he compares the dance worked by Hephaestus on the shield of Achilles to a dance made by Daidalos, because he had never seen more clever workmanship"[20].

As will be described below, a number of dances (including those associated with Ariadne and Theseus) mentioned in the ancient texts appear to have involved the winding, serpentine movement of a line of dancers. As discussed in Chapter 1, the oldest reference to Daidalos in Greek writings is in Homer's *Iliad* where he says that Daidalos built a dancing floor (or "choros") for Ariadne[21]. Homer also describes the nature of the dance performed there: "There were youths dancing and maidens of the price of many cattle, holding their hands upon the wrists one of the other. Of these the maidens were clad in fine linen, while the youths wore well-woven tunics faintly glistening with oil; and the maidens had fair chaplets, and the youths had daggers of gold hanging from silver baldrics. Now would they run round with cunning feet exceeding lightly, as when a potter sitteth by his wheel that is fitted between his hands and maketh trial of it whether it will run; and now again would they run in rows toward each other. And a great company stood around the lovely dance, taking joy therein; and two

Rationalization of the minotaur and his labyrinthine prison

As has been mentioned, Evans was convinced that the labyrinth referred to the palace at Knossos. What was striking about the palace was the profusion of bull-related symbolism such as frescoes, statues, horns of consecration and pottery decorations. The head of a sacrificed bull was also used in religious rituals which sometimes also involved men wearing bull masks. The taurokathapsia (bull-grappling sports) depicted in frescoes were particularly intriguing. These showed young men and women practising amazing, dangerous, gymnastic displays that involved grappling with, and leaping over, bulls. Did they portray sports, games or were they of religious significance? Evans believed in the religious nature of the taurokathapsia and argued that the female performers, because of their elaborate hairstyles, elegance and jewellery were aristocrats and/or priestesses. Others regard the taurokathapsia as being nothing more than a popular entertainment enacted in the central court of the palace which, perhaps, captives were forced to undertake. This could have given rise to the myth of the minotaur – a confused amalgamation of stories of a vast palace comprised of hundreds of rooms and, in the midst of it all, the horror of men wearing bull masks and potentially-lethal bull-grappling. Theseus, the great hero of Athens, could also have been mixed up with all this (Figure). The Minoans, being dominant in the Aegean at the time, may have imposed on their weaker Athenian neighbour a tribute of young men and maidens every so often. These may have been forced to participate in taurokathapsia to satisfy some tribute-demanding Minoan goddess or god and this would invariably have resulted in their death. The ability of a future king of Athens to heroically rescue these youths from a domineering, oppressive nation would have made a great story and added considerably to the stature of Athens and Athenian royalty.

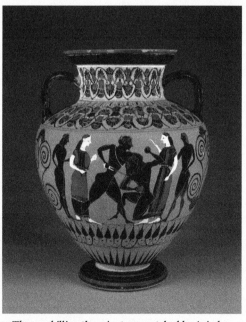

Theseus killing the minotaur watched by Ariadne. This is a terracotta, Attic black-figure neck amphora which was made in the workshop of Exekias in approximately 550 BCE.

tumblers whirled up and down through the midst of them as leaders in the dance."[21]

The scene described mirrors that portrayed in some of the frescoes (Figure 4.10) that adorn the palace of Knossos as well as on some of the seals and statues discovered there. A model of dancing women has been found in Palaikastro, a town on the East coast of Crete.

(a) Section of the Dancing Lady fresco from Knossos Palace.

(b) Reconstruction drawing of the Sacred Grove and Dance fresco from the palace of Knossos (redrawn by D. Riccardi-Percy)

Figure 4.10. Frescos from the Palace of Knossos that show dancing.

The word da-da-re-jo-de found on a clay tablet at Knossos has been translated as meaning Daidaleionde i.e. "to", "towards" or "into" the Daidaleion. It has been suggested that this refers to the choros built by Daidalos, although other interpretations have been proposed (see Chapter 1). Pausanias states that Daidalos was responsible for a depiction of the dance at Knossos "........an Athena at Cnossus, in which latter place is also Ariadne's Dance mentioned by Homer in *the Iliad*, "[19]

The choros could have been situated in the Central Court or any of the other numerous plazas within the palace at Knossos. However, another strong possibility is the theatral area to the North West of the palace. This consists of a paved area 13 x 10 m. Around it is an L-shaped area of steps which would offer standing/sitting room for an audience of about 500 people. Evans was convinced that this was the site of Ariadne's dancing floor.

The dance itself is featured on the famous Francois vase (Figure 4.11). This is a large vessel decorated in the black-figure style which has been dated to about 550 BCE. It was found in 1766 in an Etruscan tomb in the necropolis of Fonte Rotella near Chiusi and shows 270 figures, many with inscriptions. It appears to depict a dance enacted by Ariadne, Theseus and the

(a) Drawings by an unknown artist (circa 1895-1920) of the François Vase.

(b) Drawing from the Francoise vase showing a long file of men and women alternating, who hold hands. Theseus is their leader and they advance to the music of the lyre towards Ariadne. Inscriptions above their heads show their names. The original image can be seen at https://commons.wikimedia.org/ wiki/File:Kleitias,_decorazione_ del_vaso_fran%C3%A7ois,_570_ ac_ca.,_ateniesi_inviati_a_ creta_come_sacrificio_per_il_ minotauro_05.jpg

Figure 4.11. The Francois vase. This large (26 inches high) wine bowl was discovered by Alessandro Francois in Chiusi, Italy, in 1845. As stated on the vase, it was made by Ergotimos and painted by Kleitias (550 BCE). It is kept in the National Archaeology Museum in Florence.

other Athenian intended victims of the Minotaur (see also the next section below). Whether or not this dance took place on Ariadne's choros is not known.

It has also been suggested that the dance performed on Ariadne's dancing floor may have involved a line of dancers holding a python skin who followed the labyrinthine pattern designed by Daidalos[22]. Robert Graves has suggested that the maze-like pattern on the dancing floor mapped out the path of an erotic partridge dance performed in spring in honour of the goddess[23].

Daidalos as a choreographer

It would appear that Daidalos was not only responsible for constructing the dancing floor for Ariadne but it was believed by some writers that he also taught her the actual dance. Lucian of Samosata (a Greek writer from the 2nd century CE), wrote "You have read your Homer; so that I need say nothing of the Shield of Achilles, with its choral dance, modelled on that which Daidalos designed for Ariadne"[24]. Eustathius of Thessalonica (1115-1195 CE), who was Archbishop of Thessalonika and one of the most famous of the scholiasts on Homer, also says that Homer referred to Daidalos teaching the dance itself to Ariadne and "not that he worked it in either wood, stone or metal". Commenting on the relevant passage in the *Iliad* (i.e. Book II, 18.590), he states that "When Theseus came

Figure 4.12. Terracotta attic black-figure band cup from Athens, Greece (about 530 BCE). Both sides of the cup show scenes of revelry in a band with seven dancing figures on one side and six on the other. The figures are alternately male and female. Added red is used for hair, wreaths, and tunics; the white used for the women's skin has worn away.

out with the young men and women after his victory, he created for the gods this type of dancing place, circular, just like the entrance and exit of the labyrinth had been for him. Daidalos devised the choreography of the dance and taught it to them." It has been suggested that the dance mapped out the path that had to be taken to exit the labyrinth. In order to emphasise just how novel this combination of male and female dancers was, he adds: "Although men and women used to dance separately, the young men and maidens who were saved from the labyrinth with Theseus danced together."

A line of alternating men and women dancing appears on a band cup found in Athens (Figure 4.12).

In his *Life of Theseus* Plutarch also makes reference to the dance that Daidalos taught Theseus: "On his voyage from Crete, Theseus put in at Delos, and having sacrificed to the god and dedicated the image of Aphrodite which he had received from Ariadne, he danced with his youths a dance which they say is still performed by the Delians, being an imitation of the circling passages in the Labyrinth, and consisting of certain rhythmic involutions and evolutions. This kind of dance, as Dicaearchus tells us, is called by the Delians *The Crane*, and Theseus danced it round the altar called Keraton, which is constructed of horns ('kerata') taken entirely from the left side of the head."[25]. This dance (known as the "geranos" or "crane dance") is one of the most famous dances in antiquity and a considerable amount has been written about it and how it got its name. Some say it is so-called because it reminds the Delians of cranes encircling their island in flight before they land. Others say it is because the line of dancers is similar to the line formed by cranes when they migrate. One of the many frescos adorning the palace of Knossos shows a dance being performed in front of a large audience (Figure 4.10b). The remains of the original fresco show a densely-packed audience of men and women in a tree-containing outside area. Waving arms can be seen along the top of the picture. The female dancers can be seen in the bottom right-hand section of the fresco.

Pasiphae's wooden cow

This strange contraption was used to enable Pasiphae to consummate her love for a bull. As Ariadne laments in Nonnus' *Dionysiaca* (an epic poem written in the 4th century CE): "My mother too once was the menial of a farmer, [i.e. when she was disguised as a cow] and bowed her neck for a herdsman, and prattled of love to a dumb bull in the pasture and brought the bull a calf"[26]. The exact nature of the construction varies in different accounts. Apollodorus gives us the most detailed description: "He constructed a wooden cow on wheels, took it, hollowed it out in the inside, sewed it up in the hide of a cow which he had skinned, and set it in the meadow in which the bull used to graze"[27]. The scholiast of Euripides appears to agree with Apollodorus and describes it as a wooden frame over which the hide of a cow had been draped[28]. Diodorus Siculus is vaguer and simply states that it was "a contrivance in the shape of a cow"[29]. Clement of Alexandria is also not very helpful and states: "But the cow of Daedalus, made of wood, allured the savage bull..."[30]. Philo of Alexandria says that it was made of wooden planks[31].

One has to wonder why Daidalos agreed to build such a thing when he must have known that Minos would be furious with him. Was he so sure of his importance to Minos that he became over-confident? Was he perhaps in love with Pasiphae and willing to do anything for her? Did she offer him any favours for building the cow? There is no hint anywhere that he was rewarded by Pasiphae in any way. However, it is also important to remember that Pasiphae was a sorceress and so, perhaps, Daidalos was bewitched by her and simply had to do her bidding, or else he was simply afraid of her.

Then again, the scientist in him might have been intrigued by the possible outcome of such a union. What an experiment! The stories he would have been told as a child of strange hybrids such as centaurs, snake-tailed men (King Kekrops of Athens – Figure 4.13) and also legends of copulation between bulls and women, swans and women etc. may have excited his curiosity. Here was an opportunity for him to: (a) ascertain if it was biologically possible to undertake such copulation, (b) see if it resulted in offspring and (c) observe what kind of creature was produced.

The idea of using an artificial cow to enable sexual conjugation between a woman and a bull has fascinated artists over the ages and there are many images referring to this event on pottery, as mosaics and as paintings – some of these are shown in Figures 4.14.

Figure 4.13. Attic red-figure lekythos by the Selinunt painter depicting King Kekrops, the first king of Athens (440-430 BCE). Antikensammlung, Kiel, Germany.

It is a tribute to Daidalos' skills that the contraption was so life-like that it fooled the bull into mating with it: "And the cow, Daidalos, the one made out of wood, fooled a wild bull, and art deceived and coerced the beast into mounting a woman in love"[32].

(a) Daidalos presents the wooden cow to Pasiphae. Drawing of a marble Roman relief in the Palazzo Spada, Rome.

(b) An oinochoe showing Pasiphae inside the artificial cow. Attica, Greece (375-350 BCE)

(c) Daidalos helping Pasiphae to copulate with the bull.

Figure 4.14. The mating of Pasiphae with the bull. Other artworks that make reference to this event can be seen on the following websites

https://commons.wikimedia.org/ wiki/File:D%C3%A9dale_et_ Pasipha%C3%A9_-_Jean_Lemaire. jpg

https://commons.wikimedia.org/ wiki/File:Gustave_Moreau_-_ Pasiphae_and_the_Bull._(1876). jpg

https://commons.wikimedia.org/ wiki/File:Pasiphae,_Daedalus_ and_the_wooden_cow,_mosaic_ from_Zeugma,_Gaziantep_ Museum.jpg

https://commons.wikimedia. org/wiki/File:Dedalo,_pasife_e_ la_mucca_di_legno,,_da_ casa_dell%27antica_caccia_a_ pompei,_8979.JPG

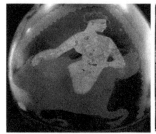

Temple of Apollo at Cumae

As mentioned in Chapter 3, Vergil tells us that Daidalos flew from Crete to Cumae and there he built a temple to Apollo and on its doors carved out images to record key events in his life (Figure 4.15). The building of this temple is also referred to by Silius Italicus[33].

In the words of Vergil[34]:

> "Here Daidalos, the ancient story tells,
>   Escaping Minos' power, and having made
>   Hazard of heaven on far-mounting wings,
>   Floated to northward, a cold, trackless way,
>   And lightly poised, at last, o'er Cumae's towers.
>   Here first to earth come down, he gave to thee
>   His gear of wings, Apollo! and ordained
>   Vast temples to thy name and altars fair.
>   On huge bronze doors Androgeos' death was
>   done;
>   And Cecrops' children paid their debt of woe,
>   Where, seven and seven, - oh pitiable sight! -
>   The youths and maidens wait the annual doom,
>   Drawn out by lot from yonder marble urn.
>   Beyond, above a sea, lay carven Crete: -
>   The bull was there; the passion, the strange guile;
>   And Queen Pasiphae's brute-human son,
>   The Minotaur - of monstrous loves the sign.
>   Here was the toilsome, labyrinthine maze,
>   Where, pitying love-lorn Ariadne's tears,
>   The crafty Daidalos himself betrayed
>   The secret of his work; and gave the clue
>   To guide the path of Theseus through the gloom.
>   o Ikaros, in such well-graven scene
>   How proud thy place should be! but grief forbade:
>   Twice in pure gold a father's fingers strove
>   To shape thy fall, and twice they strove in vain."

Figure 4.15. Woodcut illustration of the doors of Apollo's temple at Cumae from the "Strasbourg Vergil," edited by Sebastian Brant

Only four of the scenes were described by Vergil although he stated that the rest of Daidalos' story was depicted – these are shown to the right of the door.

The illustrators finish the story with four more panels to the left of the door. In the upper right of these, Theseus is shown arriving in Athens after slaying the Minotaur but his father, thinking he has failed, is about to throw himself off a cliff. In the upper left panel, Daidalos and Ikaros are shown imprisoned in the labyrinth. In the lower right panel, Daidalos and Ikaros fly away from Crete and Ikaros is shown flying upwards. The death of Ikaros is not portrayed but the fourth panel shows Daidalos consecrating a shrine to Apollo and giving the wings to the shrine.

What was missing from the temple doors, of course, was a panel showing the death of his son which, as described in Chapter 3, he could not bring himself to portray. Although the doors of the temple are described, the temple itself is not. The remains of a temple dedicated to Apollo at Cumae are shown in Figure 3.27 in Chapter 3.

Temple of Britomartis on Crete

Britomartis, which means "sweet maiden", was a Cretan goddess of mountains, hunting and fishing and was closely identified with the Greek goddess Artemis. She was also known in western Crete as Diktynna, the goddess of Mount Dikte. She was the daughter of Zeus and Carme and had temples at Khersonesos (Chersonisos/Hersonissos), which is 25 kilometres east of Heraklion and at Olous/Olus which is now a sunken city near modern-day Elounda. In both of these cities, she was often portrayed on coins.

King Minos is said to have lusted after her and pursued her all over Crete for 9 months[35]. In order to escape from him, she threw herself into the sea where she was caught by fishermen in their nets (Figure 4.16).

Gaius Julius Solinus, a Roman who lived in the 3rd century CE, implies that Daidalos built a temple for Britomartis. His most famous work was the *Polyhistor*, also known as the *Collection of memorable things* and

Wonders of the World. It described the natural history and geography of the Roman Empire but also included comments on religious and social matters. It was first translated into English in 1587 by Arthur Golding and entitled *The excellent and pleasant worke of Iulius Solinus Polyhistor Contayning the noble actions of humaine creatures, the secretes & prouidence of nature, the description of countries, the maners of the people: with many meruailous things and strange antiquities, seruing for the benefitt and recreation of all sorts of persons.* In Chapter 15, which describes Crete, he states that:

Figure 4.16. The Drowning of Britomartis from "Scenes from the Story of Diana" (1547-59 CE). A tapestry probably designed by Jean Cousin the Elder. Britomartis, pursued by Minos (in the left background), throws herself into the sea rather than succumb to him. The goddess Diana (with a crescent on her head) stands in the centre of the tapestry. To the right, the drowning Britomartis raises one hand above the water. In the middle distance, Minos, stands looking into the water with his arms raised in astonishment. Britomartis' body is fished out of the water to the right.

"The people of Crete do very devoutly worship Diana, whom in their own mother tongue they call Britomartis, which in our language means 'Sweet maid'. No man may lawfully enter the Goddess's temple unless he is bare-foot. The said temple shows the workmanship of Daidalos." However, he failed to say whereabouts on the island this temple was located and the phraseology is ambiguous, he could have been referring to a wooden statue of Britomartis which was said to have been kept in her temple in Oulos (see later in this chapter).

Daidalos the sculptor

Daidalos was famous for his ability to make statues that were extraordinarily life-like and, when describing his sculptural works, this is the characteristic feature that most commentators refer to: "In the carving of his statues he so far excelled all other men that later generations invented the story about him that the statues of his making were quite like their living models; they could see, they said, and walk and, in a word, preserved so well the characteristics of the entire body that the beholder thought that the image made by him was a being endowed with life"[36.]

A number of writers say that he was the first sculptor to produce statues with open eyes, with arms freed from the sides of the body and legs that were separated from one another[37-39]. This implies that until his time, statues would have been rather primitive and this is born out by Thermistios: "Before the time of Daidalos not only the statuary of herms [i.e. the god Hermes] was square, but also the shape of other statues"[40]. Pseudo-Apollodorus states simply that "Daidalos...... was the best builder and the first inventor of statues"[41] but, unfortunately, does not elaborate on this.

Daidalos is credited with introducing an oriental (particularly Egyptian) style to statues: "The style of old statues in Egypt is the same as those made

by Daidalos among the Hellenes"[42]. This comment
suggests that he was responsible for instigating the
particular sculptural style of young, naked boys
known as "kouroi" (singular "kouros"). These were
usually made from marble but limestone, wood,
bronze, ivory and terracotta were also used. They
are usually life-size and have the left leg extending
forwards as if they were walking (Figure 4.17). They
usually have the hairstyle, ears and large eyes characteristic of Egyptian statues. As we have seen in
Chapter 3, Daidalos was said to have visited Egypt
and so may have brought back the idea of kouroi after
studying the statues he saw there.

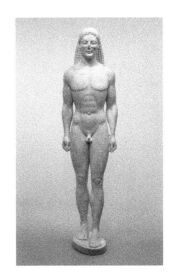

*Figure 4.17. A kouros made from
marble (about 530 BCE)*

Many writers commented on the ability of Daidalos to make statues so life-like that they appeared to
be able to walk and speak:

(i) "Don't be afraid old man, it's nothing. All the
statues of Daidalos appear to move and see, so
clever is the man"[43]

(ii) "... the statues made by Daidalos, bound in
order not to run away"[44].

(iii) "I am Hermes with a voice from Daidalos
made of wood but I came here by walking on my
own"[45]

(iv) "It is said about Daidalos that he made statues
that walked of their own accord. This seems
impossible to me, that statues should move
about spontaneously. The truth is this: in those
days the sculptors of gods and men made the
feet joined together and the arms hanging by
the sides. Daidalos first made one foot striding
forward, which is why men said, Daidalos has
made this statue walk..."[46]

(v) "... [the statues of Daidalos] could see, they
said, and walk and, in a word, preserved so well
the characteristics of the entire body that the

beholder thought that the image made by him was a being endowed with life"[47]

(vi) "**Socrates:** It's because you haven't pondered Daidalos's statues. Maybe you haven't got any up there in Thessaly.
Meno: What have they got to do with it?
Socrates: Well, they're the same: if they aren't shackled, they escape – they scamper away. But if they're shackled, they stay put."[48]

(vii) "... This is the workshop of Daidalos; and about it are statues, some with forms blocked out, others in a quite complete state in that they are already stepping forward and give promise of walking about. Before the time of Daidalos, you know, the art of making statues had not yet conceived such a thing."[49]

(viii) "Daidalos did indeed boldly advance in sculpture as far as motion, and the materials of which they were made and to move in the dance; but it was impossible and absolutely out of the question for him to make statues that could speak."[50]

In view of these abilities, it is not surprising that Daidalos was also considered to be the inventor of agalmata i.e. statues of the gods with open eyes and moveable limbs[51,52]. No wonder he was able to delight the daughters of Minos, as well as of Cocalus, by making them dolls with moveable arms and legs (Figure 4.18).

Despite the praise heaped on the statues of Daidalos for their life-like appearance, Socrates at first sight appeared to have not been impressed: "...just as the sculptors say that Daidalos, if he were to be born now and were to create such works as those from which he got his reputation, would be ridiculous"[53]. However, this comment has to be viewed in its context. In the previous section of this work, Socrates says "Then for Heaven's sake, just as the other arts have progressed,

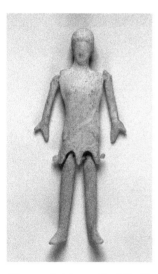

Figure 4.18. A terracotta doll with separately-made arms and legs attached with string. (5th century BCE). Traces of paint remain suggesting that it had a tunic painted onto its torso. Dolls have been found in children's graves and in religious sanctuaries. Before their marriage, girls would dedicate dolls and other toys to various goddesses.

and the ancients are of no account in comparison with the artisans of today, shall we say that your art also has progressed and those of the ancients who were concerned with wisdom are of no account in comparison with you?"[54]. What Socrates was saying was that no matter how excellent were Daidalos' statues in their time, sculptural style had changed so much that if he were to produce them now, he would be ridiculed for being so old-fashioned. Pausanias also appeared to be somewhat disappointed having viewed many of the works of Daidalos and commented, "All the works of this artist, though somewhat uncouth to look at, nevertheless have a touch of the divine in them."[55] This is a view supported by Aeschylus: "the old statues, though simply made, are thought divine; while the new, though superbly wrought, have less of the divine in them"[56]

A particular style of sculpture (in the form of reliefs and statues) proliferated during the period 650-600 BCE which was characterised by:

(a) the use of a frontal view. In statues the side elevation was compressed and in reliefs full-face heads were common

(b) a long triangular face with a low horizontal forehead, large eyes and nose, and a straight mouth

(c) a low cranium with the ears either omitted or projecting at right angles

(d) hair falling in solid masses at the front and back, relieved by horizontal grooving and sometimes a row of curls over the forehead,

(e) very long legs and a high narrow waist, which usually had a belt

(f) male figures were invariably naked, but females normally wore a heavy dress which fitted closely above the waist and became a rectangular sheath below

This style became known as "Daedalic" and should not be confused with the use of the adjective to describe "well-made objects". The term was widely used in the early 20th century but was formalized in 1936 by Jenkins[57.] Although this style derived its name from Daidalos, the time period during which it flourished was almost 1000 years after his death. An example of a statue in the so-called daedalic style is shown in Figure 4.19.

Figure 4.19. Head of a female in the Daedalic style (from Tarentum, South Italy, late 7th century BCE). Note the long, wig-like hair on either side of the face, the almond-shaped eyes and large nose – these are the main characteristics of the Daedalic style. The image shows the front, and inside, of a mould used for making Daedalic heads for statues.

At this point it is worth mentioning an interesting passage in Aristotle's *De Anima* in which he suggests the mechanism used by Daidalos to animate his statues: "An example of this is Democritus, who uses language like that of the comic dramatist Philippus, who accounts for the movements that Daidalos imparted to his wooden Aphrodite by saying that he poured quicksilver into it;"[58]. Unfortunately, no explanation is given as to why pouring mercury into the statue could possibly result in its movement. Aristotle may be using quicksilver as a metaphor for the soul's action on the body. Another possibility is that the statue had a round, hollow base which, when partially filled with mercury, would result in it wobbling back and forth when it was touched.

In contrast to his ability to make life-like statues, xoana (singular xoanon) were also associated with Daidalos. Xoanon is a term first used in the 5th century BCE to denote something made with a high degree of craftsmanship. However, it subsequently became an archaeological term used to refer to wooden objects that were sacred and very old. Most of these were very simple and were certainly not very realistic. They were usually carved from wood (usually olive, pear or oak) and so the vast majority have not survived to the present day. However, stone, ivory and marble versions were also produced and so have been preserved. In his *Description of Greece*, Pausanias described many xoana and where they were located. Examples of xoana are shown in Figure 1.11 of Chapter 1.

Works attributed to Daidalos in Sicily

Daidalos appears to be recognized more for his large-scale engineering and architectural works in Sicily than for any of his other talents and the location of these, as well as other sites associated with him, are shown in Figure 4.20.

Figure 4.20. Map of Sicily showing the location of sites associated with Daidalos

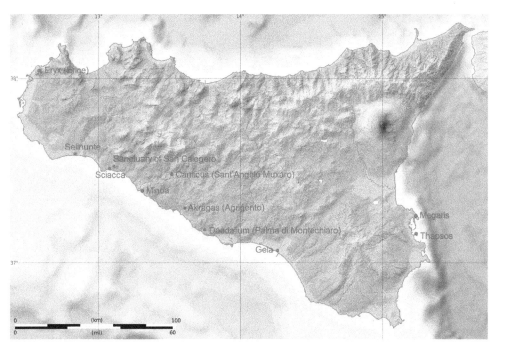

Diodorus Siculus described a number of works Daidalos carried out while staying with Cocalus[59]. Firstly, he built a city on top of a rock at Akragas on the River Camicus. This was impregnable to any attack because the ascent to it was so narrow and winding that it could be defended by only three or four men. It was considered to be the strongest city in

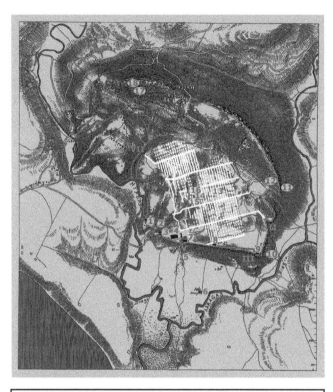

Figure 4.21. Map of Akragas showing the main archaeological sites located on the top of a steep hill. Robert Koldewey (1855-1925)

1 Temple of Hephaestus; 2 Kolymbéthra; 3 Sanctuary of the chthonic gods with Temple of the Dioscuri and Temple L; 4 Temple of Olympian Zeus; 5 Tomb of Theron and Hellenistic-roman necropolis; 6 Temple of Asclepius; 7 Temple of Hercules; 8 Temple of Concordia and Early Christian necropolis; 9 Temple of Hera; 10 Basilicula; 11 Rock sanctuary of Demeter; 12 Temple of Demeter; 13 Hellenistic-roman quarter; 14 San Nicola and Archeological Museum; 15 Ekklesiasterion and Oratory of Phalaris; 16 Bouleuterion; 17 Temple of Athena; 18 Temple of Zeus.

--- Rivers   Streets   --- Town wall
I–IX Town gates

the whole of Sicily so Cocalus moved his royal residence and treasury there.

The northern part of Akragas consists of a lofty ridge with two summits and which of these was the site of the new city is uncertain. The westernmost summit is the highest but is very small (70 m x 20 m) and therefore there would have been room for only a single building. In contrast, the easternmost (approximately 985 feet high) has a much larger area for building and is, in fact, the site of the present-day city of Agrigento (Figure 4.21). Akragas became a very important city with a population as great as 200,000 in the 5th Century BCE and from it developed the modern city of Agrigento.

In Minoan times the region was an important source of sulphur and potash which were exported from the nearby port of Porto Empedocle. Ancient Akragas comprises a large area of the modern city and on a ridge on the south side are the remains of seven large temples that were constructed during the 6th and 5th centuries BCE (Figure 4.22) which, of course, was more than a thousand years after the time of Daidalos. These are some of the largest and best-preserved ancient Greek buildings outside of Greece (Figure 4.23) and are listed as a World Heritage Site.

Interestingly, a collection of wooden xoana was discovered in 1934 at a sanctuary in Palma di Monte-

Figure 4.22. Artist's reconstruction of Akragas as it may have appeared in the 5th century BCE.

chiaro near Akragas - the ancient name for the town of Palma was Daedalium.

Next, he built a flood-control system and reservoir near Megaris (also known as Megara Hyblaea; near the modern town of Augusta) from which the River Alabon flowed into the sea (Figure 4.24).

Figure 4.23. The temple of Concordia (the Roman goddess of harmony) at Agrigento. This is regarded as being the best-preserved Doric temple in the world.

Figure 4.24. View of the remains of the ancient city of Megara Hyblaea

Interestingly, excavations carried out in 1891

discovered the northern portion of the western town wall (Figure 4.25) which acted as an embankment against floods.

Figure 4.25. Portion of the western walls of Megara Hyblea

Figure 4.26. An 18th century CE engraving advertising the stove of San Calogero.

Then, according to Diodorus Siculus: "A third construction of his, in the territory of Selinus, was a grotto where he so successfully expelled the steam caused by the fire which burned in it that those who frequented the grotto got into a perspiration imperceptibly because of the gentle action of the heat, and gradually, and actually with pleasure to themselves, they cured the infirmities of their bodies without experiencing any annoyance from the heat"[60]. This is very exciting because 25 miles from Selinus (modern-day Selinunte) on Monte Kronio is the "Sanctuary of San Calogero" where there is a karst cave system from which geothermal gas is emitted. This series of caves is referred to collectively as the "Stove of San Calogero" (Figure 4.26). Above these caves are the modern thermal baths which are a popular resort.

Figure 4.27. Interior of the Grotto di san Calogero

The first cave, known as the "Grotto del Santo" is where Saint Calogero is said to have lived and contains an altar (Figure 4.27). The next is known as the "Stufa de Animalia" and is where animals were treated for ailments. Adjacent to this is the largest cave which is named after Daedalus - "Antro di Dedalo" (Figure 4.28). This is 9.4 metres long and 4.2 metres wide and reaches a maximum height of 4 metres. Inside the temperature varies between 36 and 42°C, depending on the season and time of day. Because of the high temperature, people spent time in the cave as a cure for arthritis, rheumatism, gout and sciatica. It is paved with stone slabs and has stone benches for people to sit on as well as holes to insert diseased limbs.

Local tradition says that the caves were created by Daidalos. There is a strong possibility that this is the case because Diodorus Siculus is rather vague about the exact location of the grotto he describes and only states that it was "in the territory of Selinus". The cave system overlooks the town of Sciacca which is famous for its hot springs and by the 7th century BCE the site became a well-known thermal spa resort

Figure 4.28. Interior of the Antro de Dedalo.

Figure 4.29. Figure of Astarte made in Syria in the mid-2nd millennium BCE. This was probably used as a pendant because there are holes on either side of the body. The surface is very weathered, It may have been made of a blue-green glass which has discoloured with time.

known as Thermae Selinuntinae. The Thermal baths are still in use today and claim to be the oldest ones in Sicily.

At Eryx (modern-day Erice, near Trapani) there was a temple to Aphrodite which was an important site of pilgrimage. This had previously been a site sacred to Astarte (Figure 4.29), a Phoenician goddess, worshipped by the Elymians who were among the first settlers of the region.

The town stands on top of a very steep hill more than 2000 feet high and the temple was built on its highest point (Figure 4.30). The town was said to have been founded by Eryx, the son of Aphrodite, who offered hospitality to Hercules when he visited Sicily.

(a) The castle at Erice, built on the site of a temple dedicated to Aphrodite

(b) View from the town demonstrating its lofty position

Figure 4.30. Views of, and from, the city of Erice, Sicily

As the temple was perched precipitously on the top of a high rocky pinnacle, Daidalos rendered it safe by constructing underpinning to support it. Unfortunately, nothing remains of the temple as a castle was built on its site in the 12th Century CE. Interestingly, excavations on the north-east side of the castle hill have revealed the remains of a large platform which may have been the temple base, or even the supporting structure that Daidalos built.

Daidalos also sculpted either a golden ram or honeycomb (difficulties in translation make it impossible to ascertain which of these it was) which he placed in the temple.

Works carried out by Daidalos in Sardinia

According to Diodorus Siculus, the works Daidalos produced in Sardinia were, in his time, still known as "Daidaleia"[61]. What Diodorus was referring to are large cone-shaped towers built of stone that are extremely common on the island and can still be seen today. The towers are also called Nuraghi (Figure 4.31) after the Nuragic civilization which flourished

Figure 4.31. Nuraghe Oes. This is located on the northeastern side of Campu Giavesu in the territory of Giave, in the Valley of the Nuraghi. It is 16 metres tall and has a diameter of 11.5 metres, making it the largest Nuragic building found so far.

Figure 4.32. Roman marble statue of a young Hercules (69-96 CE).

Figure 4.33. The Feast of Peleus by Sir Edward Burne-Jones, 1881. Peleus (or Pelias) was an important Greek hero who married Thetis and their wedding was attended by many of the Olympian gods, as shown in the painting. Although they had seven sons, only one survived – Achilles.

there from the 18th century BCE to the 2nd century CE.

Daidalos also completed an ambitious building programme, although his focus appeared to have changed dramatically: "He also had large and expensive gymnasia constructed and established courts of justice and the other institutions which contribute to the prosperity of a state"[61]. His involvement in the construction of civic buildings of this type was a new departure and adds yet another dimension to his activities.

Statue of Hercules

In Chapter 3 we mentioned that Hercules found Ikaros' body and buried him. Daidalos was so grateful to him for this that he made a statue of him which was displayed in Pisa, a small town in Arcadia in the North-west Peloponnese. This was so lifelike that on seeing it, Hercules thought it was an enemy and attacked and destroyed it: "......In return Daidalos made a portrait statue of Hercules at Pisa, which Hercules mistook at night for living and threw a stone and hit it.."[62]. Figure 4.32 shows an example of one of the many statues of Hercules that have survived from ancient times.

Sword of Peleus

Peleus was the husband of Thetis (a sea goddess) and the father of Achilles (Figure 4.33).

While attending games organised by King Pelias (who sent Jason off in search of the golden fleece), the wife of Pelias' son Acastus fell in love with Peleus. When Peleus failed to respond to her she told Acastus that Peleus had propositioned her. Acastus felt that he could not kill him because he was a guest of his father but took him hunting and stole his sword while he was asleep on a mountain. The mountain was populated by centaurs and Acastus thought that Peleus would be killed by them. However, Chiron, the leader of the centaurs, protected him and found and returned his lost sword[63]. In relating this story, Pindar tells us of the provenance of Peleus' sword in the phrase "With the sword of Daedalus"[64]. What is interesting about this story is not the feud between Peleus and Acastus but rather that this is the only reference to Daidalos having made any weapons. However, even this one incidence is rather doubtful. All of the existing manuscripts use the phrase "of Daidalos" which means that the sword either belonged to him or was made by him. Unfortunately, there are no explanations as to why Peleus had a sword made by, or belonging to, Daidalos.

Apart from this one instance, there is no other mention by ancient writers of Daidalos' involvement in any form of weapons production. It is very odd that in those war-dominated days Minos, Cocalus and the Athenian patrons of Daidalos failed to make use of the talents of such an inventive and skilful technologist to make weapons and/or war machines for them. What a brilliant achievement! Although the ancient kingdoms of the Mediterranean appear to us to have been constantly engaged in warfare and pillaging, how refreshing to hear that the supreme technologist of the times was not heavily involved in the armaments industry. Nowadays it seems that almost every new invention made is eventually used to bring harm to our fellow humans in some way or other. Here we have an extremely talented individual whose inventions and skills were used for the benefit of humankind. However, perhaps this is not so surprising given the very peaceful nature of the Minoan society in which Daidalos lived for a considerable time, if not most of his life.

Statues on the Elektrides Islands

Daidalos placed two metal statues (one of tin and one of bronze), one of himself and one of Ikaros, on the Elektrides Islands which are at the mouth of the River Po (according to Appolonius of Rhodes) in the Adriatic. These islands were so-called because amber (Figure 4.34) was present in large amounts, having been deposited there by the River Po[65]. Pseudo-Aris-

Figure 4.34. Amber.

totle implied that he arrived there from Sicily. If so, he must have had a very important reason for going there as the Elektrides are about 600 miles north of this island, as the crow flies. Also, if he was planning on going home to Athens (or Crete) after his stay in Sicily then the Elektrides would not have been on a logical route to either of these places as both are directly to the east of Sicily.

Pseudo-Aristotle refers to the Elektrides as being formed by the silting up of the mouth of the River Po[65]. Such formations are, by their very nature, transient and therefore it is not surprising that they do not feature on modern or ancient maps. As can be seen from Figure 4.35, the Po delta is complex and historical records show that its structure is constantly changing. It has been estimated that the rate of extension of the delta between 1000 BC and 1200 AD was an incredible 4 metres per year. In fact, the 12 Km protrusion of the current delta into the Adriatic did not exist in 1152 CE.

I find this apparently trivial story particularly interesting – what was Daidalos doing so far away from his usual haunts? I cannot believe that the ever-inquisitive and inventive Daidalos would not have known of, or discovered for himself, the peculiar properties of amber. The Greek word for amber is "electron" (Latinised to "electrum") and it is from this word that we derive our word for electricity. However, the word elektron is itself derived from a Phoenician word, elekron, which means "shining light".

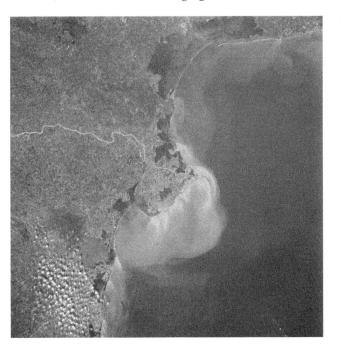

Figure 4.35. The present-day delta of the River Po.

According to Plato, static electricity was discovered in approximately 600 BCE by the Greek philosopher Thales of Miletus (Figure 4.36) who found that when

ΘΑΛΕΣ

Figure 4.36 Thales of Miletus.
Stipple engraving by J.H.
Ramberg (1763-1840).

amber is rubbed with fur, it develops the ability to attract light objects (this was mentioned by Plato[66]). It is well known that further rubbing results in a build-up of static electricity (known as the triboelectric effect) which can lead to the production of sparks.

Had Daidalos journeyed all the way to the Elektrides (which are in the far north of the Adriatic Sea), a long way from Crete (750 nautical miles) or Sicily (625 nautical miles) just to deposit statues of himself and Ikaros? I very much doubt it – he must have had a more practical reason. It's more likely that Daidalos travelled there while he was based in Knossos where for many years he would have been Minos' blue-eyed boy with considerable resources available to him. Presumably, he would have been free to come and go as he pleased but, if not, he had a family that could have been used as hostages to ensure his return. The River Po is approximately 750 nautical miles from Knossos and, according to Pliny, a sailing ship can travel at a speed of 5 knots with a favourable wind[67]. It would, therefore, have taken Daidalos 13 days to get to the Elektrides and back – assuming he sailed non-stop, day and night. A more likely journey time would have been at least double this to take account of poor weather, adverse winds and stops *en route*. That amounts to quite a journey and, therefore, he was more likely to have gone there to get large quantities of amber rather than simply to deposit a couple of statues - perhaps these were left there as a thanksgiving offering to the gods for the amber? But what did he want this amber for? In Minoan times amber was used mainly in jewellery and, although recent chemical analysis of amber jewellery from Crete has shown that a lot of the amber originated in the Baltic, some came from sources closer to Crete such as Sicily, Italy, Lebanon and Romania. Nothing in the ancient texts suggests that Daidalos was interested in jewellery or any other of the trappings of luxury. He was far more interested in machines and devices. He would certainly have come across amber in the palace and could easily have discovered its electricity-generating capacity (or been told about it) when rubbed against fur, leather or cloth. He was said to have invented the potter's wheel and so it is easy to imagine that he would have thought of a way of using this in order to mechanise the rubbing effect. Amber could be attached to the wheel and this could have been rotated rapidly against a piece of fur or leather thereby generating a huge electrostatic charge. The accumulated charge can result in sparks when discharged rapidly (e.g. by touching the surface) or can be harvested and used to drive electrical devices. In the mid-eighteenth century, a number of rotating disc devices were produced by Carl Winter (in Germany) and Benjamin Franklin (in the USA) and have been used to generate electricity ever since (see Figure 4.37).

Figure 4.37. Electricity-generating machine made by Benjamin Franklin. Turning a crank enables the glass globe at the top to rotate at high speed against a leather pad mounted below it thereby generating an electric charge. The electricity produced could be passed through metal needles close to the glass globe and stored in a Leyden jar which is a primitive battery-like device.

Such a device would not have been beyond the inventive powers of Daidalos. However, is there anything to suggest that he may have been experimenting with electricity? The answer is – possibly. There are several references to Ariadne having a "glowing crown" which she gave to Theseus before he entered the labyrinth: "... he [Dionysus] gave her this crown as a present. Delighted with it, she did not refuse the terms. It is said, too, to have been made of gold and Indian gems, and by its aid Theseus is thought to have come from the gloom of the labyrinth to the day, for the gold and gems made a glow of light in the darkness."[68]. Other writers also refer to this crown[69-71]. Although Hyginus says that the crown was a gift from Dionysus, another possibility is that it was yet another ingenious device made by Daidalos.

Figure 4.38. St. Elmo's fire on the masts of a ship at sea.

'ST. ELMO'S FIRE' ON MASTS OF SHIP AT SEA.

The accumulated static electricity on an object can result in the generation of light when the charge is dissipated. Examples of light produced in this way include lightning and the sparks generated after walking across a carpet and touching a metal door-knob. St Elmo's fire is an example of such light being generated by the discharge of electricity from a sharp object (such as a ship's mast, church spire, lightning rod) – this appears as a blue or violet glow (Figure 4.38).

It would have been possible for Daidalos to have used an amber/fur electricity-generating device to charge up a crown (like the one shown in Figure 4.39) to such an extent that St Elmo's fire would have radiated from its points thereby illuminating Theseus' passage through the labyrinth – this would match Hyginus' description. Alternatively, by touching the crown with his sword to discharge the built-up charge, Theseus could have generated light – this would not only have enabled him to see where he was but would have terrified the minotaur making him easier to kill.

Figure 4.39. Venus chastising Cupid (1st century BCE). Aphrodite is chastising her mischievous son, Eros. Note the pointed crown worn by the goddess.

Bowl in Rhodes

On the island of Rhodes is a sanctuary dedicated to Athena Lindia which dates back to the 10th century BCE (Figure 4.40). It is thought that the site originally started as a pre-Greek cult to an older Goddess called Lindia.

The Greeks then transformed the sanctuary into Athena Lindia, keeping the older name but incorporating their own goddess, Athena. What was in the sanctuary and what was offered there is described in detail on the Lindian Temple Chronicle which was written by Timakhidas and Tharsagoras on a grey marble stele erected there in 99 BCE. The sanctuary was also excavated by two Danish men (Karl Frederik Kinch and Christian Blinkenberg) in the early 20th century and they published 6 volumes containing details about everything found there – the stele (measuring 8 foot by 3 foot) is now housed in the Danish National Museum. According to the Lindian Temple Chronicle, people dedicated all kinds of jewellery and precious metals to the sanctuary as well as articles related to their trade. Other dedications include two shields from Herakles, the helmet of Alexandros from King Menelaus and Alexandra the Great also dedicated there in 331 BCE.

Figure 4.40. Remains of the temple of Athena Lindia, Acropolis of Lindos, Rhodes.

Importantly, one of the dedications describes a krater (a large vase used for mixing wine and water) which had belonged to Daidalos and had been given by him to King Kokalos as a gift: "Phalaris, the tyrant of the Akragantines, a krater, on one side of which a Titanomachy had been fashioned, and on the other Kronos taking his children from Rhea and devouring them. And upon the rim had been written, "*Daidalos gave me as a guest gift to Kokalos*, and upon the base *Phalaris from Akragas to Lindian Athena*"[72]. The bowl had eventually fallen into the hands of Phalaris who had dedicated it to the sanctuary. The fact that the krater had been owned by Daidalos would have increased its prestige tremendously. Phalaris, who died in 554 BCE was a tyrant of Akragas (present-day Agrigento) and was notorious for his cruelty. He is said to have roasted people alive in a bronze bull[73] (Figure 4.41) and to have eaten babies.

Figure 4.41. Phalaris having Perillus thrown into the bronze bull. By Stefano della Bella (17th century CE).

Egyptian works

Figure 4.42. Artist's impression of the gateway of the temple of Ptah (i.e. Hephaestus) at Memphis.

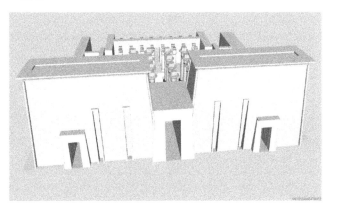

The temple of Ptah (known as Hephaestus by the Greeks) in Memphis was built by King Min (or Menes), the first King of unified Egypt, and Daidalos built a beautiful gateway and vestibule for this temple (Figure 4.42)[74]. It was also said that a wooden statue of Daidalos, which he had made himself, was placed in this temple. Daidalos was greatly honoured by the inhabitants of Memphis who considered him to be a god and built a temple for him on one of the islands near Memphis[74].

The Greeks identified Hephaestus (the god of blacksmiths, metalworking, carpenters, craftsmen, sculptors and fire) with the Egyptian god Ptah who also was the god of sculptors, craftsmen, metal-workers, architects and shipbuilders. He was the main deity worshipped in the city of Memphis which was founded in 3100 BCE.

Libyan Altar

*Figure 4.43. **Periplous** of Scylax, 1855 facsimile of a 13th-century copy of the original Greek text*

Scylax of Caryanda, (6th century BCE) was a Greek explorer who was the first Western observer to describe India. In 515 BCE the Persian king Darius I sent him to explore the Indus River. Unfortunately, few of his writings survive but he is referenced by many ancient writers. In his book *Periplous* (Figure 4.43), which describes the circumnavigation of the Mediterranean and Black Sea, Scylax states that an altar on the coast of Libya had sculptures of lions and dolphins by Daidalos[75]. This altar was dedicated to Poseidon. Other writers have stated that this altar was located in Soceis (Soluntum) near modern-day Santa Flavia near Palermo in Sicily.

Other works of Daidalos listed by Pausanias

In his *Description of Greece*, written in the 2nd century CE, Pausanias describes a number of other works of Daidalos and these include:

(a) An image of the hero Trophonios in a sacred
    cave near Lebadeia[78]; this is present-day
    Livadeia which is about 56 miles north-west of
    Athens. Trophonios was one of the five great
    Greek oracles. The site of the oracle is a few
    metres southwest of the Temple of Zeus. It
    consists of a well about 4 m deep and 2 m in
    diameter (approximately the dimensions given

Figure 4.44. Drawing of a coin from Crete showing the head of Britomartis in profile (370-320 BCE).

by Pausanias). At the bottom of the well is a cavity the width of a man's body which extends underneath the wall of the well.

(b) A wooden image of Britomartis (Figure 4.44) in her temple at Olous on Crete[79]. As described earlier in this chapter, Britomartis was a goddess venerated on Crete.

(c) A wooden image of Aphrodite on Delos. Daidalos gave this to Ariadne who took it with her when she left Crete with Theseus. Pausanias describes it as: "......a small wooden image of Aphrodite, its right hand defaced by time, and with a square base instead of feet"[80]. After he abandoned her on Naxos, Theseus took the image to Delos where he dedicated it to Apollo (Figure 4.45).

Figure 4.45. Remains of the temple of Apollo on Delos.

(d) A folding chair (a votive offering) in the temple of Athena Polias on the Acropolis in Athens[81]. This is a rather surprising offering as it is an item of furniture that was common in archaic and classical Greece (i.e. 8th-4th century BCE) but would have been unknown in the era of Daidalos.

(e) A wooden image of Hercules in the sanctuary of Athena Chalkinitis in Corinth[82]

(f) A wooden image of Hercules in the temple of Hercules at Thebes[83]

Hephaistos (Hephaestus)

Hephaistos (Figure) was the Greek god of fire, blacksmiths, craftsmen, metal-working, stonemasonry and sculpture. He is usually depicted as a bearded man holding a hammer and tongs. He was generally considered to be ugly and lame yet he married Aphrodite (arranged by the gods) despite that fact that she was in love with Ares. He made the dwellings, furnishings, and weapons of the gods and to help him he had three golden assistants.

In his workshop, Hephaistos had two golden robots as well as three Cyclops to help him. His many works included: Aphrodite's golden girdle, the bows and arrows of Artemis and Apollo, the famous Shield of Achilles, Hercules' golden breastplate, Athena's shield and spear, Apollo's chariot and the sceptre of Zeus.

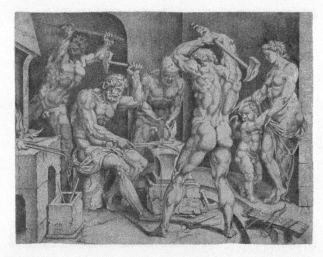

Hephaestus in his forge. Engraving by Cornelis Bos (Holland, 1546)

One of his most famous constructions was Talos, a man of bronze who he gave to Minos to protect Crete. Talos patrolled the shores of Crete three times a day and threw rocks at any ships that approached. He also had a habit of leaping into a fire until he was red hot and then clasping any intruder in his arms until they were burnt to death. He had a single vein that was filled with ichor (the blood of the gods) and this was plugged with a nail in his heel. When Jason and the Argonauts (together with Jason's wife Medea, a sorceress) tried to land in Crete, they were prevented from doing so by Talos. However, this resulted in his death as related by Apollodorus: "His death was brought about by the wiles of Medea, whether, as some say, she drove him mad by drugs, or, as others say, she promised to make him immortal and then drew out the nail, so that all the ichor gushed out and he died"[76]

There are some similarities between Hephaistos and Daidalos in terms of their skills. Indeed, some later writers suggest that Talos was made, or designed, by Daidalos.[77]

(g) A wooden image of Athena in Knossos[84]

(h) An unspecified image in Gela, Sicily. According to Pausanias: "Antiphemus the founder of Gela, after the sack of Omphace, a town of the Sicanians, removed to Gela an image made by Daidalos"[85]

Stephanius of Byzantium also mentions in his *Ethnica* a statue of Artemis made by Daidalos which was kept in her temple in Monogissa in Caria, Anatolia.

Inventions

As well as being a sculptor, architect and engineer, Daidalos was also renowned as a prolific inventor. His inventions include some of the most important in the history of humankind and contributed greatly to our advancement. According to Pliny the Elder: "Carpentry was invented by Daidalos, and with it the saw, axe, plumb-line, gimlet, glue, isinglass...."[86]

Other inventions attributed to him are: the compass (but also attributed to his nephew Talos), the adze, the auger, the hammer, masts and yards for ships, the drill and the potters wheel[87]. Pausanias says that he invented sails for ships: "fleeing from Crete in small vessels which he had made for himself and his son Ikaros, he devised for the ships' sails, an invention as yet unknown to the men of those times, so as to take advantage of a favorable wind and out sail the oared fleet of Minos"[88]. He was said to have been taught the art of carpentry by Athena: "Daidalos, son of Eupalamus, who is said to have received the art of craftsmanship from Athena...."[89].

Examples of some of these inventions from ancient times are shown in Figure 4.46.

One of Daidalos' most brilliant accomplishments was to fly away from Crete with his son, Ikaros. Most of the ancient writers describe a flight involving the use of wings but fail to specify what these were made of. The texts of five of the earliest writers who mention this story are:[1]

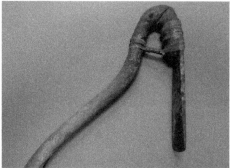

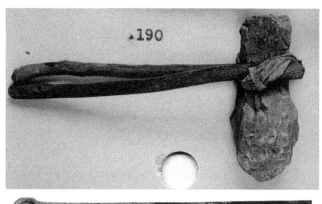

(i) 19 BCE. "Daidalos, so the story goes, fleeing from Minos's kingdom, dared to trust himself to the air on swift wings..."[90]

(ii) 13 BCE. "Daidalos tried the empty air on wings that were never granted to men:"[91]

(iii) 24 CE. "This island is named after Ikaros the son of Daidalos, who, it is said, having joined his father in flight, both being furnished with wings, flew away from Crete and fell here, having lost control of their course"[92]

(iv) 100 CE. "fashioned with amazing ingenuity wings which were cleverly designed"[93]

(v) 150 CE. "And so Daidalos made wings and fitted them to himself and to his son Ikaros, and they flew away from that place"[94]

(a) Saw found in Temple of Hatshepsut, Egypt (1479–1458 BCE).

(b) Bronze axe from Crete (ca. 1600–1450 BCE)

(c) Roman plumb bob (bronze) used to construct a plumb-line. From an unknown Dalmatian site. inv. no. AMS-H-5950. Archaeological Museum, Split, Croatia

(d) A bronze adze bound to a wooden handle with a strip of leather (1550-1295 BCE). Found in Temple of Hatshepsut, Egypt

(e) Hammer found in the Tomb of Meketre, Thebes, Egypt (circa 1990 BCE)

(f) A Roman bronze compass found in Pompeii (1st century AD)

(g) A black-figure terracotta drinking vessel depicting two ancient Greek ships with masts, yards, rigging and sails.

(h) Wall painting in the tomb of Rekhmire in Thebes (1479-1400 BCE). This shows a carpenter drilling holes in the frame of a chair. The carpenter is using a bow-drill and his adze can be seen lying on the ground behind the chair. Daidalos was credited with inventing the drill and adze and was taught carpentry by Athena.

Figure 4.46. Ancient examples of some of the inventions attributed to Daidalos.

Pictorial representations of their flight usually portray Daidalos and Ikaros wearing wings made of feathers. However, what is interesting is that none of the above accounts mention that the wings were made of feathers. Nevertheless, some writers do refer to the use of feathers. Ovid in his *Art of Love* wrote "Calling 'Ikaros', he saw the feathers on the waves....."[95]. While Silius Italicus wrote "He taught his son also to put on a counterfeit semblance of wings and attempt the flight of birds; but, when the feathery oarage melted, he saw him fall and splash the stormy sea with his ill-starred wings"[96]. Lucian of Samosata stated "To such the end soon comes: Ikaros-like, with melted wax and moulting feathers, they fall headlong into the billows"[97]

So, what are we to make of this? The idea of using feathers to make wings, while romantic, is hardly practicable and we are talking about the exploits of the greatest inventor of the ancient world. It is highly likely that Daidalos came up with a much better idea, but one that is not at variance with what most of the classical writers have reported i.e. he used wings of some sort. Daidalos would have realized that human muscles would not have been capable of generating sufficient power to flap wings to keep such heavy bodies in the air. But what about gliding rather than flapping? It has been suggested that Daidalos might have constructed gliders[98]. These could have been fabricated from cloth and wooden struts - Daidalos was well known as a carpenter and inventor of glues. These might have enabled them to island-hop from Crete to Athens in a series of gliding flights. Daidalos might have calculated that even if he couldn't make it as far as Athens, at least he would be able to glide as far as the island of Dia, which is only 11 miles north of Knossos. From there he may have been able to glide to the next island or steal a boat and sail on to Athens.

Otto Lilienthal, the German glider pioneer, showed the feasibility of such an approach. He made a number of flying machines in which the supporting framework was made from willow and the wings themselves from cotton or linen (Figure 4.47). Both willow and linen would have been available to Daidalos. Between 1891 and 1896, Lilienthal built and flew a

Figure 4.47. Otto Lilienthal performing one of his gliding experiments.

series of highly successful full-size gliders and made nearly 2,000 flights. He became known as "the flying man". Most of his gliders were monoplanes with stabilizing tail surfaces mounted at the rear. Control of the glider was achieved by shifting his body weight fore-and-aft and from side-to-side.

Modern hang gliders (Figure 4.48) can fly for several hundred miles and the current world record is 475 miles.

Figure 4.48. Hang gliding.

The warnings to Ikaros to not fly too close to the sun or too low near the sea would also be relevant to hang gliding: "But Daidalos constructed wings for himself and his son, and enjoined his son, when he took to flight, neither to fly high, lest the glue should melt in the sun and the wings should drop off, nor to fly near the sea, lest the pinions should be detached by the damp"[99]. Flying steeply up to the sun could result in the glider stalling and falling to the sea. Also, the cold air when up high may affect the performance of the glue which would result in the wooden framework collapsing and/or detachment of the cloth covering. Flying too close to the sea would mean missing out on the hot updrafts needed to stay airborne. Also, dampness would probably decrease the effectiveness of the glue.

In Chapter 3 we mentioned that alternative versions of the escape from Crete state that Daidalos sailed rather than flew from the island. We also mentioned the confusion stemming from the interchangeability of the word for sails and wings. The sails mentioned in these alternative versions may have referred to the wings of a hang glider. Interestingly, Pausanias, in describing Daidalos' escape says: "For when he was fleeing from Crete in small vessels which he had made for himself and his son Icarus, he devised for the ships' sails, an invention as yet unknown to the men of those times, so as to take advantage of a favorable wind....."[100]. Could he have been referring to the invention of the sails of a hang glider rather than those of a ship?

Daidalos had the skills, the materials and probably the knowledge necessary to build hang gliders for himself and Ikaros and we owe it to him to suggest something more ingenious than feathered wings - he would turn in his grave at being associated with such an idea.

REFERENCES

1. Diodorus Siculus. *Library*, 4.76.1.

2. Hyginus, *Fabulae*, 39

3. Athenaeus of Naucratis, *Deipnosophistae*, 7.301b.

4. Antonis Kotsonas. A Cultural History of the Cretan Labyrinth: Monument and Memory from Prehistory to the Present. *American Journal of Archaeology*, 2018; Vol. 122, pages 367-396.

5. Burrows RM, *The Discoveries in Crete and Their Bearing on the History of Ancient Civilisation*. London: John Murray, 1907.

6. Wunderlich, H.G. *The Secret of Crete*. New York: MacMillan, 1974.

7. Pliny, *Natural History*, 36.19.1

8. Diodorus Siculus, *Library*, 1.97.1

9. Herodotus, *Histories*, 2.148

10. Diodorus Siculus, *Library*, 1.96.1

11. Diodorus Siculus, *Library*, 1.97.6

12. Callimachus, *Hymns*, 4.311

13. Ovid, *Metamorphoses* 8.159–68

14. Kern, Hermann (2000). *Through the Labyrinth*. Munich, New York, London: Prestel. pp. 57–65

15. Pseudo-Apollodorus, *Library*, 3.1.4

16. S.P. Cockerell (Ed). *Travels in Southern Europe and the Levant, 1810–17 the Journal of C.R. Cockerell R.A.*, 1903.

17. Pearson, *The fragments of Sophocles III*, 141 fr 1030

18. Phrynichos, *Praeparatio Sophistica* in Bekker Anecdota Graeca I, 28, 27-28

19. Pausanias, *Description of Greece*, 9.40.3.

20. Pausanias, *Description of Greece*, 8.16.3.

21. Homer, *Iliad*, 18.590

22. Vaughan A. C., *The House of the Double Axe*, pages 159-160

23. Graves R., *The Greek Myths*. 92.2, 98.2-4

24. Lucian of Samosata, *The Dance (De Saltatione)*

25. Plutarch, *Life of Theseus*, 21

26. Nonnus of Panopolis, *Dionysiaca,* 3.390

27. Pseudo-Apollodorus, *Library,* 3.1.4

28. Scol. Eur. *Hipp.* 887

29. Diodorus Siculus, *Library,* 4.77.1

30. Clement of Alexandria, *Protrepticus,* 4.13

31. Philo of Alexandria, *De Specialibus Legibus,* 3.43-45

32. Clement of Alexandria, *Protrepticus* 4.

33. Silius Italicus, *Punica,* 12, 83-103.

34. Vergil, *Aeneid,* 6, 14-41

35. Callimachus, *Hymn to Artemis,* 134

36. Diodorus Siculus, *Library,* 4.76.2

37. Diodorus Siculus, *Library,* 4.76.3

38. Scholiast on Plato *Meno* 367

39. Scholiast on Plato *Euthyphro* 11c

40. Thermistios, *Orationes,* 15.316a

41. Pseudo-Apollodorus, *Library,* 3.15.8

42. Diodorus Siculus, *Library,* 1.97.6

43. Euripides, *Eurystheus,* fragment 188

44. Aristophanes, *Daidalos,* fragment 194

45. Plato, fragment 188

46. Palaiphatos, *De Incredibilibus* 21

47. Diodorus Siculus, *Library,* 4.76.2

48. Plato, *Meno* 97a–98b

49. Philostratus the Elder, *Imagines,* 1.16

50. Callistratus, *Descriptions,* 9

51. Donohue, Alice A. (1988). *Xoana and the origins of Greek sculpture.* Scholars Press. p. 182;

52. Deborah Steiner *Images in Mind: Statues in Archaic and Classical Greek Literature and Thought.* p. 143.

53. Socrates, *Hippias Major,* 282.a.1

54. Socrates, *Hippias Major,* 281.d

55. Pausanias, *Description of Greece*, 2.4.5

56. Porphyry, *de Abstinentia* 2.18

57. R. J. H. Jenkins, Dedalica: A Study of Dorian Plastic Art in the Seventh Century B.C., Cambridge: University Press, 1936.

58. Aristotle, *De Anima*, 1.3.9

59. Diodorus Siculus, *Library,* 4.78.1-5

60. Diodorus Siculus, *Library,* 4.78.3

61. Diodorus Siculus, *Library,* 4.30.1

62. Pseudo-Apollodorus, *Library,* 2.6.3.

63. Pseudo-Apollodorus, *Library,* 3.13.3

64. Pindar, *Nemean Odes*, 4.50

65. Pseudo-Aristotle, *On Marvelous Things Heard*. 81

66. Plato, *Timaeus*, 80c.

67. Pliny, *Natural History*, 19.1.1

68. Hyginus, *Astronomica* 2.5.1-3

69. Epimenedes, 457F19;

70. Eratosthenes, *Katasterismoi* 5;

71. Ovid, *Metamorphoses* 8.174-182

72. Josephine Shaya. *The Greek Temple as Museum: The Case of the Legendary Treasure of Athena from Lindos*. American Journal of Archaeology, 2005; 109, pages 423-442

73. Pindar, *Pythian Odes* 1.75

74. Diodorus Siculus, *Library,* 1.97.1

75. Scylax of Caryanda, *Periplous,* 112

76. Pseudo-Apollodorus, *Library* 1.9.26

77. E. T. Merrill, Commentary on Catullus, 58b

78. Pausanias, *Description of Greece*, 9.39.4

79. Pausanias, *Description of Greece*, 9.40.2

80. Pausanias, *Description of Greece*, 9.40.3

81. Pausanias, *Description of Greece*, 1.27.1

82. Pausanias, *Description of Greece*, 2.4.5

83. Pausanias, *Description of Greece*, 9.11.2

84. Pausanias, *Description of Greece*, 9.40.2

85. Pausanias, *Description of Greece*, 8.47.2

86. Pliny, *Natural History*, 7.56

87. Pliny, *Natural History*, 7.57

88. Pausanias, *Description of Greece*, 9.11.4

89. Hyginus. *Fabulae*, 39

90. Virgil, Aeneid, 6.1

91. Horace, *Odes*, 1.3

92. Strabo, *Geography*, 14.1.19

93. Pseudo-Apollodorus, *Library*, 4.77.5

94. Hyginus. *Fabulae* 40

95. Ovid, *Art of Love*, 2.90

96. Silius Italicus, *Punica* 12.96

97. Lucian of Samosata, *Essays in Portraiture (Imagines)* 21

98. Kristopher James Ide. *The Daidalos of History and Myth: The Meaning of Creation in Literature from Homer to Joyce.* University of California, Davis, USA, 2011

99. Pseudo-Apollodorus, *Library,* e.1.12

100. Pausanias, *Description of Greece*, 9.11.4

Additional Sources of Information

Our Cretan Dilemma: Labyrinth or Dancing-Place. Brewster Ghiselin. *The Sewanee Review*, 1972; Vol. 80, No. 1, pp. 39-46

Ancient Automata and Mechanical Explanation. Sylvia Berryman. *Phronesis*, 2003; Vol. 48, No. 4, pp. 344-369

The Two Labyrinths. H. R. Hall. *The Journal of Hellenic Studies*, 1905; Vol. 25, pp. 320-337

A Cultural History of the Cretan Labyrinth: Monument and Memory from Prehistory to the Present. Antonis Kotsonas. *American Journal of Archaeology*, 2018; Vol. 122, pp. 367-396

Daidalos and the Origins of Greek Art. Sarah P. Morris. Princeton University Press, 1995

The Chorus of Ariadne. Alfred Burns. *The Classical Journal*, Vol. 70, No. 2 (Dec., 1974 - Jan., 1975), pp. 1-12

The Astral Labyrinth at Knossos. Alexander MacGillivray, *British School at Athens Studies,* 2004; Vol. 12, pp. 329-338

The Geranos Dance - A New Interpretation. Lillian Brady Lawler. *Transactions and Proceedings of the American Philological Association,* 1946; Vol. 77, pp. 112-130

Chapter 5

THE LEGACY OF DAIDALOS

DAIDALOS IS DEEPLY EMBEDDED in the European consciousness. His name is a powerful "brand", to use the modern commerce-infatuated vernacular, and is currently associated with a large number of scientific and technological projects as well as being used in an emblematic fashion by many organisations and companies. His life and works have also been an inspiration to painters, sculptors, storytellers, playwrights, poets, opera-writers and film-makers over the centuries. In this chapter, some of the ways in which his name has been perpetuated will be described.

Daidalos as a challenger of the gods

It is important to appreciate just how significant Daidalos was to ancient philosophers and artists. As someone who was capable of making such lifelike statues, Daidalos and his creations were the subject of great debate as to what was "permissible" and "not-permissible". His ability to imitate life dominates all classical references to his works. For example, in a fragment of Euripides' play *Eurystheus* an old man is comforted after, apparently, being frightened by a lifelike statue: "Don't be afraid old man, its nothing. All the statues of Daidalos appear to move and see, so clever is the man"[1].

Daidalos' art and inventions were at the boundary of what was deemed to be permissible and what was not. His realistic statues, being not quite real but then again not quite inert, may have been acceptable as just being on the right side of that boundary. But, then again, others may have regarded them as being blasphemous. As Pausanias said of Daidalos' statues "All the works of this artist...... have a touch of the divine in them"[2]. This is getting dangerously close to a display of hubris i.e. a disregard for the divinely fixed limits on human action in an ordered cosmos.

Some of his other works – for example, his flight-enabling wings and the artificial cow that facilitated sex between Pasiphae and a bull – would have been judged to have definitely crossed over the boundary into what was not permissible. Euripides expressed this beautifully. In a fragment of his lost

Figure 5.1. Virgil's Tomb by Moonlight, with Silius Italicus Declaiming by Joseph Wright (Wright of Derby), 1779 CE. Metropolitan Museum of Art, New York. Virgil's tomb in Naples has been a popular touristic site for many years. Silius Italicus was a great admirer of Virgil and each year, on the anniversary of the poet's death, he read aloud some of his verses at the tomb.

play *The Cretans*, Minos says to Daidalos, with reference to the artificial cow: "You are a builder but what you did was not carpentry"[3]. That his skills may have offended the gods is suggested by Silius Italicus (a Latin poet and orator of the 1st century CE; Figure 5.1): "He dared to ascend the sky on wings not his own and to reveal to mankind the art of flying. Keeping his body poised amid the clouds, he floated on, and the strange winged creature alarmed the gods"[4]

Horace, the famous Roman poet (Figure 5.2) also implied that Daidalos had gone too far: "Daring enough for anything, the human race deals in forbidden sin......Daidalos tried the empty air on wings that were never granted to men: Hercules' labours shattered Acheron. Nothing's too high for mortal men: like fools, we aim at the heavens themselves"[5]. This is one aspect of Daidalos' life that makes it so fascinating and may, in part, account for why his name has persisted for so long.

Figure 5.2. Portrait of Horace from "Poets: twenty portraits. Engraving by J.W. Cook, 1825".

Perhaps Daidalos' greatest legacy was to challenge the power that the gods held over humanity and thereby start us off on the long path to freedom from such tyranny. Daidalos was the first human being to attempt to defy the gods by means of his skills, rather than by some simple act of disobedience. Disobeying the gods, or failing to acknowledge them sufficiently (by sacrifices etc.), was a common perceived failing of humans, for which they were punished severely. Daidalos, however, invited their displeasure not by disobedience but by using his talents and displaying his expertise. This he did in a number of ways. Firstly, the artificial cow he made for Pasiphae enabled the accomplishment of the unnatural union between a woman and a bull. It was alright, of course, for the gods (particularly Zeus) to abduct and/or have sex with human women while adopting an animal form e.g. a bull, swan, dove and even an ant. But it was clearly not permissible for humans to do likewise. Or was such an attitude simply an expression of misogyny? Perhaps it was considered unacceptable for a woman to initiate a sexual union with an animal. Next, in being able to fly, he was trespassing into the sky which was considered to be the realm of the gods and birds. What could be regarded as a third challenge to the gods is hinted at by Homer: "Therein furthermore the famed god of the two strong arms [i.e. Hephaestus] cunningly wrought a dancing-floor like unto that which in wide Cnosus Daidalos fashioned of old for fair-tressed Ariadne"[6]. The crucial words are "like unto that", because what Homer is implying is that the sculptural/architectural skills of Daidalos were so excellent that a god, Hephaestus, would want to imitate them. This would have been a huge insult to the gods, who were a very touchy lot and very prone to take offence at any implied slight. Ancient commentators expressed great consternation at the idea of a god imitating a mortal[7,8]. A fourth possibility was that he constructed a prison for the minotaur who was, after all, the offspring of a demigod (Pasiphae, daughter of Helios) and fathered by a

Figure 5.3. The Despair of Hecuba by Pierre Peyron (1784 CE).

bull who was a gift from Poseidon. So here we have a mortal colluding in the imprisonment of a creature who was descended from a god. Next, Daidalos appears to have been widely regarded as someone with magical (i.e. god-like) powers. In Euripides' play *Hekabe (Hecuba)* about the wife of King Priam of Troy, Hekabe (Figure 5.3.) makes an impassioned wish for greater eloquence so that she might persuade Agamemnon to avenge the death of her son, Polydorus: "If only I had a voice in my arms and my hands and my hair and my footsteps either through the arts of Daidalos or through some god"[9]. In this passage, she is suggesting that Daidalos' powers are equal to those of the gods. Finally, we have his numerous inventions which, being of enormous benefit to humankind, would help humanity to develop and achieve levels of accomplishment that might ultimately place them on equal terms with the gods.

Figure 5.4. Red-figured calyx krater showing armed warriors named as Daidalos and Enyalios (another name used for Ares, god of war) fighting a duel in front of Hera, who sits on her throne. Found in Bari, Italy, and made in Puglia, Italy, in 360-330 BCE. On the left is Daidalos who wears a cap made of basket-work and surmounted by a sprig. He holds a shield on his left arm and is throwing a spear with his right hand. He is wearing a mask with a snub nose and protruding lips.

At least one ancient vase-painter appears to have taken this idea literally and portrays Daidalos actually fighting Ares, the god of war (Figure 5.4). This is the only representation of Daidalos engaged in any act of violence that has ever been found. That the figure depicted is Daidalos is unmistakeable because his name is inscribed above him. He is shown sparing with Envalios which is another name used for Ares, the god of war. However, the vase is considered to be an example of a "phylax vase" i.e. one depicting a scene from a phylax play. A phylax play (also known as a hilarotragedy) was a burlesque dramatic form developed in Magna Graecia in the 4th century BCE. Its name derives from the Phlyakes or "Gossip Players" in Doric Greek. The artist might therefore have considered that to depict Daidalos as a fighter was an outrageous idea and extremely amusing. The idea that he would take on the god of war himself would have added to the comic effect.

Daidalos and the downfall of the Minoan Civilization

It is possible to argue that an important legacy of Daidalos was the key role he played in the demise of the Minoan civilization and the rise of the Mycenaeans. The following actions can be considered to have contributed to this immensely important historical turning point:

1. The construction of a wooden cow to enable Pasiphae to mate with Poseidon's bull destabilized the Minoan royal family.

2. Daidalos told Ariadne how Theseus could escape from the labyrinth. By killing the Minotaur, Theseus ended the Athenians' obligation to pay tribute to Crete.

3. The pursuit of Daidalos by Minos ended in the death of the latter so depriving the Minoans of their mighty ruler.

4. The desertion of Crete by Daidalos deprived the Minoans of the most inventive and creative figure of those times.

Figure 5.5. J.B.S. Haldane (1958).

Daidalos as a champion of science and technology

In 1923 J.B.S. Haldane (1892-1964), the famous British geneticist, biometrician, physiologist and populariser of science, delivered a talk at the University of Cambridge entitled *Daidalos or Science and the Future*[10]. This was later published and became a best-selling book.

In the talk, Haldane praised the benefits that science and technology had conferred on humankind. He went on to prophesise a number of developments which, almost 100 years later, are well on their way to being realised. A few examples of these are: (i) A decline in the energy-wasteful generation of light by heating up materials – low energy light-emitting diodes are gradually replacing electric filament lamps as light sources, (ii) the harvesting of wind as a major source of energy in the United Kingdom - in 2017 approximately 15% of the energy used in the UK was generated by wind power, (iii) the production of synthetic food by chemical and microbiological means, (iv) the increasing importance of research in the biological and medical sciences and (v) *in vitro* fertilisation.

However, he pointed out that, despite their enormous contributions to human wellbeing, scientists are generally given a hard time by always being regarded with suspicion and perceived as a challenge to some religion: "The chemical or physical inventor is always a Prometheus. There is no great invention, from fire to flying, which has not been hailed as an insult to some god. But if every physical and chemical invention is a blasphemy, every biological invention is a perversion." Prometheus was a Titan who angered the gods by teaching humans about fire. As punishment for this, he was chained to a rock and an eagle ate his liver during the day (Figure 5.6). At night his liver grew back and then was again eaten by the eagle the next day.

He then goes on to praise Daidalos who he describes as being the first modern man: "I fancy that the sentimental interest attaching to Prometheus has unduly distracted our attention from the far more interesting figure of Daedalus. It is with infinite relief that amidst a welter of heroes armed with gorgon's heads or protected by Stygian baptisms the student of Greek mythology comes across the first modern man." He celebrates him as being the first to demonstrate that the scientific researcher is not concerned with gods and points out that Daidalos was not killed by a thunderbolt despite being responsible for the death of a god's son (Minos) and engaging in the first successful venture into experimental genetics (the mating of Pasiphae and the bull).

Figure 5.6. Prometheus Being Chained by Vulcan. Dirck van Baburen, 1623 CE

His summary is full of optimism and he pointed out the enormous potential of scientific research and the excitement associated with its unpredictability: "... science is as yet in its infancy, and we can

Figure 5.7. Portrait of Bertrand Russell in 1916.

foretell little of the future save that the thing that has not been is the thing that shall be; that no beliefs, no values, no institutions are safe."

The great British philosopher Bertrand Russell (1872-1970; Figure 5.7) did not agree with this optimistic view of the benefits of science and in 1924 published a response to Haldane's book entitled *Icarus or The Future of Science*[11]. He pointed out that Ikaros, having been given the equipment to fly by his father, did not use this properly and flew so recklessly that he killed himself. He suggested that humankind, when given marvellous inventions by scientists, may similarly misuse them and suffer accordingly. His essay concluded: "Men sometimes speak as though the progress of science must necessarily be a boon to mankind, but that, I fear, is one of the comfortable nineteenth-century delusions which our more disillusioned age must discard. Science enables the holders of power to realize their purposes more fully than they could otherwise do. If their purposes are good, this is a gain; if they are evil, it is a loss. In the present age, it seems that the purposes of the holders of power are in the main evil, in the sense that they involve a diminution, in the world at large, of the things men are agreed in thinking good. Therefore, at present, science does harm by increasing the power of rulers. Science is no substitute for virtue; the heart is as necessary for a good life as the head."

This debate, of course, continues but it is interesting that two of the greatest minds in the UK in the 1920s used the story of Daidalos and Ikaros to encapsulate their contrasting views of the role of science in the modern era.

The life of Daidalos does, of course, illustrate both aspects of the above debate and shows that science and technology, while capable of providing great benefits, are also potentially dangerous. Many of his inventions (carpentry tools, masts and sails for ships etc.) continue to be of great benefit to humankind. However, his invention of wings led to the death of his son while the artificial cow resulted in the birth of a monster and, ultimately, to the death of both mother and child. Daidalos, of course, did recognise the potential dangers of his marvellous inventions and advised restraint in their use. He took pains to advise Ikaros to be cautious in using his wings: "Let me warn you, Ikaros, to take the middle way...... Travel between the extremes"[12]. This demonstrated that Daidalos' genius was tempered by sound judgement. Unfortunately, this does not mean that such advice will necessarily be followed. In contrast to his scientific and technological works, the artistic accomplishments of Daidalos resulted only in benefits. His innovative approaches to sculpture transformed the way in which the human body was represented and resulted in statues of great beauty while his wooden dolls brought delight to children.

Association of Daidalos with present-day science and technology

Daidalos has also left his mark on science and technology by having his name associated with a variety of scientific and technological developments. Some of the projects that bear Daidalos' name are highly specialised and consequently a web link has been provided in each case so that the specialist reader can access more information on the item.

Project Daedalus – interstellar mission

This was an engineering design study conducted between 1973 and 1978 to demonstrate the feasibility of interstellar travel. It was carried out by the *British Interplanetary Society* who designed an unmanned interstellar spacecraft (Figure 5.8). The design criteria specified that the spacecraft had to use existing or near-future technology and had to be able to reach the closest star in the Northern sky (Barnard's star, which is 5.9 light-years away) within a human lifetime. The use of a fusion rocket was proposed and it was estimated that the trip would take 50 years. The study remains the most complete engineering study ever undertaken for an interstellar probe.

https://www.bis-space.com/what-we-do/projects/project-Daidalos

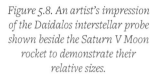

Figure 5.8. An artist's impression of the Daidalos interstellar probe shown beside the Saturn V Moon rocket to demonstrate their relative sizes.

An asteroid named Daedalus

An asteroid discovered in 1971 by the Dutch–American astronomer Tom Gehrels at the Palomar Observatory, California was named Daedalus. It is a stony asteroid approximately 3 kilometres in diameter. It is a member of the Apollo asteroids (Figure 5.9), a group of near-Earth objects, and orbits the Sun once every 645 days.

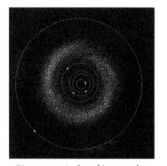

Figure 5.9. A plot of inner solar system asteroids and planets. Planets (with trajectories) are orange, Jupiter being the outer most shown. The main belt of asteroids can be seen between Mars (the fourth planet) and Jupiter (the fifth planet).

MIT Daedalus Project

In 1985 a team of undergraduate students, faculty, and recent graduates of the Massachusetts Institute of Technology started a project which aimed to use a human-powered aircraft to fly from Crete to Santorini. In 1987 work began on the construction of the aircraft which was named Daidalos 88 (Figure 5.10) – the propeller being turned by means of bicycle pedals via a gear-box. On 23rd April 1988, the aircraft flew from Heraklion on Crete to the island of Santorini, a distance of 72.4 miles in 3 hours and 54 minutes. The pilot was the Greek national cycling champion Kanellos Kanellopoulos. The flight holds official Fédération Aéronautique Internationale world records for total distance, straight-line distance and duration for a human-powered aircraft.

http://www.humanpoweredflying.propdesigner.co.uk/ html/Daidalos.html

Hellenic Airforce

In 1911 the Greek Government formed the Hellenic Aviation Service (the forerunner of the Hellenic Airforce) with the help of French specialists. Six Greek officers were sent to France for training and the first four aircraft were ordered. The first military flight was made on 13th May 1912 by Lieutenant Dimitrios Kamberos and in June of that year he flew in an aircraft called the Daedalus which was a seaplane.

Figure 5.10. The Daidalos 88 human-powered aircraft in flight during testing at NASA Dryden Flight Research Centre prior to transportation to Greece.

The Order of Daedalians

This is an American organisation founded in 1934 to honour all those who flew in the First World war (Figure 5.11). It has comprehensive awards and scholarship programmes and supports the military services and other aerospace activities.

https://daedalians.org/

Figure 5.11. Plaque honouring the Order of Daedalians at the Riverside National Cemetery in Riverside, California, with March Joint Air Reserve Base in the background.

Daedalus – a flying suit

In 2017 Richard Browning, a former Royal Marine Reserve, built a flight suit (named Daedalus) using six miniature jet engines and a specially designed exoskeleton (Figure 5.12). The Daedalus is able to take off vertically and fly using the human body to control speed. It can fly at a speed of 200mph and an altitude of a couple of thousand feet. Currently, it can fly uninterrupted for about 10 minutes.

https://en.wikipedia.orgwiki/Daidalos_Flight_Pack

Figure 5.12. Richard Browning in Daedalus, his flying suit.

Dynamics in Aircraft Engineering Design and Analysis for Light Optimized Structures (DAEDALOS) Project

European transport policy and the European aircraft industry demand safer and greener aircraft transport systems as well as reduced development and operating costs, by 20% and 50% in the short and long term, respectively. The DAEDALOS project contributes to these aims by means of an innovative design approach for aerospace structures considering dynamic effects in the loading process more realistically than at present. This project was supported by the European Commission in the 7th Framework Programme for Research and Technological Development.

https://www.daedalos-fp7.eu/

Figure 5.13. Logo of the DAEDALOS project

Daedalus – the Solent Enterprise Zone

In 1917 an RAF Seaplane Training School was established in Lee-on-Solent in Hampshire and in 1939 this was transferred to the admiralty and re-named HMS Daedalus. During the Second World War, it was home to a number of first-line squadrons and it played a key role in D-Day operations. It was demilitarised in 1996 and in 2012 it became an enterprise zone and a premier location for aviation, aerospace engineering and advanced manufacturing businesses. It consists of the Faraday Business Park, the Swordfish Business Park and Solent Airport.

http://www.solentairport.co.uk/about_Daedalos/intro.aspx

Figure 5.14. Logo of the Solent Enterprise zone

The journal *Daedalus*

The American Academy of Arts and Sciences was founded in 1870 and its aim is to "serve the nation as a champion of scholarship, civil dialogue, and useful knowledge" (Figure 5.15). It is one of America's oldest learned societies and independent policy research centres and it convenes leaders from the academic, business, and government sectors to address critical challenges facing global society. In 1955 it started publishing a quarterly journal which is called *Daedalus*. Drawing on some of the nation's foremost scholars in the arts, sciences, humanities, and social sciences the journal explores the frontiers of knowledge and issues of public importance.

https://www.mitpressjournals.org/daed

Figure 5.15. American Academy of Arts and Sciences building, Cambridge, Massachusetts, USA.

Daidalos: Berlin architectural journal

This was a quarterly journal of architecture published from 1981 to 2000. It was founded by Ulrich Conrads, Norbert Miller, Werner Oechslin, Bernhard Schneider and Anna Teut. The magazine was published by Bertelsmann Fachzeitschriften GmbH (Gütersloh), and from 1998 by the Gordon + Breach Publishing Group. Before the publishing change, the subtitle had already been changed, from the original *Daidalos - Berlin Architectural Journal* to *Daidalos – architecture, art, culture*. The magazine was discontinued with the 75th edition in 2000. It was the only bilingual architectural journal (English/German) in German-speaking countries although it was more like an encyclopaedic book series than a journal.

The journal *Icarus*

Icarus is devoted to the publication of original contributions in the field of Solar System studies. Manuscripts reporting the results of new research - observational, experimental, or theoretical - concerning the astronomy, geology, meteorology, physics, chemistry, biology, and other scientific aspects of our Solar System or extrasolar systems are welcome. The journal is endorsed by the Division for Planetary Sciences of the American Astronomical Society.

https://www.journals.elsevier.com/icarus

Daedalus Research Evaluation and Development Corporation (DREADCO).

David Edward Hugh Jones (1938-2017; Figure 5.16) was a British chemist and author who wrote a column in the journal *New Scientist* (and other publications) using the pen-name Daedalus who was supposed to be an inventor working for the company DREADCO. His columns as Daedalus were published for 38 years, starting weekly in 1964 in the *New Scientist* then in the journal *Nature* and the newspaper *The Guardian*. He continued to publish until 2002 and produced almost 1,900 columns. He also published two books of columns from these magazines, along with additional comments and implementation sketches: *The Inventions of Daedalus: A Compendium of Plausible Schemes* (1982) and *The Further Inventions of Daedalus* (1999).

Daedalus proposed many "plausible schemes" and these "thought experiments" switched between flights of fancy and satire, but they often anticipated real discoveries. For example, in 1966 he suggested the possibility of a hollow molecule of carbon. Amazingly, in 1996 the Nobel prize in chemistry was awarded to Robert Curl Jr., Harold Kroto and Richard Smalley for the discovery of such molecules – the fullerenes.

https://www.theguardian.com/science/2017/aug/18/david-jones-obituary

Figure 5.16. David Jones (the Daedalus of New Scientist*) and one of his inventions – a perpetual-motion machine for the fictitious company "Dreadco".*

Daedaleopsis and *Daedalea*

Daedaleopsis is the name of a genus of fungi that includes at least 10 species. It was named after Daidalos because of the labyrinthine appearance of its spore-forming surface on its underside (Figure 5.17). The common name of one species, *Daedaleopsis confragosa*, is the "thin-walled maze polypore" or "blushing bracket". They are usually found on decaying hardwoods but some species can attack live trees.

Figure 5.17. Daedaleopsis confragosa (Blushing bracket). The whole fungus is approximately 5 cm in diameter and its maze-like appearance is very evident.

Figure 5.18. Daedalea quercina showing the maze-like underside of the fungus.

Daedalea is another fungal genus that is, again, named on the basis of its intricate spore-forming surface. More than 37 different species have been identified. They grow on dead wood and each species tends to prefer a particular type of tree. For example,

Daedalea quercina, commonly known as the oak maze-gill or maze-gill fungus, is often found on dead oak trees (Figure 5.18).

HMS Daedalus

Four ships and three shore establishments of the British Royal Navy have borne the name HMS Daedalus. The first ship to be so-called was a 32-gun frigate launched in 1780 (Figure 5.19) while the last was a depot ship of the Royal Naval Air Service from 1916-19.

The Royal Navy also had ships named after Icarus and the minotaur (Figure 5.20).

Daedalus lunar crater

This is a large crater (Figure 5.21) on the far side of the moon and was photographed by the Apollo 11 astronauts. Because it is shielded from radio emissions from Earth, it has been proposed as the site of a future giant radio telescope.

Daedalus Reef

Daedalus Reef (also known as Abu Kizan) is a 400-metre long and 100-metre wide reef in the Red Sea approximately 90 kilometres from Marsa

Figure 5.19. HMS Daedalus and a sea serpent spotted by the crew in 1848. The ship was a nineteenth-century frigate of the British Royal Navy which had 46 guns. She was launched in 1826 but then converted in 1844 to a corvette with 19 guns and finally into a training ship in 1851. She was scrapped in 1911. On 6 August 1848, Captain McQuhae and several of his officers and crew saw a sea serpent. It was reported as having four feet of its head above the water and with another sixty feet of its body in the sea.

Figure 5.20. HMS Minotaur. This was the lead ship of the Minotaur-class armoured frigates built for the Royal Navy during the 1860s. They were the longest single-screw warships ever built. The ship spent most of her active career as flagship of the Channel Squadron. She became a training ship in 1893 and broken up in 1923.

Alam. There is a small artificial island in the centre of the reef on which a lighthouse was built in 1863 and rebuilt in 1931 (Figure 5.22). It is a marine park with an abundance of corals and attracts large fish including oceanic whitetip sharks, whale sharks and hammerhead sharks. Unfortunately, I have not been able to find out how it got its name.

Figure 5.21. The large crater in the picture is Daedalus which is located near the centre of the far side of the Moon, its diameter is about 58 miles.

Figure 5.22. Daedalus reef and its lighthouse. It is popular with divers because it is a good place for seeing hammerhead sharks.

Other uses of Daidalos' name in science and technology

(i) Daedalus, a platform for producing large quantities of recombinant proteins that can be used in structural, biophysical or therapeutic applications.
https://www.ncbi.nlm.nih.gov/pubmed/21911364

(ii) Daedalus, a curriculum mapping software.
The main mission of the Daedalus project is
to promote the development of curriculum
maps for all interested programs and academic
units. This process is about collecting enough
information so that important questions
can be answered, and important insights be
communicated to instructors and students alike.
https://www.dal.ca/sites/ Daedalus.html

(iii) Project Daedalus. The project looks at the
emerging field of 'drone cinema'. This research
is an exciting opportunity to re-purpose
drones for creative control creating multi-user
experiences and new audience environments.
*https://www.andfestival.org.uk/project Daedalus /
about/*

(iv) Daedalus - enhanced weather threat awareness
for aviation. This aims to assist airlines, air
navigation service providers and airframe
and aero-engine manufacturers to increase
operational safety and efficiency, and increase
situational awareness of stakeholders on
aircraft and the ground. Key objectives include
in-flight detection and forecasting of a range of
aviation hazards, and analytics to support flight
operations.
https://business.esa.int/projects/Daedalus

(v) The Daedalus Experiment. This is a phased
neutrino experiment whose ultimate goal is
to search for evidence of CP violation in the
neutrino sector through the oscillation of
muon antineutrinos to electron antineutrinos
over short baselines of up to 20km. This is
currently one of the most important priorities in
neutrino physics because it may help to explain
fundamentally important questions about the
development of the early universe.
https://www.nevis.columbia.edu/daedalus/index.html

(vi) Daedalus Trust. There is a growing body of opinion that the exercise of power can distort thinking and create personality changes in leaders that affect their decision making. The Daidalos Trust was founded by Lord David Owen to raise awareness of such changes and understand them better. It was a registered UK charity from 2011-2017 but was then merged with the Maudsley Philosophy Group that is likewise registered with the UK Charity Commission.

http://www.daedalustrust.com/
http://maudsleyphilosophygroup.org

(vii) Daedalus is a highly secure, multi-platform, hierarchical deterministic "wallet" for the safe storage of the Ada cryptocurrency. It will add more cryptocurrencies and will be developed over time to become a universal wallet, blockchain application platform and an app store.

https://daedaluswallet.io/

(viii) DAEDALUS (DNA Origami Sequence Design Algorithm for User-defined Structures). This free online resource is developed and maintained by the Laboratory for Computational Biology & Biophysics at the Massachusetts Institute of Technology. With this software it is possible to render nearly any target 3D geometry as a scaffolded DNA origami nanoparticle by providing only an input Computer-Aided Design (CAD) file of the object. The goal of DAIDALOS is to broaden the participation of non-experts in the design and synthesis of structured DNA assemblies by offering a fully autonomous, CAD geometry-based sequence design algorithm.

http://daedalus-dna-origami.org/about/

(ix) Daedalus – Modular, energy-independent

tracking systems. A purely satellite-based solution is only partially suitable for most tracking systems, as the high demand for electricity is a great impairment to the service life. Alternative systems based only on Radio-frequency Identification (RFID) technologies or energy-saving active communication solutions are restricted by the fact that their functionality is generally limited to a narrow geographical area. The aim of the "Daidalos" Project is therefore to find a solution that combines the benefits of satellite-based and RFID solutions, thus compensating for the disadvantages of each.

https://www.iis.fraunhofer.de/en/ff/lv/lok/proj/daedalus.html

Daidalos in the Arts

As well as being of continuing interest to scientists, engineers and inventors, Daidalos and his exploits have also been a great source of inspiration for generations of writers and artists. His name is also perpetuated in the title of a multimedia literary and arts journal - *The Daedalian*. This is published by the Texas Woman's University *https://twudaedalian.wordpress.com/*

Literature

Ancient Greek and Roman writers have written a large number of plays, stories and poems based on the life of Daidalos. Sometimes he is the focus of such writings but in others he is a secondary character in stories that are mainly about the other people who figured in his life such as Minos, Ikaros, Ariadne, Theseus, Phaedra and Pasiphae. Examples are included in Table 5.1 below. This shows that he was certainly a major inspiration for many Greek and Roman playwrights, poets and story-tellers. Unfortunately, most of these literary works have been lost, although fragments of some of them have survived. The earliest of these writings date to the 6th and 5th centuries BCE and include plays by Alcaeus, Aristophanes, Sophocles and Euripides. The way in which they are written makes them appear to refer to some actual historical figure.

Table 5.1. Greek and Roman books that feature Daidalos

Title of book	Author	Lifetime of author or publication date of book
Pasiphae	Alcaeus	620 – 580 BCE
The Thracian Women, Cressae	Aeschylus	525 – 455 BCE
Daidalos, Camici, Phaedra, Polyidus, Theseus, Cocalos, Minos	Sophocles	496 - 406 BCE
The Cretans, Cretan Women, Theseus	Euripides	480 – 406 BCE
Daidalos, Cocalus	Aristophanes	446 – 386 BCE
Daidalos	Platon (Plato Comicus)	lived around 430 BCE
Daidalos	Eubulus	4th century BCE
Minos	Antiphanes	408 to 334 BCE
The Cretans	Apollophanes	active in 388 BCE
Minos	Alexis	375 – 275 BCE
Pasiphae	Alceus	active in 388 BCE
The Cretans	Nicochares	died 345 BCE
The Aeneid, Eclogues (book 6)	Virgil	written in 19 BCE and 38 BCE respectively
The Elegies	Sextus Propertius	50-15 BCE
Metamorphoses, The Art of Love, Tristia	Ovid	43 BCE – 18 CE
Phaedra	Seneca	4 BCE – 65 CE
Concerning Astrology	Lucian	125 – 180 CE
Theseus	Aristonymus, Achaeus, Theopompus, Anaxandrides and Diphilus	various

Sometimes the interest of an author in Daidalos was very personal. For example, Ovid (Figure 5.23) appeared to have identified with him because he considered Daidalos to be a fellow exile. Ovid had been banished from Rome to Romania by the emperor Augustus and longed to return home, just as Daidalos had wanted to escape from Crete. In one of his poems in *Tristia* (written in about 9 CE while in exile) he writes:

> "now I'd wish for wings to beat in flight,
>   either yours Perseus, or yours Daidalos:
>   so the gentle air might fall beneath my swiftness
>   and suddenly, I'd see my country's sweet earth,
>   and the faces in the house I left, true friends,
>   and above all my dear wife's features.
>   Foolish, why utter childish prayers for them in
>   vain."

Daidalos was also an important figure for philosophers. Plato (428/427-348/347 BCE; Figure 5.24) refers to Daidalos extensively in his works e.g. in *Laws* and the *Republic*. He also has Socrates speaking about him in *Euthyphro* and *Alcibiades I*.

Figure 5.23. Statue of Ovid in Constanța (ancient Tomis) the city where he was exiled). Created in 1887 by the Italian sculptor Ettore Ferrari.

Figure 5.24. Marble head of Plato (3rd century CE).

Furthermore, Xenophon and Aristotle, as mentioned in Chapters 3 and 4 respectively, also refer to Daidalos in order to make important philosophical points.

Daidalos was not only a source of inspiration for classical authors, numerous later writers, poets and dramatists have written about him or have based their writings on events in his life. Examples of these are given in Table 5.2.

Table 5.2. More recent literary works that feature Daidalos or events in his life

Title of book	Author	Lifetime of author or publication date of book
The Divine Comedy	Dante Alighieri	1265 – 1321
Genealogy of the Gods	Boccaccio	1313-1375
The Legend of Good Women; The House of Fame	Geoffrey Chaucer	1343 – 1400
Henry VI	William Shakespeare	1564 – 1616
Phedre	Jean Racine	1639-1699
The Modern Daidalos	Tom Greer	1846-1904
Theseus	Andre Gide	1869-1951
A Portrait of the Artist as a Young Man; Ulysses	James Joyce	1882-1941
Daidalos in Crete	Angelos Sikelianos	1884-1951
The House of Asterion; Labyrinths	Jorge Luis Borges	1899-1986
Icaro	Lauro de Bosis	1901-31
The Wings of Daidalos	Fritz Diettrich	1902-64
The King Must Die; The Bull from the Sea	Mary Renault	1905-83
The Labyrinth	Maria Neuhauser	1906-85
Story for Ikaros. Projects, incidents, and conclusions from the life of D., engineer	Ernst Schnabel	1913-86
Testament of Daidalos; The Maze Maker	Michael Ayrton	1921-75
King Minos of Knossos	B. Cyril Windeler	written in 1935
I and the Kings	Ernst Schnabel	written in 1958
At the Palaces of Knossos	Nikos Kazantzakis	written in 1988
The Makings of Maleness: Men, Women, and the Flight of Daidalos	Peter H. Tatham	written in 1992
The Helmet of Horror	Victor Pelevin	Written in 2005

Daidalos' life has inspired a huge number of poems and a few of these are listed in Table 5.3.

Table 5.3. Examples of poems that have been written about Daidalos or his associates

Title of poem	Author	Lifetime of author or publication date of poem
Musée des Beaux-Arts	W. H. Auden	written 1938
Daidalos and Icarus	John Bliven Morin	born in 1936
Daidalos	Alastair Reid	1926-2014
Daidalos in Sicily	Joseph Brodsky	1940-96
Daidalos	Mason Lee	written 2014
Daidalos, After Icarus	Saeed Jones	written 2014
To a friend whose work has come to triumph	Anne Sexton	1928 - 1974
Icarus	Edward Field	written 1950
Waiting for Icarus	Muriel Rukeyser	written 1973
Icarus	Christine Hemp	written 1996
Icarus	Wendy A. Shaffer	written 2000

It is interesting to note that one of Brueghel the Elder's paintings, *Landscape with the Fall of Icarus* (Figure 5.37) has itself inspired no fewer than 35 poems including Auden's renowned *Musée des Beaux-Arts*.

The story of Daidalos and Ikaros was a source of inspiration for Lauro Adolfo De Bosis (1901-31) who wrote a verse-drama, *Icaro*, in 1928. This was an anti-fascist allegory. He was a fierce opponent of Mussolini and in 1930 he started to organise the distribution of anti-fascist newsletters throughout Italy. After a short course of flying lessons, on 3rd October 1931 he took off from Marseille in a small wooden plane (called *Pegasus*) and flew to Rome. There he circled over the city centre, including the Piazza Venezia where Mussolini was sitting in council, dropping thousands of anti-fascist leaflets in which he urged the Italians to rebel. He then headed out to sea for Corsica but was never to be seen again – it is thought that he crashed into the Tyrrhenian Sea. He knew that this escapade would cost him his life and so he left behind an essay entitled *The story of my death*.

Paintings and mosaics

With regard to the visual arts, from the 7th century BCE onwards many ancient pottery items featured painted scenes associated with the life of Daidalos and some of these have been included in previous chapters. In his catalogue of ancient images (on pottery, paintings, statues, reliefs etc) of Daidalos and Ikaros, Nyenhuis[13] includes more than 60 items but states that this is less than one half of the total number of such images that are listed by the German archaeologist Frank Brommer[14]. Subsequent to the publication of these catalogues, a number of other statues believed to be of Ikaros have been identified[15]. These fall into three groups in which Ikaros is depicted as standing still, getting ready to fly or actually in flight. Table 5.4 summarises the nature and origin of the various images of Daidalos and/or Ikaros produced prior to the 4th century CE that have been found so far.

One of the earliest depictions of Daidalos is on a 7th century BCE skyphos, a drinking vessel with a deep bowl and almost straight, thin walls which is in the Louvre and can be seen at *https://commons. wikimedia.org/wiki/File:Skyphos_genius_animals_Louvre_ MNB2030.jpg*

Another skyphos shows on one side Theseus fighting the Minotaur, Ariadne with her ball of thread and the fourteen young Athenians intended for sacrifice. On the reverse side is a figure of a winged man and this is thought to represent Daidalos (Figure 5.25).

A Boeotian alabastron made in 570 BCE (Figure 5.26) may depict Daidalos although debate continues as to whether this is the case. The figure is that of a young, bearded man with long hair. He carries a

Figure 5.25. Photograph of a winged figure (Daidalos?) on one side of the Rayet skyphos (ca 550 BCE). Found in Tanagra, Boeotia, Greece. Louvre Museum, Paris.

Figure 5.26. Boiotian Corinthianizing alabastron (570 BCE). Academisches Kunstmuseum, Bonn.

double-headed axe and a bucket or bag (for tools?). He is wearing wings and these are shown attached to his body by straps across his chest. Other possibilities are that the figure could represent Aristaios (a minor god) or a winged demon.[16]

Table 5.4. Representations of Daidalos and/or Ikaros painted on vases or walls or found as reliefs, statues or mosaics.

Person represented	Nature of scene depicted	Source of object			
		Etruscan	Roman	Graeco-Roman	Greek
Daidalos alone	As craftsman	4	5	2	
	Flying	6			
Ikaros alone			24	1	3
Daidalos and Ikaros together	Ikaros helping his father		1		
	Daidalos making/ fitting wings for Ikaros		14		2
	Flying	1	2		1
	Multiple scenes		1		
	Ikaros falling		10		
	Daidalos grieving over dead Ikaros				1

Ikaros is shown, and identified by the inscription "Ikaros", on a fragment of a vase found on the acropolis of Athens and dated to 570-560 BCE (Figure 5.27). Unfortunately, all that can be seen on the fragment are the legs of a running figure wearing winged boots and a short chiton. This pre-dates the earliest literary reference to Ikaros (in Euripides' play *The Cretans*) by more than 100 years.

A winged Daidalos is shown on a Boeotian terra-

Figure 5.27. A portrayal of Ikaros on a fragment of a black-figure vase depicting the birth of Athena (570-560 BCE) found on the Athenian acropolis. National Archaeological Museum, Athens.

cotta perfume container made in approximately 550 BCE (Figure 5.28).

Figure 5.28. A winged Daidalos on a terracotta tripod kothon (vessel for perfumed oil). From Boeotia, Greece (mid-6th century BCE).

Most of the earliest representations of Daidalos alone that have been found so far are on Etruscan pottery of the 5th or 4th century BCE. He is invariably shown as a craftsman with wings attached and carrying various tools such as an axe, saw, adze or hammer. In Etruscan portrayals he is always shown young, sometimes with a beard and may be clothed or naked. In contrast, Roman images invariably depict him as being bearded and clothed.

One of the earliest depictions of Daidalos and his son flying together is on a black-figure Italian neck amphora of 550 BCE (Figure 5.29). Both figures are shown flying from left to right with the first one (Ikaros) carrying two rods while the second (Daidalos) carries an axe in his right hand and a saw and an adze in his left hand.

(a) Image of the whole amphora

(b) close-up showing Daidalos on the left and Ikaros on the right

Figure 5.29. Neck amphora from Taranto, Italy (550 BCE). Antikensammlung, Kiel, Germany.

In the late 5th and early 4th centuries scenes showing Daidalos attaching wings to Ikaros begin to appear on vases made in Southern Italy. Such scenes also became common on Roman reliefs, sarcophagi, gems and cameos in the 1st and 2nd centuries CE. An example is a fragment of a late 5th century BCE Apulian skyphos in Oxford showing Daidalos attaching wings to Ikaros (Figure 5.30). Ikaros stands at the left looking back at his father who is seated behind him. One wing has already been attached while Daidalos holds the 2nd wing out, preparing to fasten it to his son.

Two pottery vessels that feature more complex scenes featuring Daidalos and Ikaros together with other characters have been described by Susan Woodford[17] although, unfortunately, no images are available. On the fragments of an Apulian calyx krater (340 BCE) in the H. A. Cahn collection in Basel, Daidalos is shown seated with his head on one hand apparently considering his options in a difficult situation. To the left a boy (Ikaros?) huddles in his cloak and looks fearfully to his left where a white-haired woman is gesticulating. Above Daidalos is part of a female figure (Pasiphae?) seated on what could be an altar. The image has been interpreted as representing a scene from *The Cretans* by Euripides (see Chapter 3). The nurse could be explaining about the birth of the minotaur to Pasiphae (seated above Daidalos). Daidalos is clearly worried about what is going to happen to him while Ikaros naturally shares his father's concern.

On a volute-krater (350-320 BCE) in the Museo Archeologico Nazionale in Naples, Ikaros stands frontally in the centre with one wing attached while Daidalos is busy attaching the second one. Athena stands to the left and below are a hammer and Daidalos' wings. There is an open box on the ground to the left of Ikaros, with some sort of container, perhaps for holding the glue used in attaching the wings.

Daidalos is rarely depicted alongside Minos but one example showing them together is on a frag-

Figure 5.30. Fragment of a late 5th century BCE Apulian skyphos showing Daidalos (only partially visible) attaching wing to Ikaros. Ashmolean Museum, Oxford.

mentary calyx (Figure 5.31). Minos (with his name inscribed) stands holding his sceptre while a woman (probably Pasiphae) stands beside him on his left. A white-haired male (Daidalos) kneels before him (unfortunately much of his head is missing) holding a suppliant's olive branch. A second olive branch is shown suggesting the presence of a second suppliant (Ikaros?). Hermes and Apollo are shown above this group. It has been suggested that the scene depicts Daidalos' first meeting with Minos in which he asks for sanctuary after his flight from Athens[18]

Figure 5.31. A fragmentary calyx-krater from Taranto, Italy (ca 350 BCE). Allard Pierson Museum, Amsterdam.

(a) View of the whole fragment showing Daidalos in the bottom left-hand corner with an olive branch.

(b) An enlarged view showing the head of Minos in the bottom left-hand corner and the top of his sceptre.

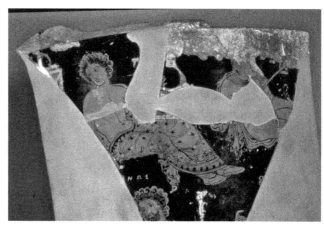

Roman artists, in particular, became fascinated with the death of Ikaros and this is featured on many wall paintings in Pompeii. A typical example can be seen at *https://commons.wikimedia.org/wiki/File:Dedalo_assiste_alla_morte_di_icaro,_da_pompei,_9506.JPG*. It is one of the four most common mythological themes in Roman wall paintings and features in 10 of the 80 examples discovered so far.

The earliest depictions of King Minos (6th century BCE) are on vases showing him as an onlooker of the fight between Theseus and the minotaur. Such representations continued to be popular on Athenian and South Italian vases throughout the 5th century and at least 11 such examples are known[19]. Figure 5.31 shows him with Daidalos. Other representations of Minos on vases show him with Scylla (3 examples) or watching Heracles capture the Cretan bull (4 examples).

(a) Oinochoe showing Pasiphae getting into the artificial cow made by Daidalos (375-350 BCE)

(b). Daedalus presents the cow to Pasiphae. A reproduction of a wall painting in the Ixion Room, House of the Vetti, Pompeii, ca. 62-68 CE

Figure 5.32. Representations of Pasiphae and the artificial cow made by Daidalos.

The earliest representation of Pasiphae is on an Etruscan cup where she is shown nursing the baby minotaur (Chapter 3). This is also one of the very few images of her on painted pottery. In contrast, she is often portrayed on wall paintings or in reliefs in both Etruscan (12 examples) and Roman (30 examples) art[20]. Roman wall painters appear to have been particularly intrigued by the wooden cow that Daidalos built for Pasiphae and this appears in 16 paintings. One of the most well-known of these can be seen at *https://commons.wikimedia.org/wiki/File:Pompeii_-_Casa_dei_Vettii_-_Pasiphae.jpg*

Other images include those shown in Figure 5.32 as well as Figures 3.11 in Chapter 3 and 4.14 in Chapter 4.

In a Roman mosaic found in Spain, Daidalos and the wooden cow are visible but, unfortunately, most of the figure of Pasiphae is missing. Pasiphae is commonly portrayed with Daidalos rather than with Minos and invariably wears a chiton underneath a himation (Figure 5.33).

(a) Chiton and himation. 19th-century engraving showing a woman with a chiton (left), and two women with a himation over a chiton (centre and right). A chiton consisted of a long and wide rectangle of fabric (wool or linen) sewn up at the sides, pinned or sewn at the shoulders and usually girded around the waist. A himation was a cloak made from large rectangular pieces of fabric (usually wool) arranged around the body in a variety of different ways, often covering the head.

(b) Terracotta fragment of a kylix (drinking cup) 480–470 BCE. The woman is wearing a chiton underneath a himation.

Figure 5.33. Ancient Greek clothing worn by women.

Daidalos is usually shown as an older man, often bearded and usually wearing an exomis i.e. a short tunic fastened over the left shoulder (Figure 5.34).

Portrayals of the minotaur are extremely common on ancient vases, wall paintings and mosaics[21]. Although literary sources tell us that he was a bull-human hybrid, how these elements were combined was not usually specified. Although he has occasionally been represented as a human-headed bull, most images show him as a bull-headed human.

In Greek art the minotaur is usually naked but sometimes he wears a short tunic. He may be shown with or without a tail and sometimes the hairiness of his body is emphasised. He does not often appear alone but is invariably shown fighting with Theseus, often in the presence of onlookers. In almost all cases, the minotaur is shown on the right of the scene while Theseus is on the left. By the beginning of the 6th century BCE, the two most commonly-depicted

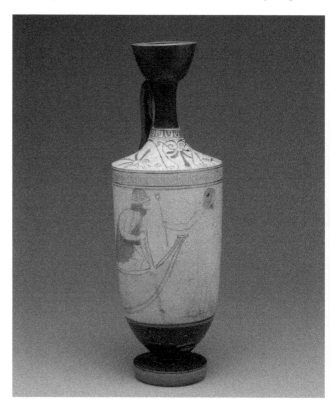

Figure 5.34. A terracotta lekythos (oil flask) portraying Charon, Hermes, and a youth (ca. 450 BCE). Hermes, in winged boots and holding a staff, beckons a young man (the deceased), toward Charon's boat. Charon is wearing the clothing typical of a Greek workman - the exomis.

scenes were of the minotaur either confronting Theseus or running away from him. His bestial nature was emphasised by showing him fighting with rocks whereas Theseus wielded a sword. At the beginning of the 5th century BCE, the minotaur was often shown dying or dead. A number of examples of portrayals of the minotaur on Greek pottery have been included in Chapter 3, other early examples are shown in Figure 5.35.

Figure 5.35. Examples of pottery depicting the fight between Theseus and the minotaur

(a) A terracotta lekythos (oil flask) from Attica showing the fight between Theseus and the minotaur (ca. 500 BCE)

(b) Attic black-figure neck amphora from Athens (about 550 BCE). Theseus has just stabbed the beast with his sword, and blood streams from the wound. A youth and a girl, representatives of the fourteen youths and maidens saved from sacrifice, stand at each side watching.

The Etruscans also showed great interest in the story of the minotaur but were more varied in the scenes they portrayed. These included: (a) the minotaur holding a dead victim under one of his arms, (b) the minotaur gnawing on the limbs of one of his victims, (c) Pasiphae nursing the baby minotaur.

Interestingly, the earliest example of pottery with the word "Minotaur" inscribed on it is the 6th-cen-

(c) Amphora with Theseus fighting the minotaur. Etruscan, 6th century BCE.

(d) Black-Figure hydria (water vessel) showing Theseus and Minotaur on the shoulder. Attica, Greece (520 BCE)

tury cup made by Archikles and Glaukytes. This was found in Etruria and is held in the Antikensammlungen in Munich and can be seen at *https://gantzmythsources.net/chapter-8-minos-and-crete/section-2-minos-pasiphae-and-the-minotaur/p-261/*

The Romans appeared to have been less interested in using the minotaur for decorating vases but his story was a popular subject in mosaics and wall paintings some of which can be seen at these websites:

https://artsandculture.google.com/asset/theseus-mosaic/ sAHPzcCsLQEyDg

https://commons.wikimedia.org/wiki/File:Teseo_in_lotta_ col_minotauro,_da_chieti,_s.n._01.JPG

https://commons.wikimedia.org/wiki/Category:Theseus_ killing_the_Minotaur,_mosaic_MANN_10016_ (from_Pompeii)#/media/File:Mosaic_from_Pompeii_ depicting_Theseus_fighting_the_Minotaur,_Naples_ National_Archaeological_Museum_(15156313689).jpg

(a) Terracotta black-figure amphora (500 BCE). Ariadne is shown as an on-looker of the fight between Theseus and the minotaur.

(b) Terracotta red-figure kylax from Anatolia, Turkey (late 5th-century BCE.–early 4th-century BCE). Ariadne is often shown lying down because she was asleep when Theseus abandoned her on Naxos. The two satyrs suggest the presence of Dionysus as does the grapevine.

(c) Terracotta black-figure amphora from Tarquinia, Italy (last quarter of 6th century BCE). Ariadne is shown with Dionysus in the presence of satyrs and maenads.

(d) Roman fresco depicting Ariadne and Dionysus (1-79 CE). Nude except for the drapery swirling around them, Dionysus and Ariadne walk with arms entwined. Ariadne lifts a drinking horn (rhyton), while Dionysus carries a kantharos (wine cup).

Figure 5.36. Representations of Ariadne.

In most of the depictions of Ariadne on vases, paintings and mosaics, she is accompanied by Theseus (Figure 5.36). In their catalogue of the 163 known representations of Ariadne described by Marie-Louise Bernhard and Wiktor A. Daszeuski, two thirds also show Theseus[22]. Most (25%) of the remaining portrayals show her abandoned on Naxos.

When it comes to paintings from the Middle Ages onwards, some of the greatest artists (van Dyck, Rubens, Breughel) have been moved to depict aspects of the life of Daidalos – particularly his flight and the death of Ikaros. Some relevant paintings have been included throughout this book.

A painting by Brueghel (Figure 5.37) departs considerably from the usual portrayal of the disastrous outcome of the escape of Daidalos and Ikaros from Crete and is worth considering in more detail (see also Auden's poem about the painting). Firstly, Daidalos does not appear in the painting at all and, with regard to Ikaros, only his legs are shown as the doomed youth disappears into the sea in the bottom right-hand corner. This is a humiliating portrayal of

Figure 5.37. Landscape with the Fall of Icarus. Pieter Brueghel the Elder (1525-69). Royal Museums of Fine Arts of Belgium, Brussels

Imitators of the flight of Daidalos through the ages

The flight of Daidalos set a dangerous precedent for other adventurous individuals throughout history.

Simon Magus, living in Rome in the time of Nero (1st century CE), used wings to try to fly to heaven but St. Peter was said to have used prayers to send him crashing down onto the temple of Romulus (Figure a).

Abbas ibn Firnas (809-887 CE; Figure b) was an Andalusian polymath who lived in Rhonda and Cordoba in Spain. His attempt at flying was described by the Algerian historian Ahmed Mohammed al-Maqqari "Among other very curious experiments which he made, one is his trying to fly. He covered himself with feathers for the purpose, attached a couple of wings to his body, and, getting on an eminence, flung himself down into the air, when according to the testimony of several trustworthy writers who witnessed the performance, he flew a considerable distance, as if he had been a bird, but, in alighting again on the place whence he had started, his back was very much hurt, for not knowing that birds when they alight come down upon their tails, he forgot to provide himself with one."[25]

According to William of Malmesbury, the eminent medieval historian (writing in 1125 CE), the Benedictine monk Eilmer of Malmesbury Abbey (Figure c): "fastened wings to his hands and feet so that, mistaking fable for truth, he might fly like Daedalus, and, collecting the breeze upon the summit of a tower, flew

Figure a. The fall of Simon Magus. Etching by Martin Speer, after Francesco Solimena, (1817 CE). A winged Simon Magus falling from the sky as a result of the prayers of St. Peter

Figure b. Portrait of Abbas Ibn Firnas (or Armen Firman) by Eulogia Merle. Spanish Foundation for Science and Technology, Alcobendas, Spain

for more than a furlong [201 metres]. But agitated by the violence of the wind and the swirling of air, as well as by the awareness of his rash attempt, he fell, broke both his legs and was lame ever after. He used to relate as the cause of his failure, his forgetting to provide himself a tail."[26]

King Bladud (Figure d), the father of King Lear and the founder of the City of Bath, travelled to Athens where he learnt the secrets of Daidalos. Geoffrey of Monmouth (writing in 1147 CE) tells us that on his return to London, Bladud made himself some wings and jumped from the temple of Apollo, known as Trinaventum. Not surprisingly, he crashed through the temple roof and was smashed to pieces.

BLADUD.
To whom the GRECIANS gave the Name of
ABARIS.

Left: Figure c. Stained glass window in Malmesbury Abbey portraying the flying monk – Eilmer of Malmesbury (1928 CE)

Right: Figure d. Bladud from "Bath and it's Environs, a descriptive poem, in three cantos. [By R. Hippesley.]

Wayland, a master blacksmith in Norse mythology, was imprisoned on an island by the Swedish King Nithad (or Nidud) who cut his hamstrings so that he could not escape and was forced to work for the king. According to the 13th century Icelandic "Edda", his brother, Egill, collected birds feathers from which Wayland made wings and flew from the island to safety.

Ikaros with comical as well as tragic aspects. The painting incorporates many of the elements of Ovid's version of the flight of Daidalos and Ikaros: "Some angler catching fish with a quivering rod, or a shepherd leaning on his crook, or a ploughman resting on the handles of his plough, saw them, perhaps, and stood there amazed, believing them to be gods able to travel the sky."[23]. Ovid also mentions "a noisy partridge poked its head out from a muddy ditch, and, called, cackling joyfully, with whirring wings"[24]. This, of course, is a reference to Daidalos' nephew, Perdix, who was transformed into a partridge when he was pushed from the Acropolis. However, although Breughel has included the fisherman, shepherd, ploughman and partridge (sitting on a branch above the fisherman), the attitudes these figures convey differ considerably from those expressed by Ovid. By and large, all four display indifference to the tragedy that is unfolding in the bottom right-hand corner of the picture. They have failed to notice anything. There is no dramatic rescue attempt. The sailors on the boat are, likewise, oblivious of the death of Ikaros. The overall impression conveyed by the painting is that nothing significant has happened and the world simply goes on with its business as usual. Only the shepherd may have seen something unusual as he looks upward – has he seen Daidalos in flight? Or else is he merely gazing into space while daydreaming? The latter seems to be the most likely as he certainly doesn't appear to be exhibiting any amazement or excitement, his posture is quite relaxed. In this painting Breughel is, perhaps, trying to convey the idea that all over the world tragedies are occurring but largely go unnoticed, life goes on and people must go about their daily business in order to survive. What is infuriating about the people portrayed in the picture is not only their indifference to Ikaros' tragic death but also their lack of awareness of a sensational technological breakthrough – the first flight of humans.

Carlo Saraceni, a follower of Caravaggio, painted a

series of three landscapes on the theme of Daidalos and Ikaros. In the first of these, Daidalos appears to be launching Ikaros into the sky, although there is a confusing entanglement of limbs and wings. In the second a group of individuals observes the tragedy of Ikaros' fall – a nobleman, fishermen and shepherds. In the final scene, Daidalos is shown burying Ikaros and gazes at a bird in flight, a reminder of both how his son died and of the death of his nephew Perdix, who was turned into a partridge by Athena. These paintings can be seen at *https://commons.wikimedia.org/wiki/ File:Paesaggio_con_volo_di_Icaro,_Carlo_Saraceni_001.JPG*

https://commons.wikimedia.org/wiki/File:Paesaggio_con_ caduta_di_Icaro,_Carlo_Saraceni_001.JPG

https://commons.wikimedia.org/wiki/File:Paesaggio_con_ sepoltura_di_Icaro,_Carlo_Saraceni_001.JPG

A painting of the minotaur by George Frederic Watts (Figure 5.38) stands out from the usual portrayals of the beast. In this painting, the Minotaur leans

*Figure 5.38. The Minotaur by George Frederic Watts (1817-1904 CE).-This is a black and white photograph of the original colour painting held in the Tate, London, which can be seen at **https://www. tate.org.uk/art/artworks/watts- the-minotaur-n01634***

out across the sea from a high parapet anticipating the arrival of the ship carrying the sacrificial victims from Athens. The sunlight glints off his shoulder and accentuates his powerful body. On the parapet, the Minotaur's hoof-like fist has crushed a small bird, a symbol of the innocence and purity of youth. Watts used the character of the Minotaur to signify man's bestiality and especially male lust. The inspiration for the painting was a series of articles on child prostitution written by WT Stead (1849-1912) which were published in the Pall Mall Gazette in July 1885 under the title 'The Maiden Tribute of Modern Babylon'. In these articles Stead referred to the Greek myth of the Minotaur: "The appetite of the minotaur of London is insatiable. If the daughters of the people must be served up as dainty morsels to minister to the passions of the rich, let them at least attain an age when they can understand the nature of the sacrifice which they are asked to make."

Other examples of relevant paintings are shown in Figure 5.39 below.

In the 20th century, events and characters from the life of Daidalos continued to be a source of inspiration for several artists including Pablo Picasso, Henri Matisse, Marc Chagall, Michael Ayrton and Leonard Baskin.

The minotaur became an obsession for one of the greatest painters of the 20th century – Pablo Picasso. He once commented, "If all the ways I have been along were marked on a map and joined up with a line, it might represent a Minotaur." He was also very keen on portraying bulls and bull-fighting. Picasso produced a huge number of paintings and drawings of the minotaur and these are on display in galleries all over the world. The three largest collections of his works are in the following museums: Museu Picasso in Barcelona, Musée Picasso in Paris and the Museum Ludwig in Cologne.

(a) *Daedalus attaching wings to the shoulders of his son Icarus. Stipple engraving by G.S. & E.G. Facius after C. Le Brun. This engraving is based on a painting by Charles le Brun in 1645 entitled "Daedalus and Icarus" which is in the Hermitage Museum, St. Petersburg.*

(b) *Daidalos and Icarus by Anthony van Dyck (1599-1641 CE). Art Gallery of Ontario, Toronto, Canada*

(c) *Daidalos and Icarus by Laurent Pêcheux (1729-1821 CE)*

(d) **Landscape with the Fall of Icarus** *by Joos de Monper (1564 – 1635 CE).*

(e) *Theseus and the Minotaur in the Labyrinth. Edward Burne-Jones (1833-1898 CE).*

(f) *Daedalus fixing wings onto the shoulders of Icarus by Pieter Thijs (17th century)*

Figure 5.39. *Images of scenes from the life of Daidalos and his associates.*

Sculpture

We have emphasised many times in this book that Daidalos was someone who changed the course of ancient art by his innovative approach to sculpture. Reference has already been made in Chapter 4 to Daidalos' name being associated with a phase of Greek sculpture in the 7th-century BCE – statues exhibiting this characteristic style are referred to as "Daidalic".

In ancient workshops, skills were transmitted to sons and apprentices who were named with reference to their master and so became known as "the sons of..." or as belonging to the "school of...". This, of course, can lead to confusion when individuals are referred to as being the "sons" of a particular craftsman/sculptor/artist as it is not always obvious as to whether they are being described as genetic sons or merely the trainees of an individual. Daidalos was no exception to this tradition and classical writers make reference to a number of individuals who were either directly taught by Daidalos or were trained in his skills by those who had been taught by him. As well as being referred to as the "sons of Daidalos", these individuals are sometimes called "daidalidai".

Pausanias mentions Dipoinos (Dipoenus) and Skyllis (Scyllis), as being two Cretan sculptors who were either pupils of Daidalos or were his sons by a woman from Gortyn in Crete[27]. They made a statue of Athena for a sanctuary in the city of Cleonae (present-day Kleonai) in Greece and several ebony statues for the temple of Castor and Pollux in Argos. Pliny also refers to these two sculptors and claimed that they were the first to produce statues made of marble[28]. He also said that they made statues of Apollo, Diana, Hercules and Minerva in the city of Sikyon near Corinth, Greece. Other daidalidai mentioned by Pausanias include Klearchos of Rhegion (present-day Reggio di Calabria, Italy), Angelion and Tektaios (who made a statue of Apollo in Delos), Dorykleides, Medon and Theokles (from Lakonia in Southern Greece), Kallon of Aegina, Daidalos of Sikyon and Endoios of Athens.

Although Endoios was said to be an Athenian, he was probably from Ionia, a region of Western Turkey around present-day Izmir (ancient Smyrna). This supposition is based on the fact that he worked in Ephesus and Erythrai and he used the Ionic alphabet in an inscription found on the Acropolis[29]. His works include: a seated statue of Athena on the Acropolis, a statue of Artemis in Ephesus, an ivory statue of Athena in Tegea (later brought to Rome by Augustus) and in Ethrai a wooden statue of Athena Polias seated on a throne with a spindle in her hand and a crown on her head

The first of these statues is interesting as well as very puzzling and worth considering in more detail. According to Pausanias: "Endoios was an Athenian by birth and a pupil of Daidalos, who also, when Daidalos was in exile because of the death of Kalos followed him to Crete. Made by him is a statue of Athena seated, with an inscription that Kallias dedicated the image, but Endoios made it"[30]. The dedicator of the statue, Kallias (or Callias), was a 5th century BCE statesman, soldier and diplomat and was extremely rich. He fought in the battle of Marathon and also negotiated a peace treaty with the Persians in 449 BCE. Endoios was also known to be active in the middle of the 5th century BCE and his name has been found inscribed on a number of statues in Athens. While Endoios is considered to have been one of the Daidalidai[27], Pausanias was incorrect in saying that he accompanied Daidalos to Crete - both Endoios and his benefactor, Kallias, lived approximately one thousand years after the time of Daidalos.

A large number of statues and reliefs of Daidalos, often accompanied by Ikaros, have been produced and some of these are discussed below. Probably the earliest of these features a winged, bearded Daidalos on a 7th century BCE ivory relief from Laconia. In this, Daidalos is shown carrying a bag, possibly containing his carpentry tools.

Daidalos is depicted on a 7th century BCE bucchero olpe excavated from a grave at Cerveteri, Italy (Figure 5.40). Bucchero pottery has a black, polished appearance and was produced in central Italy by its pre-

Roman Etruscan population. The olpe (wine jug) shows a winged man labelled "Taitale" which is Etruscan for Daidalos. This is the oldest depiction of Daidalos in which he is actually identified by an inscription. Daidalos is shown facing to the left with his left knee almost touching the ground with his arms upraised. What is also interesting about this Etruscan olpe is that it demonstrates that the story of the flight of Daidalos and Ikaros was known outside Greece in the 7th century BCE. If it was known in Italy at this time, the implication is that it must have been well-established in Greece long before this date.

Figure 5.40. A bucchero olpe (black, pear-shaped jug) which shows Jason, Medea, the Argonauts and Daidalos. In this view, the winged figure of Daidalos can be seen kneeling with his arms raised. He is nude and beardless and has large wings. His left knee touches the ground while his right knee is bent. His name is written to the right of the figure.

A winged figure appearing on a pithos that depicts the birth of Athena from the head of Zeus is thought to be Daidalos[31].

It has also been suggested that Daidalos featured

on the external Doric frieze on the Parthenon (Figure 5.41) which consisted of 92 sculptured panels (known as metopes). On the south side of the Parthenon, some of the panels are badly damaged and it is these that may have depicted episodes from Daidalos' life.

According to Martin Robertson,[32] metopes XIII to XIX depict the following scenes: Perdix and Talos in Athens, Daidalos with a young girl in Athens, Helios, Daidalos and Ikaros in Athens, Daidalos and Theseus in Knossos, Ariadne with two statues made by Daidalos, Daidalos in Athens. However, other scholars have come up with very different interpretations of what are represented on the remains of these metopes.

Both Daidalos and Ikaros appear on a 5th-century Etruscan bulla (Figure 5.42) found in Comacchio a town near the mouth of the River Po i.e. close to the Elektrides Islands mentioned in Chapter 3. A bulla is a hollow pendant that could hold perfume or a charm and is usually supplied with a removable stopper. The total height, including the stopper, is 4.0 cm, and the greatest diameter is 2.5 cm. Although it is made of gold, one side is considerably blackened suggesting

Figure 5.41. The Parthenon, Athens by Frederic Edwin Church in 1871.

that it has a high silver content. Inside it was found "labdanum", a gum found on the bark and leaves of a variety of cistus (sun rose) found around the Mediterranean. This substance was, and still is, used in perfume. This object is rightly considered to be a masterpiece of decorative design. Depicted are Daidalos (on the front) and Ikaros (on the back). This is one of the oldest representations of Daidalos in which he is identified by an inscription – "taitale", the Etruscan form of his name. Daidalos is flying to the right with his knees bent. He is carrying a saw and an adze and wears a short chiton (a sleeveless shirt made from a rectangular piece of linen or wool) which is traditionally worn by craftsmen. Ikaros (identified as "Vikare") is depicted in a similar fashion but is carrying a double axe and a carpenter's T-square. The work is very delicate with tremendous attention to detail e.g. the nails on the frame of the saw are included and different types of feathers are shown on the wings. Although used as a bulla, it could also have formed part of a necklace.

It is interesting to note that Etruscan artists often portrayed Daidalos as a beautiful youth. This is possibly because the Etruscans themselves were renowned

(a) Daidalos

(b) Ikaros

Figure 5.42. Bulla with Daidalos and Ikaros (5th century BCE). Found in Comacchio, Italy.

craftsmen and had great respect for Daidalos – they consequently portrayed him as being young, an attribute generally associated with gods. In contrast, Greek, Roman and modern artists generally portray him as an aged, experienced father while Ikaros is shown as an adventurous youth.

Figure 5.43. A recreation in modern materials of the lost colossal statue by Pheidias, Athena Parthenos by Alan LeQuire (1990) in a full-scale replica of the Parthenon in Nashville's Centennial Park.

The statue of Daidalos shown in Chapter 1 (Figure 1.7) was found in Philadelphia-Amman in 1947 and dates from around 200 CE. What is shown in the figure is thought to be only part of the original statue which probably portrayed an anguished Daidalos carrying the body of Ikaros. Daidalos was found in five main pieces and these consisted of the head and upper torso, two arms and the lower torso and legs in two parts. The left arm, raised straight upwards from the shoulder, must have supported the body of Ikaros in the hand. Unfortunately, only a foot, an arm and part of the torso of Ikaros were found and their size suggested that Ikaros was about half the size of his father.

A portrait of Daidalos was also said to be present on the shield of Athena Parthenos: "...in whose centre a portrait of Daidalos is fixed in such a manner that, if someone wanted to lift the portrait from the shield, the entire work would collapse"[33]. The Athena Parthenos (Figure 5.43) was a massive sculpture of Athena by the sculptor Pheidias/Phidias which was housed in the Parthenon in Athens.

Other examples of ancient statues and reliefs featuring aspects of Daidalos' story are shown in Figure 5.44.

(a) An Etruscan scarab made of carnallite featuring a winged Daidalos using an adze (4th century BCE).

(b) Bronze sculpture of Daidalos (3rd century CE) found in Plaošnik, Republic of Macedonia

(c) Two-handled drinking vessel with a relief showing Pasiphae, Daidalos and the artificial cow. Found in Tarsus, Anatolia (last quarter of 1st century BCE).

(d) Pasiphae entering the cow via a ladder set against its flank. Roman, 1st/2nd century CE, formerly owned by the Duke of Marlborough.Unlike most representations, this shows Pasiphae entering the artificial cow from the top rather than from its flank.

(e) Marble statue of Ikaros found in 1842-46 in a grave mound near Wagna, Austria. He is shown with long, wavy hair and his hands can be clearly seen holding handles on each of the wings. Short feathers are apparent at the top of the wings with longer ones at the bottom. It is from the Roman era but has not been accurately dated.

Figure 5.44. Examples of ancient statues and reliefs of Daidalos and his associates

A fascinating series of reliefs on funerary urns from the 2nd or 1st century BCE have been recovered from tombs in Volterra, Tuscany, which was an important Etruscan city known as Velathri or Vlathri. These are now housed in the Guarnacci Museum in Volterra. Unfortunately, no photos of any of these are available.

One relief shows Minos recoiling in horror after seeing the baby minotaur for the first time. Pasiphae and Daidalos are also shown. Another features Minos, Pasiphae, Daidalos, Ariadne and the baby minotaur in the arms of a nurse. Daidalos is bound and sits on a stool next to Pasiphae while Minos brandishes a sword. The wooden cow can also be seen behind Pasiphae and Daidalos. A third urn features a similar group of individuals but also shows Ikaros and two guards. Daidalos is, again, bound and sitting on a stool but this time a guard is clasping his shoulder and holding up a mallet as evidence of his guilt. Ikaros is standing next to Daidalos and a second guard stands by the wooden cow. In the centre, an angry Minos brandishes a sword in front of a kneeling Ariadne. A nurse is shown handing the baby minotaur to Pasiphae who is being encouraged to leave by another woman.

Nearly two thousand years after the most recent of the objects shown in Figure 5.44, Daidalos and his adventures continued to fascinate sculptors and some examples of their works are shown in Figure 5.45.

(a) Tile showing Daidalos by Andrea Pisano (1290-1348 CE) on Giotto's campanile (bell tower) in Florence. Daidalos is shown as a winged, muscular, bearded upward-soaring man whose body is covered in feathers. Pisano was one of the most important sculptors of the 14th century and worked mainly in Florence. He succeeded Giotto (who died in 1337) as the chief architect for the construction of the campanile of the cathedral of Florence. He added two stories adorned with panel reliefs, most of which depict the arts, sciences and occupations of man.

(b) The Fall of Ikaros (17th century CE), Musée Antoine Vivenel, Compiègne, France. As well as featuring both Daidalos and Ikaros, a representation of a labyrinth is also clearly visible.

(c) Labyrinth carved on a pillar of the portico of St Martin's Cathedral in Lucca, Tuscany, Italy. The Latin inscription says "This is the labyrinth built by Dedalus of Crete; all who entered therein were lost, save Theseus, thanks to Ariadne's thread." (12th-13th century CE). It pre-dates the famous Chartres maze, but has the same pattern which became a standard for all mazes.

(d) *Sculpture of Daidalos by Felipe Coscolla Plana (1880-1940 CE). Gobierno Militar building, Barcelona. Daidalos is portrayed as a modern aviator wearing a pilot's helmet. His flying ability is not denoted by the presence of wings but instead he is shown holding a model aeroplane.*

(e) *Statues of Ikaros and Daidalos at Agia Galini on the south coast of Crete which claims to be the place from which they set off on their flight from Crete*

(f). **Daedalus** *by James Walter Butler RA (2000 CE). Memorial in the Victoria Embankment Gardens, London. This statue shows Daidalos as a modern pilot reflecting on his comrades who have been killed during the war. The statue is on a column which is embedded in a plinth that resembles the prow of a ship. The inscription on the plinth reads: "To the everlasting memory of all the men and women from the United Kingdom, the British Commonwealth and the many allied nations who have given their lives whilst serving in the Royal Naval Air Service and the Fleet Air Arm. He rode upon a cherub and did fly: yea he did fly upon the wings of the wind"*

Figure 5.45. *Examples of sculptures and reliefs from the 2nd millennium CE that depict Daidalos or aspects of his life.*

Daidalos and his exploits became an obsession for the British sculptor, painter, print-maker, broadcaster and designer Michael Ayrton (1921-75). He produced more than 800 works (drawings, paintings, prints, sculptures etc) relating to Daidalos as well as two books about him (Table 5.2). Some of his works are displayed in important collections around the world including the Tate Gallery (London), the National Portrait Gallery (London) and the Museum of Modern Art (New York). Figure 5.46 shows some of his sculptures.

(a) The minotaur. Located in the Barbican, London.

(b) Icarus. Located near St. Paul's Cathedral, London

(c) Talos, the bronze guardian of Crete. Located on Guildhall Street, Cambridge.

(d) The minotaur. Located in Yorkshire Sculpture Park

Figure 5.46. Examples of sculptures by Michael Ayrton

Film and opera

A number of films related to Daidalos' life have been produced and these include those listed in Table 5.5.

Table 5.5. Films based on the life of Daidalos and his exploits

Title	Date	Director	Comments
Minotaur, the Wild Beast of Crete	1960	Silvio Amadio	Based on the legend of Theseus; starred Bob Mathias
Daidalos and Ikaros	1991	Paul Weiland	Written by Anthony Minghella; starred Michael Gambon and Derek Jacobi
Minos	2005	Juan Luis Lopez Fons	Starred Carmen Althaus, Kina Bermudez and Matthew Hammond
Minotaur	2006	Jonathan English	Written by Nick Green and Stephen McDool
Atlantis	2013-2017	Justin Molotnikov and 5 others	BBC TV series created by Johnny Capps, Julian Murphy Howard Overman
Theseus and the Minotaur	2017	Joshua Kennedy	Starred Joshua Kennedy, Marco Muñoz, Jamie Treviño & Gus Kennedy
Ariadne	2018	Adrian Rodriguez	Starred Magnea Helgadottir, Dustin Ardine and Marius Biegai

Several operas relating to Daidalos and his associates have also been produced and these include:

(i) *Theseus* composed by Jean-Baptiste Lully (1675)

(ii) *Ariadne aux Naxos* composed by Richard Strauss (1912)

(iii) *The Wings of Daidalos* composed by Maurizio Squillante (1978)

(iv) *The Minotaur* composed by Harrison Birtwistle (2008)

(v) *Ikaros* composed by David Blake (2016)

Some final thoughts

Daidalos has been an important figure throughout history. Firstly, he was very important in shaping the identity of Athens in the Classical era because it helped to give it a history that incorporated such a well-known and talented figure. Consequently, in the fifth century BCE, he was given an identity that included being Athenian, a descendant of Athenian royalty, a relative and associate of Theseus and a famous sculptor, craftsman and inventor. He is also an important "bridge" between the classical and modern worlds as Aristotle, reflecting on the works of Daidalos, appears to anticipate the world in which we now live: "For if each instrument were able to accomplish its own task, either in obedience or anticipation of others, like the works of Daidalos or the autokinetic tripods of Hephaistos which, as the poet says, 'of their own accord entered the assembly of the gods', then, in the same manner, shuttles would weave and plectra play the lyre on their own, master builders would not need apprentices, nor masters, slaves." (*Politics*, 1.4). But throughout all ages, Daidalos has been an inspiration to humanity because he was the first person to attempt the impossible and take humankind beyond its self-imposed limitations.

Some writers have argued that despite being renowned as a famous sculptor (even as being the "inventor" of sculpture) there is little evidence to support the existence of Daidalos as a real person. However, this should not surprise us as nearly four millennia have passed since his era. Even if we go back to times that are not so distant, such as classical Greece, it is worth noting the comment of Andrew Stewart in his book *One Hundred Greek Sculptors, Their Careers and Extant Works*: "Though the names of well over a thousand Greek sculptors have survived, very few emerge as concrete personalities through either securely attributed works, or extended treatment in ancient texts, or (very occasionally) both". Likewise, there is little hard evidence of the existence of figures such as King Arthur, Robin Hood, Beowulf, William Tell, Prester John and Saint Christopher who loom large in our culture. Perhaps all we can say is that if there was no such person as Daidalos, humanity would have needed to invent him because of the important role he serves – his existence is an emotional truth.

The purpose of this book was not to try to establish whether or not Daidalos actually existed. Many other attempts have been made to do this and have reached different conclusions. Its purpose was to summarise his story and to remind us of his legacy. Few individuals from so long ago have captured the public's imagination so strongly and remained in their consciousness for so long. Following the demise of the Minoan and Mycenaean civilisations, the European world entered a dark age that lasted approximately 4 centuries until the emergence of Archaic Greece in the 8th century BCE. It is intriguing that one story that survived through those times, and continues to fascinate us thousands of years later, was that of Daidalos.

The adventures and achievements of Daidalos have echoed down the millennia and he will always be remembered for as long as humanity continues to delight in listening to stories. His lasting legacy to us is his appearance in our history as the first "modern man". He challenged the gods and initiated the long and noble quest to free ourselves of their tyranny. But what of the future? In the essays of Haldane and Russell, we have seen two very contrasting views of the effects of scientific and technological developments – one full of glorious optimism while the other portrays doom and gloom. I feel we should take the advice of Daidalos: "'Let me warn you, Ikaros, to take the middle way...... travel between the extremes'[34]. Yes, science will assuredly produce many more wonders but humanity will have to develop more collective wisdom to ensure that these are not misused and can lead to the utilitarian ideal of "the greatest good for the greatest number". I will finish with a poem quoted by Haldane in his essay "Daidalos or Science and the Future" which portrays Daidalos and his daidalidai (in the sense of his scientific/technological descendants) beavering away in the background for the benefit of humanity:

> "Black is his robe from top to toe,
>   His flesh is white and warm below,
>   All through his silent veins flow free
>   Hunger and thirst and venery,
>   But in his eyes a still small flame
>   Like the first cell from which he came
>   Burns round and luminous, as he rides
>   Singing my song of deicides."

(author unknown)

Their work enables the realisation of humankind's greatest aspirations (eradication of disease, elimination of hunger, colonisation of other planets etc.), giving us hope and lifting us far above the stifling trivia of our daily lives.

Thank you Daidalos.

REFERENCES

1. Euripides, *Eurystheus*, Fragment 372N

2. Pausanias, *Description of Greece*, 2.4.5

3. Euripides, *The Cretans*, F988

4. Silius Italicus, *Punica*, 12.90-103

5. Horace, *Odes*, 1.3.

6. Homer. *The Iliad*, 18.587.

7. Nicanor, *Venetus Graecus* 822;

8. Erbse, *Scholia Graeca in Homeri Iliadem* 4:564-65A

9. Euripides, *Hekabe*, 836-40

10. J.B.S. Haldane. *Daedalus or Science and the Future*. Kegan Paul, Trench, Trubner & Co., 1925

11. Bertrand Russell. *Icarus or the Future of Science*. Spokesman Books; Facsimile of 1924 edition, 2005

12. Ovid, *Metamorphoses*, 8.183-235

13. J.E. Nyenhuis: *Daidalos et Ikaros*. In: *Lexicon Iconographicum Mythologiae Classicae (LIMC)*. Book III, Artemis-Verlag, Zurich and Munich 1986, pages 313-342

14. Brommer, Frank. Denkmalerlisten Zur Griechischen Heldensage. N.G. Elwert Verlag, 1974

15. Sanader M. *Contribution to the sculpture of Icarus from Daruvar*. Opusc. Archaeol. 2012; 36: 105–142

16. Erika Simon, *Early Images of Daidalos in Flight*. In: *The Ages of Homer*, edited by JB Carter and SP Morris, The University of Texas Press, 1995

17. Woodford S. Daidalos and Ikaros on an Apulian fragment newly acquired by the British Museum. *Bulletin of the Institute of Classical Studies*, 2009; 52; 93-101

18. J. D. Beazley, Ikaros. *The Journal of Hellenic Studies*, 1927; 47; 222-233

19. Jan Bazant: Minos. In: *Lexicon Iconographicum Mythologiae Classicae* (LIMC). Book VI, Artemis-Verlag, Zurich and Munich 1992, pages 57-574

20. John K. Papadopoulos: Pasiphae. In: *Lexicon Iconographicum Mythologiae Classicae (LIMC)*. Book VII, Artemis-Verlag, Zurich and Munich 1994, pages 193-200

21. Susan Woodford: The minotaur. In: *Lexicon Iconographicum Mythologiae Classicae (LIMC)*. Book VI, Artemis-Verlag, Zurich and Munich 1992, pages 574-581

22. Marie-Louise Bernhard and Wiktor A. Daszeuski: Ariadne: In: *Lexicon Iconographicum Mythologiae Classicae (LIMC)*. Book III, Artemis-Verlag, Zurich and Munich 1992, pages 1050-1077

23. Ovid, *Metamorphoses*, 8.217-220

24. Ovid, *Metamorphoses*, 8.236-38

25. Lynn Townsend White, Jr. *Eilmer of Malmesbury, an Eleventh Century Aviator: A Case Study of Technological Innovation, Its Context and Tradition. Technology and Culture* 1961, 2, pages 97-111

26. William of Malmesbury, *The history of the English kings*, ed. and trans. R. A. B. Mynors, R. M. Thomson, and M. Winterbottom, 2 vols., Oxford Medieval Texts, 1998–9

27. Pausanias, *Description of Greece*, 2.15.1

28. Pliny, *Natural History*, 36.4.1.

29. Jones, H. S. *Greek Sculpture*. Page 7-8. Macmillan and Company, London, 1895

30. Pausanias, *Description of Greece*, 1.26.4-5

31. Sarah P. Morris. *Daidalos and the Origins of Greek Art*. Princeton University Press, 1995, page 99

32. Martin Robertson, *The South Metopes: Theseus and Daidalos*, in E. Berger, Der Parthenon-Kongress Basel. Referate und Berichte 4. bis 8. April 1982, Mayence, von Zabern, 1984

33. Lucius Ampelius, *Liber Memorialis* 8.10

34. Ovid, *Metamorphoses*, 8.200

Additional sources of information

Bruegel on Icarus: Inversions of the Fall. Karl Kilinski II. *Zeitschrift für Kunstgeschichte*, 2004; 67. Bd., H. 1, pp. 91-114

The Testament of Daedalus. Michael Ayrton. *The Massachusetts Review*, 1962; Vol. 3, No. 4, pp. 733-752

The Maze Maker. Simone Oettli. *The Kenyon Review*, 1983; Vol. 5, No. 1, pp. 67-84

Legend Builders of the West. Arthur Milton Young. University of Pittsburgh Press; 1958

Daedalus and Icarus Within: The Literature/Art/Writing Connection. Gabriele Lusser Rico. *The English Journal*, 1989; Vol. 78, No. 3, pp. 14-23

IMAGE CREDITS

Note: All uncredited photographs are from the author's personal collection.

Figure 1.2

By Unknown photographer (Beeld & Geluid Wiki Dutch TV, 7 June 1968, Fenklup) (https://creativecommons. org/licenses/by-sa/3.0), via Wikimedia Commons.

Figure 1.3

Image courtesy of Rijksmuseum, Amsterdam, Public domain.

Figure 1.4

By Future Perfect at Sunrise CC0 1.0, via Wikimedia Commons

The Labyrinth (insert)

(a) Image courtesy of Rijksmuseum, Amsterdam, Public domain.

(b) JamesJen (https:// creativecommons.org/licenses/ by-sa/3.0)

Herodotus (insert)

(a) Metropolitan Museum of Art, New York. Gift of George F. Baker, 1891. CC0 1.0.

(b) By Cush [Public domain], via Wikimedia Commons.

Figure 1.5

By O. Von Corven, Colorized by K. Vail Abdelhamid [CC0], via Wikimedia Commons.

Figure 1.6

Public domain via Wikimedia Commons.

Figure 1.7

(a) Scanned photograph from a book. Public Doman via Wikimedia Commons.

(b) Rogers Fund, 1972, Metropolitan Museum of Art, New York. CC0 1.0.

Figure 1.8

Rijksmuseum, Amsterdam. CC0 1.0

Homer and the Iliad (Insert)

(a) Walters Art Museum, Baltimore. CC0.

(b) Walters Art Museum, Baltimore. CC0.

Figure 1.9

John Flaxman, designer; Rundell, Bridge, and Rundell, mfg / CC0 via Wikimedia Commons.

Figure 1.10

Digital image courtesy of the Getty's Open Content Program, J. Paul Getty Museum, Los Angeles, USA

Pausanias (Insert)

By Tomisti (https://creativecommons. org/licenses/by-sa/4.0), from Wikimedia Commons.

Figure 1.11

(a) Digital image courtesy of the Getty's Open Content Program, J. Paul Getty Museum, Los Angeles, USA.

(b) Metropolitan Museum of Art, New York. The Cesnola Collection, Purchased by subscription, 1874–76. CC0 1.0.

Figure 1.12

Christoffer Wilhelm Eckersberg, Socrates and Alcibiades, 1813-1816, Thorvaldsens Museum, *www.thorvaldsensmuseum.dk*. CC0 1.0

Diodorus Siculus (Insert)

British Library Arundel Collection. Public domain

Lucius Mestrius Plutarchus (Insert)

Odysses / CC BY-SA (https://creativecommons.org/licenses/by-sa/3.0).

Figure 1.13

Walters Art Museum, Baltimore. CC0.

Figure 1.15

Nome: The Burning of Troy with the Flight of Aeneas and Anchises, Nationalmuseum, Sweden (photo: Erik Cornelius), public domain.

Figure 1.16

The Wellcome Collection. Attribution 4.0 International (CC BY 4.0).

Gaius Julius Hyginus (Insert)

Rijksmuseum, Amsterdam. Public domain.

Figure 1.17 Leen van Dorp / CC0 via Wikimedia Commons.

Figure 1.18

By Internet Archive Book Images [No restrictions], via Wikimedia Commons.

Figure 1.19

By Wilhelm Heinrich Roscher [Public domain], via Wikimedia Commons.

Figure 1.21

Metropolitan Museum of Art, New York. Rogers Fund, 1972. CC0 1.0.

Figure 2.1

Modification of map by Nzeemin (https://creativecommons.org/licenses/by-sa/4.0), via Wikimedia Commons.

Figure 2.2

Brooklyn Museum, Charles Edwin Wilbour Fund, 35.763. CC BY 3.0.

Figure 2.4

Public domain, via Wikimedia Commons.

Figure 2.5

(a) The Wellcome Collection. Attribution 4.0 International (CC BY 4.0).

(b) Institute for the Study of the Ancient World from New York, United States of America (The Acropolis (XXVI)) (https://creativecommons.org/licenses/by/2.0), via Wikimedia Commons.

Figure 2.6

Image courtesy of Dimitrios Tsalkanis – www.AncientAthens3d.com.

Figure 2.9

Drawing attributed to artist Evangelos Olympios. Photograph by Ken Russell Salvador, Flickr username flypegassus (http://creativecommons.org/licenses/by/2.0), via Wikimedia Commons.

Figure 2.10

By Janmad (Own work) https://creativecommons.org/licenses/by-sa/4.0-3.0-2.5-2.0-1.0), via Wikimedia Commons.

Figure 2.11

By Spiridon Ion Cepleanu (Own work) https://creativecommons.org/licenses/by-sa/3.0), via Wikimedia Commons.

Figure 2.12

Metropolitan Museum of Art, New York. Gift of Bashford Dean, 1924. CC0 1.0.

Figure 2.13

(a) Unknown author. Public domain via Wikimedia Commons.

(b) Scan from a book, courtesy of n·e·r·g·a·l, Public domain via Wikimedia Commons.

Figure 2.14

(a) Walters Art Museum, Baltimore. CC0.

(b) Metropolitan Museum of Art, New York. Gift of the Greek Government, 1927. CC0 1.0.

Figure 2.15

(a) Metropolitan Museum of Art, New York. Rogers Fund, 1954. CC0 1.0.

(b) Metropolitan Museum of Art, New York. Fletcher Fund, 1939. CC0 1.0.

(c) Metropolitan Museum of Art, New York. Rogers Fund, 1923. CC0 1.0.

(d) Metropolitan Museum of Art, New York. Rogers Fund, 1923. CC0 1.0.

(e) Metropolitan Museum of Art, New York. Fletcher Fund, 1939. CC0 1.0.

Figure 2.16

Image courtesy of Fotocollectie Van de Poll, The National Archives of the Netherlands. Public domain.

Figure 2.17

Metropolitan Museum of Art, New York. Fletcher Fund, 1935. CC0 1.0.

Figure 2.18

Metropolitan Museum of Art, New York. The Cesnola Collection, Purchased by subscription, 1874–76. CC0 1.0.

Figure 2.19

George Douros, Vectorization: MagentaGreen / Public domain via Wikimedia Commons.

Figure 2.20

Alexikoua (https://creativecommons.org/licenses/by-sa/3.0), from Wikimedia Commons.

Figure 2.21

User:Bibi Saint-Pol (https://creativecommons.org/licenses/by-sa/2.5), via Wikimedia Commons.

Figure 2.22

Wellcome Collection. Attribution 4.0 International (CC BY 4.0).

Figure 2.23

Photograph from: *"The palace of Minos: a comparative account of the successive stages of the early Cretan civilization as illustrated by the discoveries at Knossos"* by Sir Arthur Evans and Joan Evans. London: Macmillan and Co., 1921

A. J. Evans/public domain.

Figure 2.24

Metropolitan Museum of Art, New York. Rogers Fund, 1931. CC0 1.0.

Figure 2.25

Image courtesy of Alex Swanston, the Map Archive (https://www.themaparchive.com/).

Figure 2.26

By Martin Belam from Chania, Crete (Replica Minoan ship) (https://creativecommons.org/licenses/by-sa/3.0), via Wikimedia Commons.

Figure 2.27

By Mmoyaq (Own work) (https://creativecommons.org/licenses/by-sa/3.0), via Wikimedia Commons

Bull-leaping (Insert)

Photograph from: Daniel Baud-Bovy and Frédéric Boissonnas "Des Cyclades en Crète au gré du vent", Geneva, Boissonnas & Co, 1919. Aikaterini Laskaridis Foundation Library. Public domain.

Figure 2.28

Antonios Triantafyllakis (https://creativecommons.org/licenses/by-sa/3.0).

Figure 2.29

(a) Photograph from: Encyclopædia Britannica (11th ed.), v. 7, 1911, "Crete," Plate II (between pp. 424 and 425), Fig. 4. Public domain via Wikimedia Commons.

(b) Scan of a photograph from: "A Short History of the World" by H. G. Wells, 1922

H. G. Wells / Public domain via Wikimedia Commons.

Figure 2.30

Walters Art Museum, Baltimore. CC0.

Figure 2.31

Digital image courtesy of the Getty's Open Content Program, J. Paul Getty Museum, Los Angeles.

Figure 2.32

Photograph from: The palace of Minos: a comparative account of the successive stages of the early Cretan civilization as illustrated by the discoveries at Knossos by Sir Arthur Evans and Joan Evans, 1893-1977; London: Macmillan and Co., 1921. A. J. Evans/public domain.

Figure 2.33

From: Encyclopædia Britannica (11th ed.), v. 7, 1911, "Crete," Plate I (facing p. 424), Fig. 2. A. J. Evans / Public domain.

Figure 2.34

Photograph from: *The palace of Minos: a comparative account of the successive stages of the early Cretan civilization as illustrated by the discoveries at Knossos* by Sir Arthur Evans and Joan Evans, 1893-1977; London: Macmillan and Co., 1921. A. J. Evans/public domain.

Figure 2.35

Image courtesy of Professor Jan Driessen.

Figure 2.36

Photograph from: *The palace of Minos: a comparative account of the successive stages of the early Cretan civilization as illustrated by the discoveries at Knossos* by Evans, Arthur, Sir, Evans, Joan, 1893-1977; London: Macmillan and Co., 1921. A. J. Evans/public domain.

Figure 2.37

Photograph from: *The palace of Minos: a comparative account of the successive stages of the early Cretan civilization as illustrated by the discoveries at Knossos* by Evans, Arthur, Sir, Evans, Joan, 1893-1977; London: Macmillan and Co., 1921. A. J. Evans/public domain.

Figure 2.38

Photograph from: *The palace of Minos: a comparative account of the successive stages of the early Cretan civilization as illustrated by the discoveries at Knossos* by Evans, Arthur, Sir, Evans, Joan, 1893-1977; London: Macmillan and Co., 1921. A. J. Evans/public domain.

Figure 2.39

Photograph from: *The palace of Minos: a comparative account of the successive stages of the early Cretan civilization as illustrated by the discoveries at Knossos* by Evans, Arthur, Sir, Evans, Joan, 1893-1977; London: Macmillan and Co., 1921. A. J. Evans/public domain.

Figure 2.40

(a) Metropolitan Museum of Art, New York. Bequest of Richard B. Seager, 1926. CC0 1.0.

(b) Metropolitan Museum of Art, New York. Rogers Fund, 1922. CC0 1.0.

(c) Gift of American Exploration Society, 1907. The Metropolitan Museum of Art, New York. CC0 1.0.

(d) Metropolitan Museum of Art, New York. The Cesnola Collection, by exchange, 1914. CC0 1.0.

(e) Metropolitan Museum of Art, New York. CC0 1.0.

(f) Metropolitan Museum of Art, New York. Gift of Alastair Bradley Martin, 1973. CC0 1.0.

(g) Brooklyn Museum, Charles Edwin Wilbour Fund, 37.13E. Creative Commons-BY

Minoan writing (Insert)

(a) Photograph from: *The palace of Minos: a comparative account of the successive stages of the early Cretan civilization as illustrated by the discoveries at Knossos* by Evans, Arthur, Sir, Evans, Joan, 1893-1977; London: Macmillan and Co., 1921. A. J. Evans/public domain.

(b) Evans, Arthur, Sir (1851-1941) / Public domain via Wikimedia Commons

Minoan seals (Insert)

(a) Walters Art Museum, Baltimore. CC0.

(b) Metropolitan Museum of Art, New York. Gift of Nanette B. Kelekian, in memory of Charles Dikran and Beatrice Kelekian, 1999. CC0 1.0.

Figure 2.41

By http://de.wikipedia.org/w/index.php?title=Diskussion:Purpur_%28Farbstoff%29 (http://creativecommons.org/licenses/by-sa/3.0/), via Wikimedia Commons.

Figure 2.42

By H. Zell (https://creativecommons.org/licenses/by-sa/3.0), from Wikimedia Commons.

Figure 2.43

By Encyclopædia Britannica, 1911 [Public domain], via Wikimedia Commons.

Figure 2.44

Metropolitan Museum of Art, New York. Bequest of Richard B. Seager, 1926. CC0 1.0.

Figure 2.45

Walters Art Museum, Baltimore,. CC0

The Uluburun ship-wreck (Insert)

(a) By Martin Bahmann (https://creativecommons.org/licenses/by-sa/2.5), from Wikimedia Commons.

(b) By Ra'ike (https://creativecommons.org/licenses/by-sa/3.0), from Wikimedia Commons.

Figure 2.46

By Soprani (Self-published work by Soprani) (http://creativecommons.org/licenses/by-sa/3.0/), via Wikimedia Commons.

Figure 2.47

By Carlo Columba from Palermo, Italia (Panoramica su Sant'Angelo) (https://creativecommons.org/licenses/by-sa/2.0), via Wikimedia Commons.

Figure 2.48

By Davide Mauro (https://creativecommons.org/licenses/by-sa/4.0), from Wikimedia Commons.

Figure 2.49

By Codas2 (https://creativecommons.org/licenses/by-sa/4.0), from Wikimedia Commons.

Figure 2.50

By Codas2 (Own work) (https://creativecommons.org/licenses/by-sa/4.0), via Wikimedia Commons.

Figure 2.51

By Archeo (Own work) (https://creativecommons.org/licenses/by-sa/3.0), via Wikimedia Commons.

Figure 3.1

Public domain, via Wikimedia Commons.

Figure 3.2

By Zde https://creativecommons.org/licenses/by-sa/3.0), from Wikimedia Commons.

Figure 3.3

Rijksmuseum, Amsterdam. Public domain.

Figure 3.4

Public domain via Wikimedia.

Figure 3.5

Digital image courtesy of the Getty's Open Content Program, J. Paul Getty Museum, Los Angeles.

Figure 3.6

Digital image courtesy of the Getty's Open Content Program, J. Paul Getty Museum, Los Angeles

Zeus (Insert)

Metropolitan Art Museum, New York. The Elisha Whittelsey Collection, The Elisha Whittelsey Fund, 1949, CC0 1.0.

Figure 3.8

Classical Numismatic Group, Inc. http://www.cngcoins.com (https://creativecommons.org/licenses/by-sa/2.5), via Wikimedia Commons.

Figure 3.9

(a) Cleveland Museum of Art, USA. Purchase from the J. H. Wade Fund. CC0 1.0.

(b) Walters Art Museum, Baltimore. Public domain.

(c) Walters Art Museum, Baltimore. Public domain.

(d) Walters Art Museum, Baltimore. Public domain.

Figure 3.10

Metropolitan Art Museum, New York. Purchase, Edward C. Moore Jr. Gift, 1924. CC0 1.0

King Minos (Insert)

Public domain via Wikimedia Commons

Pasiphae (Insert)

Christine de Pizan, British Library Harley Collection. http://creativecommons.org/publicdomain/mark/1.0/.

Figure 3.11

Courtesy of the Beazley Archive, University of Oxford (photo: C. Wagner).

Figure 3.12. Yale University Art Gallery. Public Domain.

Figure 3.13

Digital image courtesy of the Getty's Open Content Program, J. Paul Getty Museum, Los Angeles. Gift of Leon Levy

Palaiphatos (Insert)

By Johann Heinrich Friedrich Meineke (Transferred from de.wikipedia) Public domain, via Wikimedia Commons.

Heracles and the Cretan Bull (Insert)

(a) Metropolitan Museum of Art, New York. Rogers Fund 1941. CC0 1.0.

(b) Metropolitan Museum of Art, New York. Rogers Fund 1906. CC0 1.0.

Figure 3.14

(a) Photograph from: *The palace of Minos: a comparative account of the successive stages of the early Cretan civilization as illustrated by the discoveries at Knossos* by Evans, Arthur, Sir, Evans, Joan, 1893-1977; London: Macmillan and Co., 1921. A. J. Evans/public domain.

(b) Metropolitan Art Museum, New York. Gift of L. P. di Cesnola, 1876. CC0 1.0.

Figure 3.16

The New York Public Library http://digitalcollections.nypl.org/items/510d47e4-5510-a3d9-e040-e00a18064a99.

Figure 3.17

Metropolitan Art Museum, New York. Rogers Fund, 1941. CC0 1.0.

Figure 3.18

Metropolitan Art Museum, New York. Rogers Fund, 1941. CC0 1.0.

Figure 3.19

(a) Metropolitan Art Museum, New York. Fletcher Fund, 1956. CC0 1.0.

(b) Walters Art Museum, Baltimore. Public domain.

(c) Metropolitan Museum of Art, New York. Rogers Fund, 1905, CC0 1.0

Minos' feud with Athens (Insert)

Digital image courtesy of the Getty's Open Content Program, J. Paul Getty Museum, Los Angeles.

Figure 3.20

Pietro da Cortona: Ariadne and Theseus; Nationalmuseum (Foto: Erik Cornelius), public domain.

Figure 3.21

(a) Metropolitan Museum of Art, New York. Rogers Fund, 1909. CC0 1.0.

(b) Metropolitan Museum of Art, New York. Rogers Fund, 1909. CC0 1.0.

(c) Metropolitan Museum of Art, New York. Fletcher Fund. 1956, CC0 1.0.

(d) Digital image courtesy of the Getty's Open Content Program, J. Paul Getty Museum, Los Angeles.

Figure 3.22

Digital image courtesy of the Getty's Open Content Program, J. Paul Getty Museum, Los Angeles. Gift of Seymour Weintraub.

Figure 3.23

(a) Metropolitan Museum of Art, New York. Gift of Samuel P. Avery, 1897. CC0 1.0.

(b) Digital image courtesy of the Getty's Open Content Program. J Paul Getty Museum, Los Angeles.

(c) Severance and Greta Millikin Trust. Image courtesy of the Cleveland Museum of Art. CC0 1.0

Theseus (Insert)

(a) Image courtesy of the National Gallery of Denmark. CC0 1.0.

(b) Digital image courtesy of the Getty's Open Content Program, J. Paul Getty Museum, Los Angeles.

Figure 3.24

Image from "The life, letters and work of Frederic Leighton" by Russell Barrington. Internet Archive Book Images. Public Domain via Wikimedia Commons.

Figure 3.25

Modified from a map of the Aegean by Rostislav Botev (Own work) (https://creativecommons.org/licenses/by-sa/3.0), via Wikimedia Commons.

Figure 3.26

(a) Rijksmuseum, Amsterdam. Public domain.

(b) Metropolitan Museum of Art, New York. Fletcher Fund, 1924. CC0 1.0.

Figure 3.27

By Carole Raddato from FRANKFURT, Germany https://creativecommons.org/licenses/by-sa/2.0), via Wikimedia Commons.

Figure 3.28

By GianlucaIsidoro (Own work) (https://creativecommons.org/licenses/by-sa/4.0), via Wikimedia Commons.

Figure 3.29

Rijksmuseum, Amsterdam. Public domain.

Figure 3.30

Image courtesy of the British Museum. © The Trustees of the British Museum.

Figure 3.31

Digital image courtesy of the Getty's Open Content Program, J. Paul Getty Museum, Los Angeles.

Figure 3.32

© José Luiz Bernardes Ribeiro / CC BY-SA 4.0.

Figure 3.33

By Future Perfect at Sunrise [Public domain], from Wikimedia Commons.

Figure 3.34

Rijksmuseum, Amsterdam. Public domain.

Figure 3.35

National Gallery of Denmark, Copenhagen. CC0 1.0.

Figure 3.36

By MrPanyGoff (https://creativecommons.org/licenses/by-sa/3.0), from Wikimedia Commons.

Figure 3.37

By Map_Anatolia-fr_draft.svg: Bibi Saint-Polderivative work: Keltorrics (Map_Anatolia-fr_draft.svg) (https://creativecommons.org/licenses/by-sa/2.5), via Wikimedia Commons.

Figure 3.38

By Lori (Flickr: Lycian rock tombs, Myra) (https://creativecommons.org/licenses/by-sa/2.0), via Wikimedia Commons.

Figure 3.39

Reproduced with the permission of the publishers, John Wiley & Sons Ltd., from *Narrative of a Survey of Part of the South Coast of Asia Minor; And of a Tour into the Interior of Lycia in 1840-1; Accompanied by a Map*. Richard Hoskyn, *The Journal of the Royal Geographical Society of London*, 1842: 12; 143-161.

Figure 3.40

Image courtesy of the Wilson sisters.

Figure 3.43

Reproduced from *Stadiasmus Patarensis. Itinera Romana Provinciae Lyciae* by Sencer Sahin and Mustafa Adak with the kind permission of Ege Yayinlari / Zero Books Inc., Istanbul, Turkey.

Figure 3.44

From: Paavo Roos. Topographical and other notes on South-eastern Caria. Opuscula Atheniensia IX, 1969, 59-93.

Figure 4.1

United States Library of Congress's Prints and Photographs division. Public domain.

Figure 4.2

(a) Brooklyn Museum, Charles Edwin Wilbour Fund, 35.775. CC BY 3.0.

(b) Photograph from: *"The palace of Minos: a comparative account of the successive stages of the early Cretan civilization as illustrated by the discoveries at Knossos"* by Sir Arthur Evans and Joan Evans. London: Macmillan and Co., 1921.

Figure 4.3

By Karl Richard Lepsius (1810–1884) (Lepsius-Projekt Sachsen-Anhalt) [Public domain], via Wikimedia Commons.

Figure 4.4

Metropolitan Museum of Art, New York. Gift of Dr. and Mrs. Thomas H. Foulds, 1924. CC0 1.0.

Figure 4.5

Image courtesy of the Petrie Museum, University College London, London.

Figure 4.6

(a) Metropolitan Museum of Art, New York. Rogers Fund, 1911. CC0 1.0.

(b) Metropolitan Museum of Art, New York. Rogers Fund, 1911. CC0 1.0.

Figure 4.7

Image from: Mazes and labyrinths; a general account of their history and developments by William Henry Matthews (1922) via Wikimedia Commons.

Figure 4.8

By Franz Wilhelm Sieber (http://www.wkistler.de/more4/gall_f10.html) [Public domain], via Wikimedia Commons.

Figure 4.9

Photograph from: *"The palace of Minos: a comparative account of the successive stages of the early Cretan civilization as illustrated by the discoveries at Knossos"* by Sir Arthur Evans and Joan Evans. London: Macmillan and Co., 1921.

Rationalization of the minotaur and his labyrinthine prison (Insert)

Digital image courtesy of the Getty's Open Content Program, J. Paul Getty Museum, Los Angeles, USA.

Figure 4.10

(a) Photograph from: "Des Cyclades en Crète au gré du vent" by Daniel Baud-Bovy and Frédéric Boissonnas, Geneva, Boissonnas & Co, 1919. Aikaterini Laskaridis Foundation Library. *http://creativecommons.org/publicdomain/mark/1.0/*

(b) Image courtesy of Professor Jan Driessen.

Figure 4.11

(a) Public domain via Wikimedia Commons.

(b) Image from page 269 of "The antique Greek dance, after sculptured and painted figures" (1916) by Emmanuel, Maurice, 1862-1938. Public domain.

Figure 4.12

Digital image courtesy of the Getty's Open Content Program, J. Paul Getty Museum, Los Angeles, USA. Gift of Carlos Luis Campillo,.

Figure 4.13

Image courtesy of Dr. Manuel Flecker, Antikensammlung – Kunsthalle zu Kiel.

Figure 4.14

(a) From: "Otto's Educational Vocabulary: An Illustrated Encyclopædie of General Knowledge". Publisher Jan Otto, Czechoslovakia (1893 AD)". Public domain via Wikimedia Commons.

(b) Image courtesy of the John Elliott Classics Museum, University of Tasmania.

(c) Photo of a drawing in "Picta poesis: ut pictura poesis erit" by Barthélemy Aneau, Pierre Eskrich and Bernard Salomon (1552 AD). Publisher: Lugduni: Apud Mathiam Bonhomme. Public domain.

Figure 4.15

Heidelberg University Library, Publii Virgilii Maronis Opera cum quinque vulgatis commentariis expolitissimisque figuris atque imaginibus nuper per Sebastianum Brant superadditis (Strasbourg: Johannis Grieninger, 1502), fol. 253r, – CC-BY-SA 3.0. *http://digi.ub.uni-heidelberg.de/diglit/vergil1502/0259.*

Figure 4.16

Metropolitan Museum of Art, New York. Gift of the children of Mrs. Harry Payne Whitney, 1942. CC0 1.0.

Figure 4.17

Digital image courtesy of the Getty's Open Content Program, J. Paul Getty Museum, Los Angeles, USA.

Figure 4.18

Digital image courtesy of the Getty's Open Content Program, J. Paul Getty Museum, Los Angeles, USA.

Figure 4.19

Digital image courtesy of the Getty's Open Content Program, J. Paul Getty Museum, Los Angeles, USA.

Figure 4.20

Based on a map by © Sémhur / Wikimedia Commons, via Wikimedia Commons. CC BY SA 3.0.

Figure 4.21

Robert Koldewey (https://creativecommons.org/licenses/by-sa/2.5), via Wikimedia Commons.

Figure 4.22

By Davide Mauro (https://creativecommons.org/licenses/by-sa/4.0), from Wikimedia Commons.

Figure 4.23

By General Cucombre from New York, USA (Valle dei Templi 3214Uploaded by Markos90) (https://creativecommons.org/licenses/by/2.0), via Wikimedia Commons.

Figure 4.24

By Davide Mauro (https://creativecommons.org/licenses/by-sa/4.0), from Wikimedia Commons.

Figure 4.25

By Davide Mauro (https://creativecommons.org/licenses/by-sa/4.0), from Wikimedia Commons.

Figure 4.26

By Incisione firmata: "Pietro Trombetto Architetto Pal<atino> dis<egnò>". (Archivio privato della famiglia Riggio.) [Public domain], via Wikimedia Commons.

Figure 4.27

By Ravenclaraw (https://creativecommons.org/licenses/by-sa/4.0), from Wikimedia Commons.

Figure 4.28

Image from "The "Progetto Kronio: History and problems of an extreme exploration in an intact Archaeological deposit" Badino G., Torelli L. 2014, 31-42. Archivio Istituzionale Open Access dell'Università di Torino.

Figure 4.29

Digital image courtesy of the Getty's Open Content Program, J. Paul Getty Museum, Los Angeles, USA.

Figure 4.30

(a) By Dedda71 (Own work) (http://creativecommons.org/licenses/by-sa/3.0/), via Wikimedia Commons.

(b) By Bjs (https://creativecommons.org/licenses/by-sa/2.5), from Wikimedia Commons.

Figure 4.31

By Gianni Careddu (https://creativecommons.org/licenses/by-sa/4.0), from Wikimedia Commons.

Figure 4.32

Metropolitan Museum of Art, New York. Gift of Mrs. Frederick F. Thompson, 1903. CC0 1.0.

Figure 4.33

Image courtesy of Birmingham Museums Trust. CC0.

Figure 4.34

By Hannes Grobe (https://creativecommons.org/licenses/by-sa/2.5), from Wikimedia Commons.

Figure 4.35

Image courtesy of NASA. Public domain.

Figure 4.36

The Wellcome Collection. Attribution 4.0 International (CC BY 4.0).

Figure 4.37

Electrostatic Generator (FI Cat. #768) from the collections of The Franklin Institute, Philadelphia, PA.

Figure 4.38

In *The Aerial World*, by Dr G. Hartwig, London, 1886. P. 310. Public domain, via Wikimedia Commons.

Figure 4.39

Digital image courtesy of the Getty's Open Content Program, J. Paul Getty Museum, Los Angeles, USA.

Figure 4.41

Metropolitan Museum of Art, New York. The Elisha Whittelsey Collection, The Elisha Whittelsey Fund, 1949, by exchange 1968. CC0 1.0.

Figure 4.42

By Neithsabes (https://creativecommons.org/licenses/by/3.0), via Wikimedia Commons

Hephaistos (Hephaestus) Insert Metropolitan Museum of Art, New York. Bequest of Phyllis Massar, 2011. CC0 1.0.

Figure 4.43

Public domain via Wikimedia Commons.

Figure 4.44

Image from page 743 of "The museum of classical antiquities: being a series of essays on ancient art" (1860) by Falkener, Edward, 1814-1896 Wood, J. E Davies, Benjamin Rees. Longman, Green, Longman, and Roberts.

Figure 4.45

By Institute for the Study of the Ancient World from New York, United States of America (The Temple of Apollo (II)) (https://creativecommons.org/licenses/by/2.0), via Wikimedia Commons.

Figure 4.46

(a) Metropolitan Museum of Art, New York. Rogers Fund, 1925. CC0 1.0.

(b) Metropolitan Museum of Art, New York. Rogers Fund, 1925. Gift of American Exploration Society, 1907. CC0 1.0.

(c) By Gaius Cornelius (https://creativecommons.org/licenses/by-sa/4.0), from Wikimedia Commons.

(d) Metropolitan Museum of Art, New York. Rogers Fund, 1925. CC0 1.0.

(e) Metropolitan Museum of Art, New York. Rogers Fund and Edward S. Harkness Gift, 1920. CC0 1.0.

(f) Digital image courtesy of the Getty's Open Content Program, J. Paul Getty Museum, Los Angeles, USA.

(g) CC0, via Wikimedia Commons.

(h) Metropolitan Museum of Art, New York. Rogers Fund, 1931. CC0 1.0.

Figure 4.47

United States Library of Congress's Prints and Photographs division. Public domain.

Figure 4.48

Scheffer, Public domain via Wikimedia Commons.

Figure 5.1

Metropolitan Museum of Art, New York, CC0 1.0. Purchase, Lila Acheson Wallace Gift, Gifts of Mrs. William M. Haupt, Josephine Bay Paul, and Estate of George Quackenbush, in his memory, by exchange, The Morris and Alma Schapiro Fund Gift, and funds from various donors, 2013.

Figure 5.2

Wellcome Collection. Attribution 4.0 International (CC BY 4.0).

Figure 5.3

Metropolitan Museum of Art, New York, Rogers Fund, 1965, CC0 1.0.

Figure 5.4

Image courtesy of the British Museum. © The Trustees of the British Museum.

Figure 5.5

Image courtesy of the Esther M. Zimmer Lederberg Trust, http://www. estherlederberg.com/home.html.

Figure 5.6

Rijksmuseum Amsterdam. Public Domain.

Figure 5.7

Public domain via Wikimedia Commons.

Figure 5.8

Image courtesy of the British Interplanetary Society and Adrian Mann.

Figure 5.9

This work has been released into the public domain by its author, Mdf at English Wikipedia. This applies worldwide.

Figure 5.10

By National Aeronautics and Space Administration (en:NASA) / Beasley [Public domain], via Wikimedia Commons.

Figure 5.11

By MissionInn.Jim [Public domain], from Wikimedia Commons.

Figure 5.12

Image courtesy of Richard Browning

https://en.wikipedia.org/wiki/Daidalos_Flight_Pack.

Figure 5.13

Daedalos Project https://www. daedalos-fp7.eu/

Figure 5.14

Solent Local Enterprise Partnership http://www.solentairport.co.uk/about_Daidalos/intro.aspx.

Figure 5.15

By Daderot [Public domain], from Wikimedia Commons.

Figure 5.16

Image courtesy of Conor Lawless: *https:// www.flickr.com/conchur.*

Figure 5.17

By Martin Cooper from Ipswich, UK (Blushing Bracket (Daedaleopsis confragosa) pores) (https://creativecommons.org/licenses/ by/2.0), via Wikimedia Commons.

Figure 5.18

By Patrick Harvey (pg_harvey) at Mushroom Observer, a source for mycological images. (https://creativecommons.org/licenses/ by-sa/3.0), via Wikimedia Commons.

Figure 5.19

Image from: "Monsters of the Sea: Legendary and Authentic" by Gibson, J. (1887). Thomas Nelson and Sons, London. Public domain via Wikimedia Commons.

Figure 5.20

By unattributed; probably Royal Navy. Public domain via Wikimedia Commons.

Figure 5.21

Image courtesy of NASA.

Figure 5.22

Derek Keats from Johannesburg, South Africa *(https://creativecommons.org/licenses/ by/2.0).*

Figure 5.23

By Kurt Wichmann (https:// creativecommons.org/licenses/by/3.0), from Wikimedia Commons.

Figure 5.24

 Digital image courtesy of the Getty's Open Content Program, J. Paul Getty Museum, Los Angeles.

Figure 5.25

Image courtesy of Cambridge University Press from: Beazley, J. (1927). Ikaros. *The Journal of Hellenic Studies,* 47(2), 222-233 © The Society for the Promotion of Hellenic Studies 1927, published by Cambridge University Press.

Figure 5.26.

Image courtesy of Patrick Schwarz, Akademisches Kunstmuseum, Universitat Bonn.

Figure 5.27

Image courtesy of Cambridge University Press from: Beazley, J. (1927). Ikaros. *The Journal of Hellenic Studies,* 47(2), 222-233 © The Society for the Promotion of Hellenic Studies 1927, published by Cambridge University Press.

Figure 5.28

Metropolitan Museum of Art, New York, Fletcher Fund, 1960. CC0 1.0.

Figure 5.29

Image courtesy of Dr. Manuel Flecker, Antikensammlung – Kunsthalle zu Kiel.

Figure 5.30

Image reproduced with kind permission of the Ashmolean Museum, University of Oxford.

Figure 5.31

Images courtesy of the Allard Pierson Museum, Amsterdam. Attribution 3.0 Netherlands (CC BY 3.0 NL).

Figure 5.32

(a) Image courtesy of the John Elliott Classics Museum, University of Tasmania.

(b) The Miriam and Ira D. Wallach Division of Art, Prints and Photographs, Picture Collection, The New York Public Library. Public domain.

Figure 5.33

(a) Unknown author, public domain via Wikimedia Commons.

(b) Metropolitan Art Museum, New York. Gift of Dietrich von Bothmer, Distinguished Research Curator, Greek and Roman Art, 2011. CC0 1.0.

Figure 5.34

Metropolitan Museum of Art, New York. Rogers Fund, 1921. CC0 1.0.

Figure 5.35

(a) Metropolitan Museum of Art, New York. Gift of Dietrich von Bothmer, 1964. CC0 1.0.

(b) Digital image courtesy of the Getty's Open Content Program, J. Paul Getty Museum, Los Angeles, USA.

(c) Thorvaldsen Museum, Copenhagen, Denmark *www.thorvaldsensmuseum.dk* CC0 1.0.

(d) Cleveland Museum of Art. Purchase from the J. H. Wade Fund. CC0 1.0.

Figure 5.36

(a) Metropolitan Museum of Art, New York. Rogers Fund, 1962. CC0 1.0.

(b) Metropolitan Museum of Art, New York. Rogers Fund, 1962. CC0 1.0.

(c) Metropolitan Museum of Art, New York. CC0 1.0.

(d) Digital image courtesy of the Getty's Open Content Program, J. Paul Getty Museum, Los Angeles, USA.

Figure 5.37

Public domain via Wikimedia Commons.

Imitators of the flight of Daidalos through the ages (Insert)

(a) Rijksmuseum Amsterdam. Public Domain.

(b) By Eulogia Merle (Fundación Española para la Ciencia y la Tecnología) (https://creativecommons.org/licenses/by-sa/4.0), via Wikimedia Commons.

(c) By Radicalrobbo (https://creativecommons.org/licenses/by/3.0), from Wikimedia Commons.

(d) British Library, Public Domain.

Figure 5.38

Photo published in "A Wanderer in London" by E. V. Lucas in 1906. Public Domain via Wikimedia Commons.

Figure 5.39

(a) Wellcome Collection. Attribution 4.0 International (CC BY 4.0).

(b) Anthony van Dyck [Public domain], via Wikimedia Commons.

(c) Laurent Pêcheux [Public domain], via Wikimedia Commons.

(d) Nationalmuseum, Stockholm, Sweden. CC0.

(e) Birmingham Museum and Art Gallery. CC0 1.0.

(f) Agnews Gallery, London.

Figure 5.40

Museo Nazionale Etrusco di Villa Giulia, Rome.

Figure 5.41

Metropolitan Art Museum, New York. Bequest of Maria DeWitt Jesup, from the collection of her husband, Morris K. Jesup, 1914. Co 1.0.

Figure 5.42

Walters Art Museum, Baltimore, USA.

Figure 5.43

Photograph by Dean Dixon, Sculpture by Alan LeQuire, Free Art License (http://artlibre.org/licence/lal/en/) via Wikimedia Commons.

Figure 5.44

(a) Digital image courtesy of the Getty's Open Content Program, J. Paul Getty Museum, Los Angeles, USA.

(b) Reprinted with permission from "Macedonian Cultural Heritage. OHRID world heritage site" by the Ministry of Culture of the Republic of Macedonia – Cultural Heritage Office.

(c) Los Angeles County Museum of Art, Public domain.

(d) Image courtesy of the Beazley Archive, University of Oxford (photo: C. Wagner).

(e) By IKAl (https://creativecommons. org/licenses/by-sa/2.5), from Wikimedia Commons.

Figure 5.45

(b) Image courtesy of Musée Antoine Vivenel, © musée Antoine Vivenel, Compiègne.

(c) Photo: Myrabella via Wikimedia Commons. CC BY-SA 3.0.

(d) By Jordiferrer (Own work) (https:// creativecommons.org/licenses/ by-sa/3.0), via Wikimedia Commons.

(e) By Sanpi (Own work) (https:// creativecommons.org/licenses/ by-sa/4.0), via Wikimedia Commons.

(f) By Dahn (Own work) [CC0], via Wikimedia Commons.

Figure 5.46

(a) By Metro Centric (The Minotaur, Barbican) (https://creativecommons. org/licenses/by/2.0), via Wikimedia Commons.

(c) Dr Zak at the English language Wikipedia (http://creativecommons. org/licenses/by-sa/3.0/), via Wikimedia Commons.

(d) Malcolm Morris / Yorkshire Sculpture Park / CC BY-SA 2.0 via Wikimedia Commons.

CPSIA information can be obtained
at www.ICGtesting.com
Printed in the USA
LVHW072334280920
667372LV00005B/435